Leveraging Migration for Africa

Leveraging Migration for Africa

Remittances, Skills, and Investments

Dilip Ratha

Sanket Mohapatra

Çağlar Özden

Sonia Plaza

William Shaw

Abebe Shimeles

THE WORLD BANK
Washington, DC

ISBN: 978-0-8213-8257-8
eISBN: 978-0-8213-8718-4
DOI: 10.1596/978-0-8213-8257-8

Library of Congress Cataloging-in-Publication Data

Leveraging migration for Africa : remittances, skills, and investments / edited by Dilip Ratha.
     p. cm.
   Includes bibliographical references and index.
   ISBN 978-0-8213-8257-8 — ISBN 978-0-8213-8718-4 (electronic)
   1. Emigrant remittances—Africa.   2. Africa—Emigration and immigration—Economic aspects.   3. African diaspora—Economic aspects.   4. Investments, Foreign—Africa.
5. Economic development—Africa.   I. Ratha, Dilip.
   HG3982.L48 2011
   338.96—dc22

                                                                      2011012319

Cover painting: Diana Ong/SuperStock by Getty Images
Cover design: Drew Fasick

Table of Contents

Figures

Tables

Foreword

Every country in Africa has been affected by international migration, in all its forms. Some people choose to migrate; others are forced to do so by natural disasters or conflict. Migration has often been viewed as a "brain drain" rather than an opportunity. Technological progress has made it easier for migrants to stay in touch with the country they left behind and to contribute to its social and economic development. Until recently, few governments and institutions in Africa recognized the potential contribution that the diaspora could make, if properly managed, to the economic transformation of the continent.

The projected rise in the labor force in poor regions and decline in rich and some emerging economies in the next few decades are expected to create substantial imbalances in the global labor market. If not addressed, these imbalances could have negative long-term economic consequences in both regions. Climate change, which can be addressed only through early preparedness and innovative solutions, is also expected to drive increases in migration from the most populated areas in Africa. Despite pressures for migration and rapid improvements in transportation and communication technology, global migration is occurring at a much slower pace than the movement of goods and capital across the globe, owing to the presence of barriers to migration. And these barriers are likely to rise going forward, as recent increases in immigration and the financial crisis have made migration a sensitive issue in the minds of the public as well as policy makers in the developed and developing worlds.

This flagship report by the African Development Bank and the World Bank comes at a time when countries are grappling with difficult choices on how to manage international migration. Both institutions place great emphasis on the role of migrants in social and economic development. They work in close collaboration with African governments, private sector operators, diaspora associations, and other stakeholders to create an environment that encourages the mobilization and effective utilization of the financial and intellectual resources of migrants for the development of Africa.

Most countries in Africa face severe financing gaps that impede their development and are in need of finance for infrastructure and the transfer of technology. Traditional sources of finance, such as official development assistance and foreign direct investment, have generally proven to be inadequate and unpredictable. By contrast, remittances have increased strongly over the past decade, easing the foreign exchange constraint facing most countries and becoming a reliable source of external finance. Leveraging the developmental impact of remittances is high on the agenda of both the African Development Bank and the World Bank. Innovative financing mechanisms such as securitization of future remittance flows and issuance of diaspora bonds could help finance big-ticket projects, such as railways, roads, power plants, institutions of higher learning, institution building, and related projects that are critical for Africa's economic transformation.

Migration is an integral part of the agenda for regional economic integration that has made headway in the past decade. This report provides a wealth of information on migration and remittance trends, as well as an analysis of the determinants of migration and a discussion of policies that Africa and its partners should adopt to improve the developmental impact of migration. The report also outlines various means through which diaspora resources can be harnessed to promote economic development in Africa.

The report is a product of a longstanding joint effort by the African Development Bank and the World Bank that exemplifies solid partnership built on mutual respect, collegiality, and professionalism.

Shantayanan Devarajan
Chief Economist, Africa Region
The World Bank

Mthuli Ncube
Chief Economist and Vice President
African Development Bank

Hans Timmer
Director
Development Prospects Group
The World Bank

Acknowledgments

Canadian International Development Agency

Agence canadienne de développement international

MINISTRY OF FOREIGN AFFAIRS OF DENMARK

DANIDA INTERNATIONAL DEVELOPMENT COOPERATION

DFID Department for International Development

This report was prepared by the Migration and Remittances Unit of the World Bank and the Development Research Department of the African Development Bank. The lead author of the report is Dilip Ratha. The principal authors of the chapters are Abebe Shimeles and William Shaw (chapter 1), Sanket Mohapatra (chapter 2), Çağlar Özden (chapter 3), and Sonia Plaza (chapter 4). William Shaw provided comments and suggestions on all the chapters throughout the preparation of the report. Uri Dadush, Shantayanan Devarajan, Louis Kasekende, Mthuli Ncube, Leonce Ndikumana, John Page, and especially Hans Timmer provided guidance to the team at various stages of the study. Manolo Abella, Richard Adams, Jr., Abdousalam Drame, Marguerite Duponchel, Suhas Ketkar, Anthony Kusi, Loren B. Landau, David McKenzie, Birgitte Mossin Brønden, John Oucho, Peter Hansen, Nauja Kleist, Elina Scheja, William Shaw, Lars Trans, Simon Turner, and Ida Vammen prepared background papers for the report.

Special thanks are due to Johannes Koettl, Subha Nagarajan, Désiré Vencatachellum, and Peter Walkenhorst for contributions to chapter 1; Jose Anson and Nils Clotteau for information on the role of post offices in remittances in chapter 2; Mirvat Sewadeh for significant contributions; David McKenzie for the box on the emigration of Ghana's best and brightest

Enabling poor rural people
to overcome poverty

Liberté • Égalité • Fraternité
RÉPUBLIQUE FRANÇAISE

MINISTRY OF THE INTERIOR,
OVERSEAS FRANCE, LOCAL AUTHORITIES AND IMMIGRATION

THE WORLD BANK

in chapter 3; Chris Parsons and Frédéric Docquier for their help with datasets in chapter 3; and Jacqueline Irving and Seifu Mehari for chapter 4.

Kaouther Abderrahim, Manka Angwafo, Sohini Chatterjee, Aymen Dhib, Farai Jena, Onitola Oni, Carly Petracco, Ani Silwal, and Zhimei Xu provided research assistance. Neil Ruiz provided excellent assistance in project coordination throughout.

David McKenzie, Mustapha K. Nabli, and David Olusanya Ajakaiye served as peer reviewers during the project's advisory committee meeting. Shanta Devarajan, Punam Chuhan-Pole, Maureen Lewis, Benjamin Musuku, and Raju Singh served as internal peer reviewers of the consultation draft. Special thanks to Michael Clemens, Uri Dadush, Sarah Lahmani, Thomas Melonio, Leonce Ndikumana, and Rosemary Vargas-Lundius for serving as external referees of the consultation draft.

Barfour Osei was a part of the team during the initial stages of the project and provided guidance and support. For their generous comments and support, special thanks go to Martin Alsop, Jeff Dayton-Johnson, Thomas Debass, Pedro de Lima, Rick Erlebach, Tim Green, Robert Holzman, Bela Hovy, Arun Kashyap, Sarah Lahmani, Robert E. B. Lucas, Leonce Ndikumana, Kerry Nelson, David Olusanya Ajakaiye, and Rosemary Vargas-Lundius.

The report draws on primary surveys of migrants' households in Burkina Faso, Kenya, Nigeria, Senegal, South Africa, and Uganda, managed by Sonia Plaza and with administrative aspects coordinated by Neil G. Ruiz. Advice on survey methodology came from Richard Adams Jr., Richard Bilsborrow, Juan Muñoz, and Mario Navarrete, and is gratefully acknowledged. The surveys were conducted by the Université de Ouagadougou (for Burkina Faso), the Consortium pour la Recheche Economique et Social (CRES) (for Senegal), the Human Sciences Research Council (HSRC) (for South Africa), Makerere Statistical Consults Ltd. (for Uganda), the University of Nairobi School of

Economics (for Kenya), and Zibah Consults Ltd. (for Nigeria). Carly Petracco and Adriana Castaldo helped with the analysis of the survey data.

The report also draws on surveys of remittance service providers conducted in Burkina Faso, Cape Verde, Ethiopia, France, Ghana, Kenya, Nigeria, Uganda, Senegal, and the United Kingdom, which were managed by Sanket Mohapatra, with the administrative aspects coordinated by Neil Ruiz. The surveys were conducted by Yiriyibin Bambio in Burkina Faso, Georgiana Pop in Cape Verde, Alemayehu Geda and Jacqueline Irving in Ethiopia, Frédéric Ponsot in France, Peter Quartey in Ghana, Rose Ngugi in Kenya and Uganda, Chukwuma Agu in Nigeria, Fatou Cisse in Senegal, and Leon Isaacs in the United Kingdom. Thanks also go to Antonio C. David, for his invaluable contributions to the surveys at the initial stage of the project.

The report benefited from interviews with government officials, embassy and consulate staff, and leaders of the diaspora associations conducted in 2009 in Abu Dhabi, London, New York, Paris, Philadelphia, Pretoria, and Washington, DC.

This study was made possible by the financial support of the African Development Bank; the Canadian International Development Agency (CIDA); the U.K. Department of International Development (DFID); the French Ministry of Immigration, Integration, Asylum and Solidarity Development; the Danish International Development Agency (DANIDA), part of the Ministry of Foreign Affairs of Denmark; the International Fund for Agricultural Development (IFAD); and the Swedish International Development Cooperation Agency (SIDA).

Book design, editing, and production were coordinated by Fayre Makeig and by Steven McGroarty, Aziz Gökdemir, Mary Fisk, and Denise Bergeron of the World Bank Office of the Publisher.

Abbreviations

(all dollar amounts are in U.S. dollars)

ADB	Asian Development Bank
ADHA	Additional Duty Hours Allowance
AIDS	acquired immune deficiency syndrome
AKPA	Association of Kenyan Professionals in Atlanta
AML-CFT	anti–money laundering and combating the financing of terrorism
API	Agency for Promotion of Investments (Mali); Agency for the Promotion of Industry (Tunisia)
ARI	African Remittances Institute
ATM	automatic teller machine
AU	African Union
AUC	African Union Commission
BIS-CPSS	Bank for International Settlements—Committee on Payment and Settlement Systems
BRIDGE	Building Remittance Investments for Development, Growth and Entrepreneurship
CEMAC	Communauté Économique et Monétaire de l'Afrique Centrale (Economic and Monetary Community of Central Africa)
CEPEX	Centre de Promotion des Exportation (Export Promotion Centre)
CGAP	Consultative Group to Assist the Poor
COMPAS	Centre on Migration, Policy and Society

DCI	Development Corporation for Israel
DNA	Diaspora Networks Alliance
DUTFS	Diaspora Unit Trust Funds Schemes
EAC	East African Community
ECA	Economic Commission for Africa
ECOSOCC	Economic, Social and Cultural Council of the African Union
ECOWAS	Economic Community of West African States
e-money	electronic money
EU	European Union
FAR	Future of African Remittances
FDI	foreign direct investment
GCC	Gulf Cooperation Council
GDDA–UK	Ghanaian Doctors and Dentists Association United Kingdom
GDP	gross domestic product
HIV	human immunodeficiency virus
HTA	hometown association
ICMPD	International Centre for Migration Policy Development
IFAD	International Fund for Agricultural Development
ILO	International Labour Organization
IMF	International Monetary Fund
INEC	Independent National Electoral Commission
IOM	International Organization for Migration
IT	information technology
KAIF	Kenyans Abroad Investment Fund
KEPSA	Kenya Private Sector Alliances
MIDA	Migration for Development in Africa
MME	Migration, Mobility, and Employment
NEC	National Electoral Commission
NHS	National Health Service
NIDO	Nigerians in Diaspora Organization
NIDOE	Nigerians in Diaspora Organisation Europe
NIPC	Nigerian Investment Promotion Commission
NRI	nonresident Indian

OCI	overseas citizenship of India
OECD	Organisation for Economic Co-operation and Development
OSIC	One Stop Investment Centre
PATC	Project Advice and Training Centre
PIO	person of Indian origin
R&D	research and development
RISE	Regional Initiative in Science and Education
RSP	remittance service provider
SAFE	Strategy for Assuring Financial Empowerment
SANSA	South African Network of Skills Abroad
TOKTEN	Transfer of Knowledge through Expatriate Nationals
UNDP	United Nations Development Programme
UNESCO	United Nations Educational, Scientific and Cultural Organization
UNHCR	United Nations High Commissioner for Refugees
UNPD	United Nations Population Division
USAID	United States Agency for International Development
WALTPS	West African Long-Term Perspective Study
WITS	World Integrated Trade Solution

Introduction and Summary

International migration has profound implications for human welfare, and African governments have had only a limited influence on welfare outcomes, for good or ill. Improved efforts to manage migration will require information on the nature and impact of migratory patterns. This book seeks to contribute toward this goal, by reviewing previous research and providing new analyses (including surveys and case studies) as well as by formulating policy recommendations that can improve the migration experience for migrants, origin countries, and destination countries.

The book comprises this introduction and summary and four chapters. Chapter 1 reviews the data on African migration and considers the challenges African governments face in managing migration. Chapter 2 discusses the importance of remittances, the most tangible link between migration and development; it also identifies policies that can facilitate remittance flows to Africa and increase their development impact. Chapter 3 analyzes high-skilled emigration and analyzes policies that can limit adverse implications and maximize positive implications for development. Chapter 4 considers ways in which Africa can leverage its diaspora resources to increase trade, investment, and access to technology.

TRENDS IN AFRICAN MIGRATION

According to official statistics, about 30 million Africans—about 3 percent of the population—have migrated internationally (including within Africa). This figure—which includes both voluntary migrants and international refugees—almost certainly underestimates the size and importance of migration from and particularly within Africa.

Figure 1 Stock of Emigrants from Africa, 2010 *(percent of population)*

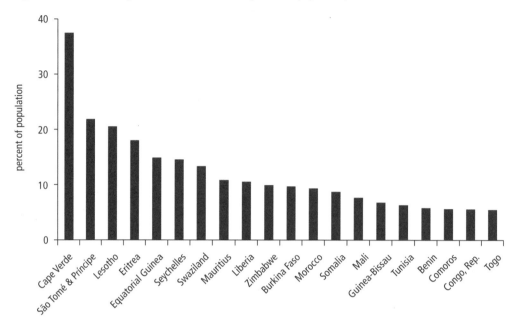

Source: Authors, based on data from World Bank 2011.

The percentage of a country's population that has emigrated varies greatly across Africa (figure 1). It is particularly large in countries with small populations (because of limited diversification of economic activities within national borders) or histories of conflict.

About two-thirds of migrants from Sub-Saharan Africa, particularly poorer migrants, go to other countries in the region; the bulk of migrants remain within their subregions. In West Africa, for example, more than 70 percent of intra-African emigration was within the subregion. In contrast, more than 90 percent of migrants from North Africa travel to countries outside the region. Migrants from middle-income countries disproportionately migrate to destinations outside Africa, whereas emigrants originating from poorer countries generally go to neighboring countries.

New data on migration from household surveys conducted in Burkina Faso, Ghana, Nigeria, and Senegal indicate that migrants tend to be young adults (two-thirds of Burkina Faso's emigrants were between the ages of 15 and 40) and male (more than 90 percent in Burkina Faso), generally with some education beyond primary school. Migration from these countries resulted in significant occupational changes, in particular a transition from farming to trading, semi-skilled employment, and professional jobs.

Official statistics indicate that migration rates are not particularly high in African countries on average. But migration touches the lives of hundreds of millions throughout the continent. Many Africans have moved to new countries, in most cases neighboring ones, without bothering to cross at border posts or register with officials. Each migrant may support a significant network of family members in the home country through remittances; in areas of heavy out-migration, economic activity is often highly dependent on these inflows. Demographic factors are likely to increase migration substantially over the next decade, particularly to countries in the Organisation for Economic Co-operation and Development (OECD), as the working-age population is projected to grow significantly in Africa and to decline in the OECD.

Improving the gains from migration will require an understanding of where and how African governments should intervene, given their limited resources, and what destination countries can do, given their different interests and policy constraints. This volume therefore focuses on four key policy areas where governments can make a difference: managing migration, improving the efficiency of migrant remittances, addressing high-skilled migration, and eliciting contributions from diasporas.

MANAGING MIGRATION

Limited financial and technical resources, borders that are long and difficult to police, and ethnic ties across borders have combined to establish a relatively control-free environment for cross-border migration within Africa. The lack of an effective legal and institutional framework to govern migration significantly increases the risks and costs facing migrants. Many migrants from Africa are vulnerable to traffickers, in physical danger during desert or sea crossings, and largely at the mercy of exploitative practices in destination countries. In several African countries, inadequate legislation, poor enforcement, and social attitudes make trafficking difficult to combat, a situation that is exacerbated by rules in destination countries that leave migrants, particularly women, in the power of employers and border officials. Engaging in stricter law enforcement, providing information on the dangers of migration, improving regulation of intermediaries, and ensuring that children have adequate support at home (so they do not have to migrate) would help fight trafficking. But rules that seek to protect or control women by restricting their right to migrate can force them into illegal channels, increasing rather than decreasing their vulnerability to traffickers. Some African governments have exacerbated the difficulties facing migrants through mass expulsions, the use of violence against unauthorized migrants, and their failure to limit the depredations of the police and other officials against undocumented migrants.

Bilateral agreements supporting temporary migration programs can be used to increase legal migration from African countries. But these programs require careful monitoring to protect migrants from exploitation by employers and intermediaries. The resources required to oversee such programs mean that they can cover only a small proportion of undocumented migrants.

IMPROVING THE EFFICIENCY OF MIGRANT REMITTANCES

Remittance inflows to Africa quadrupled in the 20 years since 1990, reaching nearly $40 billion (2.6 percent of GDP) in 2010. They are the continent's largest source of net foreign inflows after foreign direct investment (FDI) (figure 2).

Remittance receipts generate large benefits for emigrants' countries of origin. At the macro level, remittances tend to be more stable than other sources of foreign exchange; their variation is often countercyclical, helping sustain consumption and investment during downturns; and they improve sovereign creditworthiness, by increasing the level and stability of foreign exchange receipts.

At the micro level, both country studies and cross-country analyses have shown that remittances reduce poverty. They also spur spending on health and education, as a result of both higher household incomes and—according to some studies—the devotion of a larger share of remittances than other income sources to these services. In addition, remittances provide insurance against adverse shocks by diversifying the sources of household income. For example, a recent study finds that Ethiopian households that receive international remittances are less likely than other households to sell their productive assets, such as livestock, to cope with food shortages.

Large remittance inflows can present a macroeconomic challenge, however, by causing the exchange rate to appreciate, potentially reducing the production of tradable goods. Policy makers in countries that receive very large remittance inflows should be alert to their impact on the exchange rate, particularly where supply constraints are a significant hindrance to the expansion of the nontradable sector and a significant portion of remittances are spent on domestic nontradables. In addition to maintaining a flexible exchange rate and considering the true level of remittance inflows when crafting targets for reserves policies and money supply growth, policy makers can implement microeconomic interventions aimed at easing

Figure 2 Remittances and Other Resource Flows to Africa, 1990–2010

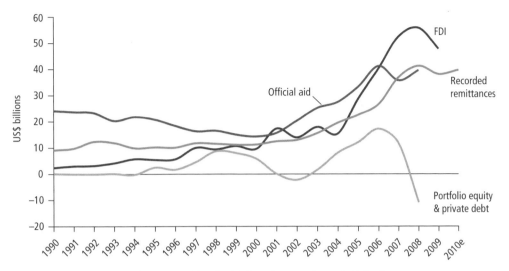

Source: Authors, based on data from the World Bank Global Development Finance 2010 database.

e = estimated.

labor market rigidities and reforms aimed at improving competitiveness to limit the potential danger of excessive exchange rate appreciation. Large remittance inflows could also impair growth by reducing the supply of labor, although there is little evidence of this effect.

Remittance flows are likely significantly underestimated: only about half of the countries in Sub-Saharan Africa collect remittance data with any regularity, and some major receivers of remittances report no data at all. Few African countries report monthly or quarterly data on remittances. African central banks and statistical agencies can improve the woefully inadequate collection of data on remittances by expanding the reporting of remittances from banks to other providers of remittance services, such as companies that facilitate money transfers, post offices, savings cooperatives, and microfinance institutions. They can use household surveys and surveys of emigrants to estimate remittance flows through formal and informal channels. Labor ministries and embassies in destination countries can also help estimate the volume and costs of remittance transactions.

Policy makers need to increase the transparency and efficiency of the markets for remittance services. The cost of sending remittances to Sub-Saharan Africa averaged almost 12 percent of a $200 transaction, compared with less than 8 percent for most other developing regions. The cost of cross-border remittances within Africa, if permitted at all, tends to be even higher. Governments in both sending and receiving countries (in Africa and elsewhere) should discourage exclusive agreements between providers of remittance services (such as commercial banks, post offices, credit and savings cooperatives, microfinance institutions, and mobile money transfer services) and international money transfer agencies, which keep costs high. Providing information on available remittance channels, maintaining databases of the prices charged, and promoting the financial literacy of prospective migrants can strengthen competition in the market and encourage the use of formal channels. Over the long term, financial development should reduce remittance costs by increasing access to financial services in rural areas and poor communities and reducing the costs of opening bank accounts.

Post offices, credit cooperatives, rural banks, and microfinance institutions have large networks (particularly among the poor), providing a unique opportunity to expand formal remittance markets and improve access to financial services among the poor and in rural areas. A recent survey found that 81 percent of post offices in Sub-Saharan Africa are located outside the three largest cities, where more than 80 percent of Africans live (by contrast, mainstream commercial banks in Africa are usually concentrated in the largest cities). Consistent with financial stability, the regulatory framework should support the provision of money transfer services by these institutions, which should be encouraged to partner with banks and money transfer operators. Such partnerships should not be exclusive agreements with a single money transfer operator, as such limits on competition tend to raise the cost of remittances.

Technological advances have enormous potential to improve competition and broaden the reach of formal remittance markets. Money transfer services through mobile phone networks have increased significantly in Africa, especially for internal remittances in Kenya (the use of mobile phones to transfer international remittances is limited by concerns over money laundering). Governments can support this process by improving their telecommunications infrastructure; harmonizing banking and telecommunications regulations to enable mainstream African banks to participate in mobile money transfers; and—to the extent consistent with public safety—simplifying anti-money laundering and combating the financing of terrorism (AML-CFT) regulations for small-value transfers, which would facilitate mobile-to-mobile cross-border transactions.

Governments can potentially improve their access to international capital markets by issuing bonds that are securitized by future remittance inflows. Such transactions have been limited in African countries because of the overall low level of financial development; weak protection of creditor rights; volatile macroeconomic environment; lack of relationships with international banks; and high fixed cost of legal, investment banking, and credit-rating services. Measures to improve the potential for remittance securitization include improving the measurement of remittances and encouraging flows through formal channels, obtaining sovereign ratings, and implementing a securitization law. Multilateral and bilateral donors can play a role in facilitating such transactions. Any increase in foreign currency debt, however, should be accompanied by prudential risk management.

ADDRESSING HIGH-SKILLED MIGRATION

The emigration of skilled workers can generate substantial benefits for origin countries through remittances, contacts with foreign markets, technology transfer, enhanced skills of returning emigrants, and perhaps increased demand for education in the origin country. However, high-skilled emigration can also impair development by reducing the supply of critical services; limiting productivity spillovers to both high- and low-skilled workers; reducing the potential for innovative and creative activities that are at the core of long-term growth; and limiting contributions to the health of social, political, and economic institutions. The loss of workers educated at public expense can represent a substantial fiscal drain, and the many university-educated African emigrants who fail to obtain skilled jobs in high-income destination countries represent a lost investment in human capital (a recent study of the U.S. job market finds that immigrants with bachelor's degrees from 7 of 15 African countries surveyed have less than a 40 percent chance of ending up in a skilled job).

Skilled migration rates are particularly high in Africa. In 2000 one out of every eight Africans with a university education lived in a country in the OECD, the highest rate among developing regions except the Caribbean, Central America, and Mexico. Small and poor countries have lost an unusually large share of their skilled workforce (figure 3); the stock of skilled emigrants averages 30 percent of the skilled workforce in small countries and almost 25 percent in low-income countries—and these figures understate the impact of high-skilled migration if the most qualified workers migrate. In a survey of the top five students graduating from the top 13 high schools in Ghana between 1976 and 2004, three-quarters had emigrated at some point between secondary school and age 35. The low supply of skilled workers in African economies reflects limited educational opportunities and, in many countries, low returns to education, as a result of difficult working conditions, an unfavorable investment

Figure 3 High-Skill Migration Rates in Africa, by Country Size and Income Level, 2000

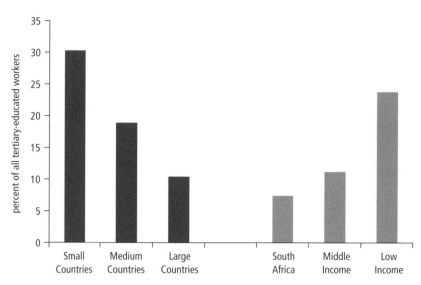

Source: Authors, based on data in Docquier and Marfouk 2004.

climate, or a small economy. Addressing the lack of skills in African workforces requires increasing opportunities for—and thus increasing the return to—education and training rather than limiting emigration.

A variety of educational policies could be designed to address the disadvantages of tertiary-educated migration. Each has problems, however. Increasing tuition for publicly funded tertiary education would reduce the fiscal loss involved in the emigration of highly educated workers, but it is not in the interest of African economies to restrict the supply of graduates or limit education to the rich by raising tuition levels. An alternative approach would be to determine eligibility for free education through academic testing and charge lower-scoring applicants full tuition.

Imposing service requirements as a condition of education or professional registration could increase the availability of professionals. It could also encourage emigration to gain professional credentials and discourage return, however. Graduates might agree to provide a few of years of service in underserved communities as a reasonable cost for subsidized education; some might even consider it an opportunity for postgraduate experience. Ghana experimented with requiring some medical professionals to pay back a portion of their government-funded tuition if they failed to work in the country for a specified time following graduation. Most doctors working abroad paid off the bond rather than complete the service requirement.

Countries could educate students in lower-level skills (for example, nurses' or physicians' assistants rather than nurses and physicians), which would reduce costs and the demand for graduates' services in destination countries. Such (controversial) programs imply a trade-off between quantity and quality of service provision, however. They should be designed with regard to the country's need for specialists rather than the implications for emigration.

An option worth considering involves getting hiring institutions (for example, public or private hospitals) in receiving countries to open training facilities in Africa. More intrusive policies, such as the imposition of a tax on professionals who emigrate and travel restrictions on educated workers, require the effective support of destination governments and may violate human rights.

Some countries have offered incentives, such as higher salaries, help in finding employment, or subsidies for housing and return expenses, to encourage the return of professionals. It is unclear whether such incentives are effective, as motivations for migration often include professional advancement and the quality of the research environment. Financial incentives for returnees may also penalize professionals who remained in the country or subsidize the return of people who would have returned in any event. The removal of biases against returning professionals, involving the recognition of foreign qualifications and experience, could help facilitate return with limited fiscal costs. Destination countries (for example, France) and international organizations (for example, the United Nations Development Programme's Transfer of Knowledge Through Expatriate Nationals [TOKTEN] program) have taken steps to encourage return. These programs have covered only a limited number of migrants, however, and their effectiveness has not been evaluated.

Destination-country policies encourage high-skilled emigration, by offering visas for temporary work or permanent settlement and by actively recruiting some professionals (particularly healthcare workers). Destination countries that benefit from skilled immigration could be asked to compensate origin countries for this practice, in a way that does not simply replace existing aid flows. The controversy over the emigration of health professionals has encouraged public agencies in some countries to limit their foreign recruitment, but the impact of such restraint on overall recruitment levels has not been significant.

ELICITING CONTRIBUTIONS FROM DIASPORAS

About half of Africa's emigrants live outside Africa, primarily in Europe. The main extraregional destinations for African migrants include France

Figure 4   Major Destination Countries for Emigrants from Africa, 2010

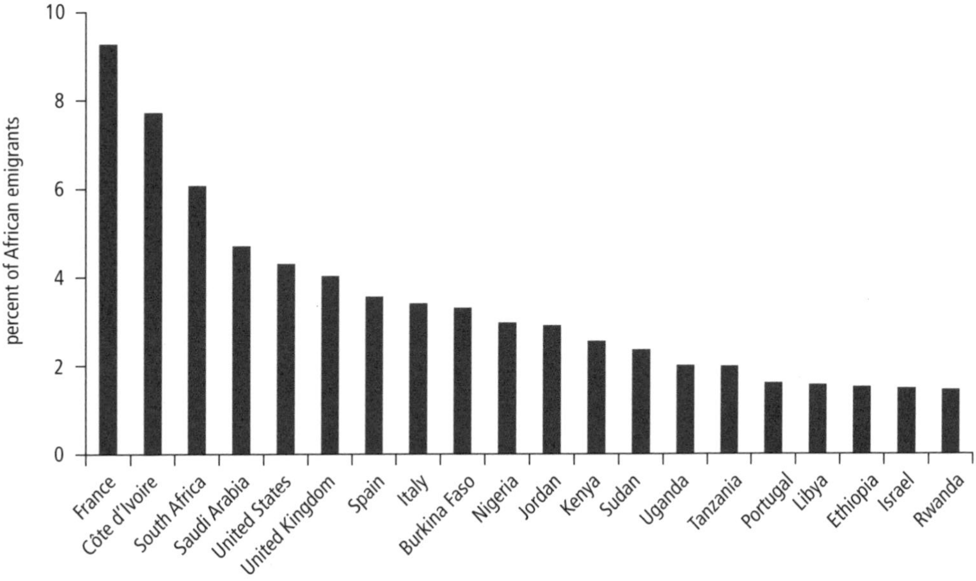

Source: Authors, based on data from World Bank 2011.

(9 percent of total emigrants), Saudi Arabia (5 percent), and the United States and the United Kingdom (4 percent each) (figure 4).

Destination countries' growing diasporas offer a significant opportunity to improve development by increasing direct investments, improving access to foreign capital markets through investment funds and diaspora bonds, providing grants for development, establishing contacts to promote trade and investment, increasing demand for a country's exports, and transferring technology (through, for example, professional associations that provide expertise to origin-country firms, temporary assignments of skilled expatriates in origin countries, and the return of emigrants with enhanced skills).

Allowing for dual citizenship can encourage greater participation by diasporas in their origin countries by facilitating travel; avoiding the constraints foreigners face on some transactions (for example, temporary work, land ownership); and providing access to public services and social benefits. More broadly, dual citizenship can help maintain emotional ties with the origin country, thus encouraging continued contact and investment. Despite these benefits, only 25 of Africa's 54 countries allow dual citizenship.

Facilitating voting by citizens of the origin country who reside abroad also can help solidify ties. Where such voting is permitted, improvements in registration processes and voting procedures (such as increasing the number of locations or allowing for voting by post) may be required.

A few African countries have established government agencies to encourage diasporas to invest, assist local communities, and provide policy advice. Such agencies are also involved in the collection of data on diasporas, the provision of information and counseling services, and the provision of consular services. The results of a recent survey of efforts by embassies from African governments to engage their diasporas found that several have little information on the number of diaspora members, that coordination between the embassies and government ministries is poor, and that there is an urgent need for orienting and training embassy staff on how to work with diaspora members.

Governments can help facilitate diaspora networks by supporting professional associations and arranging cultural events. In some countries, encouraging the growth of private sector networks may be more effective than involving the government directly in establishing links to the diaspora. Investments in modern communications technology can help the private sector maintain links with diasporas.

Emigrants' better access to information on their home countries and their greater tolerance of currency devaluation (because they hold local currency liabilities) can induce them to purchase bonds issued by public or private sector entities ("diaspora bonds"). A few governments have also encouraged investment in origin countries by allowing emigrants to enjoy continued social security coverage and to remain eligible for local savings schemes while abroad. Countries with large numbers of emigrants, including Ghana, Nigeria, Senegal, and South Africa, have developed plans to incorporate diaspora communities as partners in development programs. The effectiveness of such efforts has yet to be evaluated.

THE WAY FORWARD

International migration has tremendous potential to improve development and welfare in origin countries. African governments can play a significant role in securing the benefits of migration by strengthening ties to diasporas, improving competition in remittance markets, designing educational policies in light of the challenges surrounding high-skilled emigration, and providing information and protection for emigrant workers. But limited fiscal and technical resources in African origin countries constrain the effectiveness of such policies and reduce the gains from migration while exposing migrants to severe risks. African governments also face significant difficulties in managing immigration, which can engender resentment and lead to repressive policies, such as mass expulsions, that impose heavy costs on migrants and disrupt African economies.

Africa is a continent of many small countries, which creates significant pressures for international migration. Africa's population is smaller than that of India, yet movements of people within Africa cannot occur within a common legal and political framework. This problem implies significant political challenges to governments and higher costs for migrants, who face different legal and regulatory systems, higher fees for remittances, and risks associated with undocumented migration.

Substantial efforts are required to reduce the costs and risks facing African migrants and to improve the benefits of migration to countries in the region. This book is an attempt to improve the information base so that African governments, destination countries, and the international community can improve migration policies.

BIBLIOGRAPHY

Docquier, Frédéric, and Abdeslam Marfouk. 2004. "Measuring the International Mobility of Skilled Workers (1990–2000). Release 1.0." World Bank Policy Research Working Paper 3381, Washington, DC.

World Bank. 2011. *Migration and Remittances Factbook 2011*. Washington, DC: World Bank.

CHAPTER 1

Migration Patterns and Policies in Africa

Africa is known for its long history of migration within and beyond the vast continent. The number of people of African descent that live outside the continent is estimated at almost 140 million, most of them in the Western Hemisphere (Shinn 2008). Many of these people are not emigrants but members of families that have lived in destination countries for many generations and may have few ties to Africa. By contrast, migrants that left their country in recent decades—conservatively estimated to number more than 30 million—have been able to keep in close contact with their relatives and maintain economic, social, and political relationships with their country of origin, mainly thanks to globalization and improvements in communications technology.

This chapter presents a broad description of international migration from Africa, based on studies, cross-country data, and household surveys.[1] It focuses on differences in migration rates between Africa and other regions as well as on migration within regions and countries in Africa; the choice of destination country by African emigrants; the potential for increasing migration from Africa in the coming years; and the socioeconomic characteristics of migrants and migrant households. The analysis is based on official data, which likely underestimate actual migration flows, particularly within Africa. Several conclusions emerge from this analysis:

- The majority of international migrants from Africa (particularly from the poorer countries) go to other African countries, as most potential emigrants lack both the financial resources to travel to distant continents and the education and skills required to succeed in rich countries' labor markets. In contrast, 90 percent of North African emigrants go to destinations outside of Africa, predominantly Europe, the Middle East, and North America.

- African migration has been heavily influenced by the continent's history of conflict, coups, insurgencies, dictatorships, war, and natural disasters. Past emigration to the Organisation for Economic Co-operation and Development (OECD) countries appears to facilitate current emigration through network effects.
- Colonial ties continue to exert an influence on the choice of destination countries, with half of African countries reporting that the most common destination for emigrants is the former colonizer.
- Recent household surveys of a few countries (Burkina Faso, Nigeria, and Senegal) provide some tentative information on the profile of African emigrants. Migrants from these countries tend to be young, relatively well educated, and predominantly male. The probability of a household having a member abroad is positively related to family size, education, and wealth. The majority of migrants from the households surveyed left their country to obtain employment. Migration tends to have a dramatic impact on the labor market status of migrants, often reflecting a shift from self-employment to wage employment. The rate of return migration from households in these surveys is relatively low (less than 10 percent of total emigrants in Nigeria and Senegal).
- Large differences in potential earnings, the aging of populations in high-income countries, the rapid increase in working-age cohorts in Africa (and the decline of such cohorts in Europe and North America),[2] and the importance of network effects will continue to boost pressures for emigration from Africa to high-income countries. Whether these increases in the demand for and supply of migrants result in more migration will depend, in part, on policy decisions. The willingness of high-income countries to accept migrants, and their ability to effectively control their borders, will be tested in the years to come. Potential migrants will need to obtain the skills required to make them competitive in high-income labor markets: poor African laborers who lack education and language skills have little ability to secure jobs in Europe or the United States. Migration decisions will also be affected by the ability of African governments to establish the framework required for rapid development and income-earning opportunities. Migration can provide enormous welfare benefits to developing countries, but ultimately development should reduce the need for migration.
- African governments face major challenges in managing migration. Governments could help protect migrants by improving regulation of intermediaries, strengthening legal safeguards against trafficking, and providing information on the potential dangers involved in illegal bor-

der crossings and exploitative practices by destination country officials and employers. Undocumented migration is accepted in many areas—particularly where migrants come from contiguous areas of neighboring countries and have ethnic ties to people in their new country—but can be a source of considerable social tension. Coping with undocumented migration is a daunting challenge in both rich and poor countries. At a minimum, governments should prevent violent or exploitative practices such as mass expulsions or tolerance of corrupt officials who prey on undocumented immigrants. International cooperation can support better management of migration through well-regulated temporary migration programs, which need to be carefully supervised to avoid the exploitation of migrants. The substantial resources required to effectively supervise such programs means that they can cover only a very small proportion of potential emigrants.

The chapter is organized as follows. The first section documents migration trends from and within Africa. The second section looks at immigration to Africa. The third section examines cross-country migration patterns. The fourth section identifies the socioeconomic characteristics of migrants from Africa. The last section suggests what countries can do to manage migration.

MIGRATION FROM AND WITHIN AFRICA

Emigration from Africa has increased substantially over the past several decades (see Russell, Jacobsen, and Stanley 1990 for an early survey and World Bank 2011 for recent data). Nevertheless, the migration rate (the ratio of emigrants to the total population of the country of origin) remains low on average, albeit with marked variation across countries (table 1.1).

According to the World Bank's bilateral migration matrix data, in 2010 about 30.6 million African people (3 percent of the world's population) were living in countries other than the one in which they were born. However, official data on migration in Africa significantly understate the actual movement of people (box 1.1). The actual number of African emigrants is likely to be significantly larger.

At the country level, France stands out as the leading destination for emigrants from Africa (9 percent of total emigrants), followed by Côte d'Ivoire (8 percent), South Africa (6 percent), Saudi Arabia (5 percent), and the United States and United Kingdom (4 percent each) (figure 1.1). In most OECD countries, the share of African emigrants is less than 3 percent. Western Europe, the United States, Canada, and Australia account

Table 1.1 Emigrants as Percentage of the Population in Selected World Regions, 2010

Region	Emigrant stock (millions)	Population (millons)	Emigrants/population (percent)
Africa	30.6	1,032	3.0
North Africa	8.7	170	5.1
Sub-Saharan Africa	21.9	862	2.5
East Asia and Pacific	21.7	1,974	1.1
Europe and Central Asia	43.0	404	10.7
Latin America	30.2	581	5.2
South Asia	26.7	1,644	1.6
World	215.8	6,909	3.1

Source: World Bank 2011.
Note: Figures include intraregional migration.

Box 1.1 Problems with Data on African Migration

Data on migration in Africa are often missing, out of date, or inconsistent with definitions used in other countries. Intraregional migration flows are often informal and not captured in official statistics. Data on seasonal and transit migration remain a big challenge. The recording of refugee flows by the United Nations High Commissioner for Refugees (UNHCR) is more accurate and timely.

Although 49 of Africa's 54 countries provide data from a national census on immigrants by source country, the data on intra-African migration suffer from significant gaps. Only 15 African countries have data for the period after 2000, 24 countries have data for the 1990s but not later, and 10 countries have no data even for the 1990s. Coverage varies across subregions. Data for the 1990s are available for all southern African countries, three-quarters of East and West African countries, and half of Central and North African countries. Central Africa has the weakest data, with no country providing data after 2000. Throughout Africa many countries report migrants only from the major source countries.

Data on emigration from Africa to high-income countries belonging to the Organisation for Economic Co-operation and Development (OECD) are of significantly better quality and are more current than data on intra-African migration. Immigration data from the OECD national censuses conducted in 2000 were augmented by labor force and population surveys in 2005–07.

The migration data for all destination countries were used to construct a bilateral matrix of migration stocks for 2010 (Ratha and Shaw 2007; World Bank 2011). The migrant stocks for each destination country—and a breakdown by source country—were scaled to the UN Population Division's latest estimates of immigrant stocks in each destination country for 2010.

The reliance on infrequent census data particularly impairs knowledge of migration flows in countries affected by significant economic or political shocks. Côte d'Ivoire, for example, a major destination for migrants from neighboring countries, may have become less attractive after the 2002–04 civil war. Similarly, the latest South African census does not fully capture the surge in immigrants from Zimbabwe since that country's economic crisis began almost a decade ago. Overall, migration data in Africa, especially on intra-African migration, require substantial improvement in availability, timeliness, quality, and cross-country comparability.

Figure 1.1   Major Destination Countries for Emigrants from Africa, 2010
(share of African emigrants)

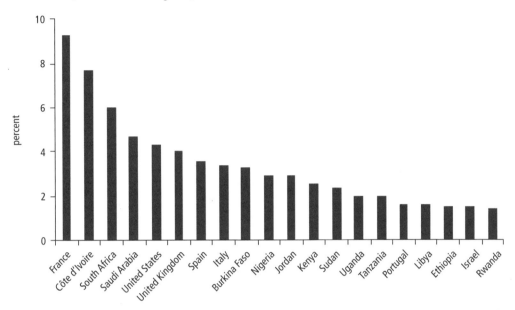

Source: Authors, based on data in World Bank 2011.

for only about 37 percent of total African migrants (65 percent if intra-African migration is excluded).

Many African countries have experienced sharp changes in net migration rates (the difference between immigration and emigration as a share of origin country population) since the late 1970s, reflecting the tumultuous events in the continent's history during this period.[3] In part, these wide variations in net migration rates were caused by civil and external conflicts. For example, net migration rates have been particularly volatile in Eritrea, Liberia, Malawi, Mozambique, Rwanda, Sierra Leone, and Somalia (see annex table 1A.1).[4] For Africa as a whole, however, net migration rates have been stable over time, ranging from –0.4 percent to –0.6 percent across five-year periods from 1975 to 2010. As a large percentage of African migration is within the continent, the cross-country average tends to be close to zero. Patterns since 2006 indicate some decline in the average net migration as well as its variability across countries.

The rate of emigration varies significantly across countries. Some of the smaller countries (for example, Cape Verde, Equatorial Guinea, Lesotho, Mali, São Tomé and Príncipe, and Seychelles) have gross emigration rates that exceed 10 percent (figure 1.2). This high level of emigration partly reflects limited livelihood opportunities and a high variability of income

Figure 1.2   Rate of Migration, by Country, 2010

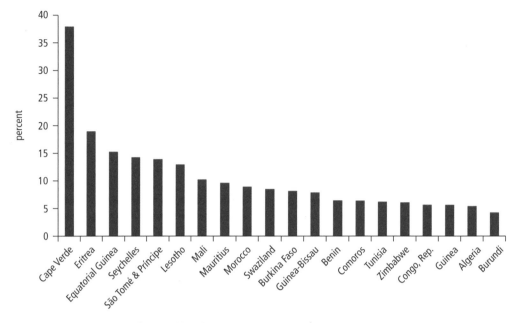

Source: Authors, based on data from World Bank 2011.
Note: Figures show stock of emigrants divided by population.

as a result of dependence on primary commodities (Docquier and Schiff 2009). Several countries suffering civil disorder also have high emigration rates. For example, after more than three decades of war, Eritrean emigrants represent almost 20 percent of the country's population.

A marked feature of the movement of people across the globe is that at least half of it takes place within the same continent (except for emigrants from Latin America and the Caribbean, most of whom go to North America, and for East Asia and Pacific) (table 1.2).[5] The intra-Africa emigration rate is about 50 percent, which is similar to intraregional rates for developing countries in Europe and Central Asia (59 percent) and the Middle East (45 percent).

There is a significant difference between Sub-Saharan Africa and North Africa in this regard. Intraregional emigration in Sub-Saharan Africa accounts for almost 65 percent of total emigrants, the largest intracontinental or South-South movement of people in the world. In contrast, more than 90 percent of emigrants from North Africa head to countries outside Africa (table 1.3). Intra-African emigration is driven largely by a search for job opportunities in neighboring countries. It is also driven by the complexities of historical state formation—colonial borders often overlooked linguistic and ethnic commonalities—as well as by waves of internal and cross-border conflicts (box 1.2).

Table 1.2 Origin and Destination of Emigrants, by World Region, 2010
(percent of total emigration)

Source region	Destination region						
	Africa	East Asia and Pacific	Europe and Central Asia	Latin America and the Caribbean	Middle East	South Asia	High-income countries
Africa	50	0	0	0	4	0	46
East Asia and Pacific	0	15	0	0	1	0	83
Europe and Central Asia	0	0	59	0	0	0	41
Latin America and the Caribbean	0	0	0	13	0	0	87
Middle East	2	0	1	1	45	0	51
South Asia	0	2	0	0	8	30	61
High-income countries	1	1	3	5	2	0	87

Source: World Bank 2011; Ratha and Shaw 2007.
Note: Rows may not sum to 100 percent because of rounding errors.

The bulk of intra-African emigration has occurred across neighboring countries. In West Africa, more than 70 percent of emigration took place within the same subregion; in southern Africa 66 percent of emigration was intra-African, reflecting the strong pull of South Africa (see table 1.3).

The predominance of cross-border emigration reflects common linguistic and historical roots. For example, a large number of emigrants from Djibouti, Eritrea, Ethiopia, and Somalia are found in the same region because of strong ethnic, religious, and linguistic ties along the

Table 1.3 Migration within and outside Africa *(percent of all emigrants)*

Origin subregion	Destination subregion					
	Central Africa	East Africa	North Africa	Southern Africa	West Africa	Out of Africa
All Africa	3	13	2	11	21	50
Central Africa	23	26	0	9	3	39
East Africa	1	52	3	3	0	41
North Africa	0	0	6	0	0	93
Southern Africa	0	7	0	66	0	28
West Africa	5	0	0	0	71	24
Other regions	0	0	0	0	0	100

Source: World Bank 2011.
Note: Includes only identified sources and destinations. Rows may not sum to 100 percent because of rounding errors.

Box 1.2 Forced Migration in Africa

Nearly 2.2 million Africans living in countries other than the ones in which they were born are recognized as refugees, displaced mainly by war or drought and other natural disasters (UNHCR 2010). About half of these refugees are in Kenya, Chad, the Democratic Republic of Congo, and Sudan (box figure 1.2.1). The main sources of international refugees are Somalia, the Democratic Republic of Congo, Sudan, and Eritrea (box figure 1.2.2). Another 6.5 million people are considered internally displaced persons, who were forced to move within African countries.

Box figure 1.2.1   Cross-Border Refugees in Selected African Countries, End 2009

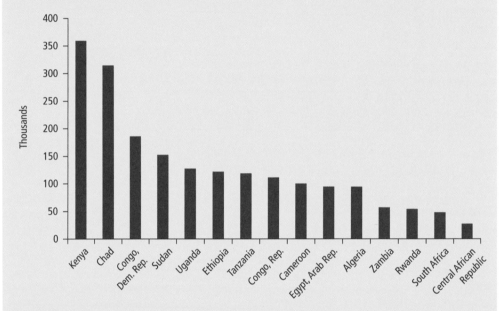

Source: UNHCR 2010.

The number of refugees has declined sharply from the late 1990s, when their numbers reached about 5 million and 1 out of every 5 Africa migrants was a refugee (Hatton and Williamson 2003; Lucas 2006). The decline reflects the lower frequency of coups, guerilla insurgency, government collapse, and civil war.

Refugees can impose a substantial burden on host countries by requiring additional public expenditures, putting pressures on infrastructure, and contributing to environmental degradation (Puerto Gomez and Christensen 2010). For example, the presence of Eritrean and Ethiopian refugees was perceived by their Sudanese hosts to pose an enormous strain on the fragile Sudanese economy (Ek and Karadawi 1991). A large influx of refugees can lead to the transformation of forest and rural land into camps and settlements, and displaced people may resort to unsustainable activities in absence of other means of survival (Hugo 2008). The social and economic impact of a protracted refugee presence can be addressed by targeting development assistance to affected areas, as in the Zambia Initiative, which used community development projects to cope with the impact of more than 100,000 Angolan refugees (Puerto Gomez and Christensen 2010).

Box 1.2   Forced Migration in Africa *(continued)*

Box figure 1.2.2   Cross-Border Refugees from Selected African Countries, End 2009

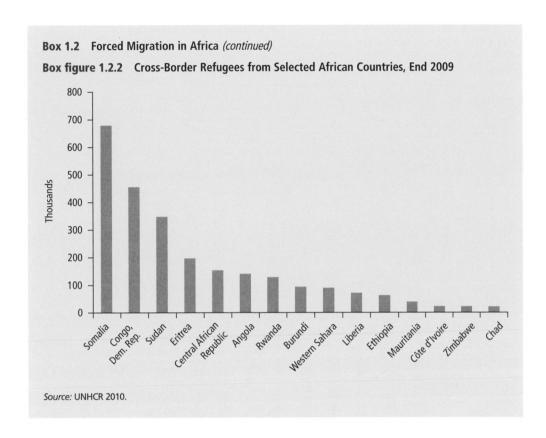

Source: UNHCR 2010.

vast borders these countries share. Kenya is a common destination for emigrants from Tanzania and Uganda. Sudan is a principal destination of emigrants from Chad, Eritrea, and Ethiopia. Emigrants from Burundi and Rwanda often speak the same language as or share historical ties with natives of Tanzania and Uganda. Côte d'Ivoire is a melting pot for neighboring countries, as most migrants are able to communicate with people in the surrounding countries and share religious and historic bonds. Emigrants from Benin, Ghana, and Niger head to Nigeria for similar reasons. In southern Africa, migrants from Botswana, Lesotho, Mozambique, and Swaziland can blend into communities in South Africa, making mobility and settlement comparatively easy.

Intra-African migration flows are affected by income differences, as the large immigration to the relatively prosperous South Africa suggests. There are, however, exceptions. Tanzania, for example, is the most common destination for emigrants from Burundi, the Democratic Republic of Congo, and Zambia, despite the fact that the difference in per capita gross domestic product (GDP) is negligible or favors the source country (figure 1.3).

Figure 1.3   Major Migration Corridors in Sub-Saharan Africa, 2010

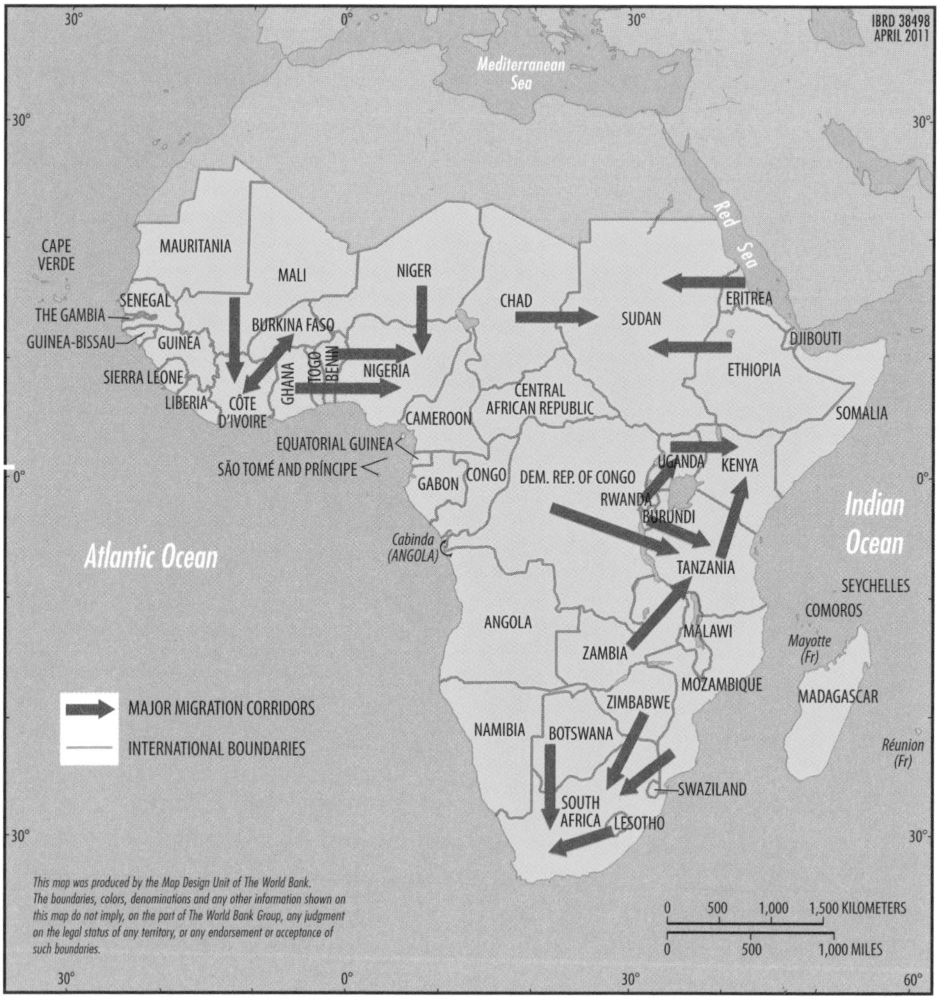

Source: Authors, based on data from World Bank 2011.

More than 90 percent of emigrants from North Africa end up outside Africa (see table 1.3). In contrast, only 41 percent of emigrants from East Africa, 24 percent from West Africa, 39 percent from Central Africa, and 28 percent from Southern Africa end up outside Africa. These figures suggest that people from North Africa, and to some extent East Africa, have better access to opportunities in OECD and Middle Eastern countries than do people in other parts of Africa.

Demographic changes (coupled with network effects) may further boost emigration from Africa to OECD countries in coming years. The working-age population is set to decline between 2005 and 2050 in Europe and the United States and to increase sharply (doubling the labor

Table 1.4 Projected Changes in the Size of the Working-Age Population in Selected World Regions, 2005–50 *(millions)*

Age group	Sub-Saharan Africa	Middle East and North Africa	South Asia	East Asia and Pacific	Eastern Europe and Central Asia	European Union and other Europe	North America
15–24	163	10	27	–78	–26	–18	–7
25–39	262	53	178	–65	–14	–37	–6
40–64	274	124	450	215	15	–33	1
Total working age (15–64)	699	187	655	72	–26	–88	–12
Total population	951	270	863	321	–7	–57	22

Source: Koettl 2010.

force) in Sub-Saharan Africa (table 1.4). Although the impact of a declining population on labor demand in industrial countries is uncertain, the aging of their populations will increase the demand for personal and healthcare services. At the same time, the growth of employment in Africa may not be strong enough to absorb all of the new entrants to the labor force. Thus both the demand for and supply of migrants are likely to rise in the future. Even if Africa achieves rapid growth, the income gap with industrial countries will remain a substantial incentive to migrate for the foreseeable future.

IMMIGRATION TO AFRICA

Immigration to Africa by people born outside Africa was estimated at about 618,000 in 2010, about 4 percent of total immigration in the continent, with the rest accounted for by migrants from within the region. The most common destinations for immigrants from Africa are Côte d'Ivoire (16 percent), South Africa (12 percent), and Burkina Faso (6 percent) (figure 1.4). South Africa and the Arab Republic of Egypt lead in the number of immigrants from outside Africa. Both have large communities of migrants from Australia, Lebanon, the Philippines, the West Bank, and Yemen.

UNDERSTANDING CROSS-COUNTRY MIGRATION PATTERNS

Differences in the ability to migrate account for a significant part of the variation in intra-African migration rates.[6] Emigrants from poorer countries tend to remain in Africa, often in neighboring countries. Figure 1.5 compares per capita income with the share of a country's emigrants that go to other African countries. A 10 percent difference in per capita GDP

Figure 1.4 Rate of Immigration to African Countries, 2010

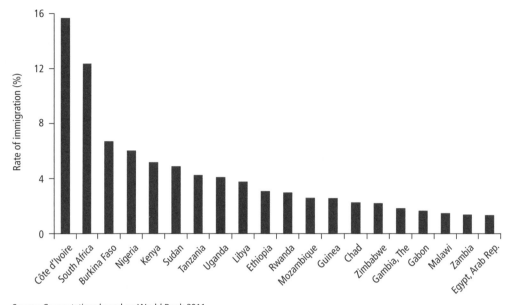

Source: Computations based on World Bank 2011.
Note: Figures show stock of immigrants divided by population.

Figure 1.5 Relationship between Intra-African Migration and per Capita GDP, 2006

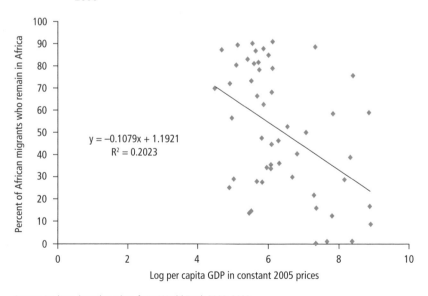

Source: Authors, based on data from World Bank 2008, 2009.

is associated with a 1 percentage point difference in the proportion of emigrants staying in Africa.[7] Emigrants from middle-income countries disproportionately tend to migrate to destinations outside of Africa; African emigration rates to the OECD countries are strongly correlated with per capita GDP (figure 1.6). Emigrants from middle-income countries are more likely to have the resources to pay for transport to and resettlement expenses in the OECD countries, and they are more likely to have the education and other skills required to find jobs there.

Many African countries maintain close economic, political, and cultural ties with their former colonial rulers. France, Belgium, and the United Kingdom in particular cultivated special relationships with their former colonies in Africa that included opportunities for travel, study, and business. Language is also an important link: it is easier for migrants from francophone areas to travel to France and Belgium and those from anglophone areas to travel to the United Kingdom.

Colonial ties continue to play a role in influencing the choice of the destination country. The vertical axis of figure 1.7 plots the share of a country's emigrants to former colonizers; the horizontal axis measures the share of a country's emigrants to the most common destination. If the most common destination is the former colonizer, then the value for the x and y axes would be equal (the point would lie on the 45-degree line

Figure 1.6 Relationship between Emigration Rates to OECD Countries and Log per Capita GDP in Africa, 1990–2000

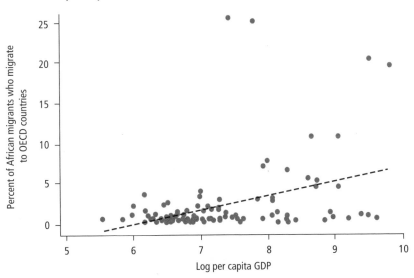

Source: Authors, based on data from World Bank 2008, 2009.

Figure 1.7 Relationship between Colonial Links and Emigration Patterns in Africa

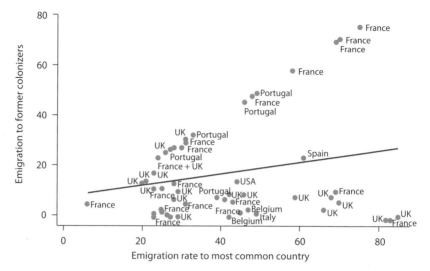

Source: Authors, based on data from World Bank 2011.

from the origin). The large number of observations below the 45-degree line implies that the former colonizer is sometimes, but not always, the most favored destination. Although the trend line shows a limited relationship between former colonial power and the most common destination country for emigrants, a significant share of emigrants from Sub-Saharan Africa remain within the region. (The colonial tie would have a stronger impact on choice of destination if only emigration outside of Africa were considered.)

This relationship does not appear to have changed greatly over time: a study conducted in 1990 (Russell, Jacobsen, and Stanley 1990) also found that trans-African emigrants tended to migrate to former colonizers. The fact that the choice of destination country has not changed partly reflects immigrants' ability to assist aspiring emigrants from origin countries (Hatton and Williamson 2009). Immigrants help new immigrants by financing trips, facilitating legal entry through family reunification programs, and providing information and other assistance that reduce the burden of resettlement.

SOCIOECONOMIC CHARACTERISTICS OF MIGRANTS FROM AFRICA

Understanding the determinants of migration in Africa is difficult because of the lack of descriptive information on migrants and their households in the origin country. Some detailed evidence on the determinants of internal migration in Africa is available, but there is little information on international migration.[8] It is only recently that household surveys have begun to capture characteristics of households that have a member living in another country. This section presents results from the 2005/06 Living Standard Measurement Survey for Ghana and more recent surveys of Burkina Faso, Nigeria, and Senegal completed for the Africa Migration Project.

Analysis of these household survey data shows that migrants from the countries surveyed tend to be young, predominantly male adults with some education beyond primary schooling (table 1.5). The sex, age, and educational composition of migrants vary by destination. Not surprisingly, migrants to OECD countries tend to be older and better educated, and more than 70 percent are men. There are some differences in the motive for migration among the countries covered in the survey. Employment is the predominant reason for emigration from Burkina Faso, whereas education and family reunion are cited as the reason for emigration by almost half of households interviewed in Nigeria and Senegal.

Table 1.5 Characteristics of Migrants from Selected African Countries *(percent)*

Characteristic/ destination	Burkina Faso	Ghana	Nigeria	Senegal
Age (middle 50 percent)				
Migrants in OECD countries	35	37	33	38
Intra-African migrants	32	35	28	35
Internal migrants	32	35	27	32
Gender (percent male)				
Migrants in OECD countries	79	70	72	80
Intra-African migrants	90	63	75	86
Internal migrants	82	62	62	75
Education (percent with given level of education)				
Migrants in OECD countries	52 secondary	61 secondary	45 tertiary	44 tertiary
Intra-African migrants	65 primary	45 secondary	38 secondary	48 primary
Internal migrants	45 secondary	54 secondary	49 secondary	35 primary
Reason for emigration				
Employment	78	..	48	48
Education	8	..	29	29
Family	10	..	20	20
Others	4	..	4	3

Source: Authors, based on data from Plaza, Navarette, and Ratha 2011.
Note: .. = negligible; OECD = Organisation for Economic Co-operation and Development.

Both the Living Standard Measurement Survey of Ghana and the surveys of Burkina Faso, Senegal, and Nigeria conducted for the Africa Migration Project find that larger household size increases the probability that a household member emigrates and remains abroad. This relationship may simply reflect the fact that among a larger number of household members, it is more likely that someone had the desire and ability to migrate. It is also consistent with the view that, often, migration is a decision made by households to diversify their income sources in a risky environment in which insurance is unavailable or unaffordable (larger households have greater opportunities for diversification) (Hoddinott 1994). The likelihood that a household has sent a migrant abroad is also correlated with the average age in the family, a reflection of life-cycle effects. This effect is captured clearly in the case of Nigeria and Senegal, where both internal and external migrants come from older families.

In Ghana, the higher the education of the head of household (and that of the parents of the head of household), the higher the probability that a household member has emigrated. The marginal increase in the probability of sending a migrant is about 8 percent for each additional year of schooling of the head of household. This effect is dampened for households with relatively high wage rates. One way to explain the correlation between education and migration is that a higher level of education makes it easier to gather and process the information necessary for international migration. This trend is observed in Nigeria, where the probability of migration increases with education—up to a point. This effect is not seen in Burkina Faso, where obtaining an education was a more important reason for internal than international migration. This result reflects the fact that data were collected in predominantly rural areas, where secondary schooling may not have been available. Richer families in Burkina Faso are more likely to have a member abroad, but the effect may result from higher incomes from remittances. Income levels are not related to internal migration.

In Ghana, families that earn higher pay have a lower probability of having a member abroad. Controlling for the level of education attained and employment status, however, the level of earnings is not significantly related to the probability of migration. Some areas of Ghana (Greater Accra, Ashanti) have substantially higher international migration rates than others, which may reflect the importance of network effects in facilitating migration.

The survey data also provide information on the dramatic labor market effects of migration. In Burkina Faso and Nigeria, migration allowed a shift from self-employment, often in farming, to wage employment.

Migration appears to have differing implications for women's labor market status in these countries. In Burkina Faso and Nigeria, the share of housewives is higher in the sample after migration; in Senegal migration appears to have helped some women change their status from housewife to some form of employment (table 1.6). In Senegal, the shift in labor market status is significant for students, many of whom were able to find wage employment after migrating (table 1.7).

The Burkina Faso survey shows a significant change in labor market status following migration. Nearly all migrants were farmers in their original place of residence, which is not surprising given that the survey was administered predominantly in rural areas. Migration frequently resulted in changes in occupation. After internal migration, which was often from rural to urban areas, only one-third of internal migrants remained farmers (about half of international migrants continued as farmers). Although

Table 1.6 Occupation of Individuals from Burkina Faso before and after Migrating, 2009

	Before migration		After migration	
Occupation	Internal	International	Internal	International
Farmer	85.7	91.6	36.4	58.8
Trader	4.5	2.4	20.9	6.8
Professionals (managers)	4.1	2.1	16.0	23.0
Semiskilled workers	2.5	1.6	6.1	1.3
Unstable occupations	2.1	1.8	10.6	5.8
Other	1.1	0.5	10.0	4.3

Source: Authors, based on data from Plaza, Navarette, and Ratha 2011.

Table 1.7 Labor Market Status of Individuals from Selected African Countries before and after Migrating, 2009 *(percent)*

	Burkina Faso		Nigeria		Senegal	
Labor market status	Before	After	Before	After	Before	After
Self-employed	80.3	64.1	15.7	25.6	42.2	42.7
Student	10.2	5.4	42.5	23.2	20.6	7.6
Housewife	2.9	5.1	1.3	4.9	9.4	7.6
Full-time wage earner	2.5	8.8	13.9	33.5	9.0	24.3
Part-time wage earner	1.5	12.2	2.7	4.1	3.3	4.2
Unemployed	1.9	1.5	22.0	4.3	8.9	3.4
Other	1.0	3.0	2.0	4.0	7.0	10.0

Source: Authors, based on data from Plaza, Navarette, and Ratha 2011.

Table 1.8 Return Migration in Selected African Countries *(percent)*

Item	Burkina Faso	Nigeria	Senegal
Returnees as a share of migrants	25	3	9
of which:			
Returned in less than 4 years	67	69	32
Returned in 5–15 years	16	23	2
Returned after more than 15 years	16	8	66

Source: Authors, based on data from Plaza, Navarette, and Ratha 2011.

many internal migrants became traders and some even mid-level managers, others ended up in unstable or casual employment.

The survey data show low rates of return migration: the share of emigrants who returned was only 3 percent in Nigeria, 9 percent in Senegal, and 25 percent in Burkina Faso (table 1.8). The majority of those who did return in Burkina Faso and Nigeria came back in less than four years. In contrast, in Senegal two-thirds of returnees had spent 15 or more years abroad.[9]

MANAGING MIGRATION

African governments have done little to increase the benefits of migration or reduce the risks migrants face. The potential economic benefits of migration are impaired by the lack of support for migrants in key markets and insufficient flows of information. Migration also has important social implications for African societies that cannot be evaluated purely in economic terms (box 1.3). Subsequent chapters discuss key policy areas where governments can make a difference—remittances, high-skilled migration, and diaspora resources. The remainder of this chapter focuses on the principal challenges African governments face in protecting migrants, managing immigration within Africa, and encouraging greater legal migration to high-income countries.

EXPLOITATION

Migrants may be subject to exploitation by intermediaries and employers. They may suffer physical deprivation during illegal border crossings and be vulnerable to traffickers. The common practice of migration by children and the phenomenon of "child fostering" in West Africa (where children leave home for a period of years) increases the vulnerability of children to traffickers and makes it difficult to identify the victims

Box 1.3 The Social Costs and Benefits of Migration

Migration in Africa has important effects on social issues that cannot be evaluated purely in economic terms. These benefits include their effects on gender roles, family cohesion, and health.

Changes in Gender Roles

Migration shapes values and attitudes toward gender roles within the household (Ghosh 2009). When women move, their role as caregiver changes; as a result, men are more likely to engage in traditionally female activities such as caring for children and the elderly (King and Vullnetari 2006). When men emigrate, women are empowered to take a more prominent part in community decision making, controlling their own income, and expanding their role in the domestic sphere (Deshingkar and Grimm 2005).

Recent migration flows have included a larger number of women who are migrating independently rather than following fathers or husbands (ECA 2006). Migration provides women with new economic opportunities and sometimes escape from a failed marriage, particularly in societies in which divorce is not an option. Interpreting high divorce rates among migrants is not always straightforward. In traditional societies, where divorce is highly uncommon or not possible, migration has been associated with a higher probability of family breakdown. Although protracted separation can take its toll on family cohesion, Lucas (2005) points out that men and women whose marriages were unstable to begin with are more likely to migrate.

Gender differences are apparent in other ways as well. Manuh (2001) finds that Ghanaian men in Canada are more likely than Ghanaian women to return home. For men the attractiveness lies in the opportunity to go back to a patriarchal society; women do not relish losing the independence they have experienced in Canada.

Migration can entail substantial risks for women and children, who often find themselves victims of traffickers. Some research also indicates that migrants' fertility patterns tend to shift toward those of natives of the destination country, either through social adaptation or self-selection of migrants by fertility preferences (Kulu 2005). These changes may affect the broad population in migrant-sending areas.[a]

Effects on Family Cohesion

Migration may spread attitudes and behaviors from democratic host countries to less-democratic sending countries through returning migrants, cross-border communications from diaspora members, and information networks in migrant-sending communities (Perez-Armendariz and Crow 2010). Although the decision to migrate may be made in the interest of household welfare, separation from one's immediate family often entails considerable emotional cost and can erode family structures and relationships (D'Emilio and others 2007). A breakdown of family ties because of emigration can impose significant emotional costs on children (McKenzie and Rapoport 2006).

To some extent, e-mail, Skype, and affordable telephone calls may allow transnational families to thrive even at a distance (UNDP 2009). Recent evidence from Mozambique suggests that migration may also strengthen social networks by enabling households that receive remittances to participate more actively in their communities (Gallego and Mendola 2010). Closer interfamily collaboration can, to some extent, remedy the absence of within-family cohesion and safety nets.

(Box continues on next page)

Box 1.3   The Social Costs and Benefits of Migration *(continued)*

Effect on Spread of HIV/AIDS and Other Diseases

Several studies have focused on the link between migration and the rapid spread of HIV/AIDS in different parts of Africa (Decosas and others 1995; Lurie and others 2000; Brummer 2002). Several studies have shown that migrant laborers tend to have higher HIV infection rates than nonmigrants (UNFPA 2006).[b] Some researchers contend that South Africa has been turned into an AIDS hot spot primarily because of the nature and magnitude of circular labor migration in the region (Barnett and Whiteside 2002). HIV prevalence has been observed to rise with migration, a situation exacerbated by laws, regulations, and policies that present obstacles to effective HIV prevention, treatment, care, and support for migrants (UNAIDS 2008). Temporary circular migration also increases the risk of family breakdown, the fragmentation of social networks, and psychosocial stress (Kahn and others 2003). The effects of migration on tuberculosis and pneumoconiosis have been documented in Lesotho, Malawi, Mozambique, South Africa, and Zambia (Packard 1989; Leger 1992).

---

a. Fargues (2006) finds that fertility patterns in Egypt, Morocco, and Turkey were influenced by fertility patterns in destination countries (Western Europe versus the Persian Gulf). Beine, Docquier, and Schiff (2009) find that a 1 percent decrease in the fertility norm in the destination country reduces fertility rates in the origin country by about 0.3 percent.

b. In a detailed study by Kane and others (1993), 27 percent of male Senegalese migrants were HIV positive compared with 1 percent of nonmigrant men from the same area. Migration from neighboring countries was observed to contribute to a rise in HIV infections and AIDS cases in Mali (World Bank 1993).

---

of abuse.[10] A range of coercive and misleading practices are used in the trafficking of women, which can be compounded by rules in destination countries that leave women in the power of their employers. Inadequate legislation, poor enforcement, flawed or nonexistent birth registration systems, and social attitudes make trafficking difficult to combat.

The absence of domestic antitrafficking legislation in several countries offers law enforcement agencies little incentive to pursue criminal syndicates (Martens, Pieczkowski, and van Vuuren-Smyth 2003). Stricter enforcement of existing laws and the enactment of new laws could help control trafficking, but law enforcement is only part of the answer. Some countries have initiated programs to protect children from traffickers. To fight trafficking, in 2002 Burkina Faso introduced a new travel document that requires the name of the adult accompanying a fostered child and the adult who is to shelter the child (Wouterse and van den Berg 2004). Save the Children developed a program in Burkina Faso and Mali to provide children with alternative economic activities and training in their home villages. In general, addressing the root causes of child migration is likely to be more successful than attempts to regulate the employment of children away from home (Delap, Ouedraogo, and Sogoba 2005).

Governments could enhance protection of potential victims by maintaining lists of legitimate recruitment agencies, publicizing the terrible experiences of victims and the kinds of offers that might leave migrants vulnerable to traffickers, assisting parents in obtaining information on child-fostering opportunities, and assisting potential migrants to investigate the legitimacy of offers. Information campaigns could also be used to change public attitudes toward the exploitation of women and children.

A few African governments have assisted potential emigrants by providing information on migration opportunities and counseling them about the risks involved in migration. Ethiopia, Kenya, and Senegal provide predeparture orientation seminars to inform migrants about potential abuses. The Ethiopian government has also established an office to regulate private recruitment agencies, which are required to obtain a one-year, renewable license, to report the status of their work, and to submit to audits to ensure that workers are not being cheated by the agencies or foreign employers.[11] Overall, however, African governments have invested only limited resources in protecting migrants. In contrast, agencies in several Asian countries have been created to promote and regulate migration (Wongboonsin 2003). Passing legislation is not enough; it must be accompanied by enforcement of laws that protect migrants.

A few African countries restrict the right of women to emigrate, in part as a means of protecting them.[12] These laws actually increase vulnerability to trafficking, by forcing some women to migrate illegally and limiting their ability to call on the authorities for help (Black, Hilker, and Pooley 2004).

Bilateral agreements between origin and destination countries can be used to protect migrants. For example, some African countries have entered into agreements with France to enable their workers to receive benefits under French social safety net provisions (see, for example, the discussion of Senegal in Ammassari 2005). Algeria, Morocco, and Tunisia have entered into agreements with the main destination countries to ensure that emigrants are provided social security and to shield them against racism and xenophobia (Musette 2006). But African countries have only limited ability to influence the immigration policies of high-income destination countries.

Destination countries can also help protect migrants. In the Middle East, rules that treat migrants who leave their job—in particular women who leave their work as domestic helpers—as illegal aliens increase migrants' vulnerability to physical abuse and exploitation. In some countries, migrants may not understand or be aware of the terms of the contracts they are forced to sign on arrival, leaving them at the mercy of employers through prohibitions on leaving the house without permission, heavy penalties for quitting their jobs, or requirements that large debts to traffickers must be worked off before leaving. The regulation of recruitment and the monitoring of working conditions by destination countries would help curb abuse of migrants.

MANAGING IMMIGRATION WITHIN AFRICA

Limited resources, weak public institutions, and long land borders severely impede the control of migration in many African countries, resulting in large numbers of undocumented migrants. Although African countries generally have laws regulating who may immigrate, such laws are often enforced only at formal entry places, such as airports and ocean ports, and are easily evaded by migrants who take informal routes from contiguous countries. The large informal sector in most African economies means that it is difficult to regulate immigrants' participation in the domestic economy.[13] In South Africa, many immigrants remain undocumented because of the considerable cost and time required to be regularized, even with the support of an employer.[14]

In some respects, the ineffectiveness of immigration restrictions may have a positive impact on development by permitting migration. Even where income differences between countries are not great, cross-border migration can improve welfare by diversifying income sources, facilitating trade, and exploiting differences in seasonal patterns. The West African Long-Term Perspective Study (WALTPS) concludes that the ability of West Africa to increase its agricultural production at the same rate as population growth may be attributable in part to migration to areas with high agricultural potential. The artisanal marine fishing industry in West Africa is thriving because of the ease of crossing borders at sea (Odotei 2006). In some cases (for example, migration between Ghana and Togo and between Benin and Nigeria), undocumented migration simply reflects uncontrolled but generally accepted movements across borders set by European colonial powers that divide ethnic groups accustomed to close communication (Adepoju 2005).

Some African countries do experience difficulties stemming from their inability to manage migration. Undocumented migration may result in large numbers of residents being perceived as foreigners, who often live in lower-income urban neighborhoods. Large numbers of undocumented immigrants may contribute to lawlessness and can undercut attempts to regulate labor market conditions and protect workers. Martin (2010) notes that cash grants in South Africa designed to support poor workers' incomes are evaded by hiring undocumented immigrants, who can become the focus of random violence and police harassment. Mass expulsions of immigrants—from Ghana in 1969, Nigeria in 1983, and Côte d'Ivoire early in the past decade—resulted in economic disruptions and severe hardships.[15]

Coping with undocumented immigration involves extremely difficult social choices that have confounded governments in both rich and poor countries. At a minimum, governments should avoid violent or exploitative practices, such as mass expulsions or tolerance of corrupt officials who prey on undocumented immigrants. Some countries where migrants have suffered from violence have made efforts to restore social peace. For example, Côte d'Ivoire's 2008 anti-xenophobia law imposes sanctions on conduct that incites violence; South Africa set up the "No to Xenophobia" emergency phone line following violence in May 2008 (UNDP 2009).

ENCOURAGING LEGAL MIGRATION

Temporary migration programs may help reconcile the desires of migrants and destination country employers to reap economic benefits with the broader society's concern over the social implications of permanent immigration. A survey by the OECD (2007) found that programs in 57 of 92 countries using temporary employment schemes were managed through bilateral agreements. The Global Forum on Migration and Development (2008) outlined a set of best-practice recommendations for such agreements. Topics covered include matching the demand for and supply of workers, involving all stakeholders in recruitment, encouraging circular migration, recognizing skills and qualifications, respecting workers' rights and protecting them from high transportation and recruitment costs, ensuring equal access for and treatment of women, providing appropriate training, and encouraging return by easing reintegration and allowing for repeat migration. The close supervision of employers is essential to the success of such programs. As migrants' authorization to work in the destination country is linked to a specific employer, it is important to monitor working hours, compensation, and conditions to avoid exploitation. Reliance on private intermediaries also requires close monitoring to ensure that migrants are treated fairly.

Some temporary migration programs have had success in encouraging legal, temporary immigration with minimal visa overstays. However, the supervision required to limit overstays and ensure against exploitation of migrants means that successful programs cover only a small number of migrants (World Bank 2006). Morocco's agreement with Spain, for example, allowed for the movement of only 700 workers at a time when there were more than 200,000 Moroccan workers in Spain (Collyer 2004).

Box 1.4 The Evolution of European Policies toward Migration from Africa

The need to reduce undocumented migration has become a dominant theme of European policy making toward Africa since the early 1990s, particularly in the Mediterranean states—France, Greece, Italy, Portugal, Spain, and, more recently, Malta. The approach to undocumented migration has evolved over the past two decades, from bilateral readmission agreements with origin and transit states (which proved difficult to ratify, because they were politically unpopular in the origin countries) to policies aimed at preventing conflicts, supporting peacekeeping, tying foreign aid to development strategies directed at the root causes of emigration, and imposing migration-related conditions on trade concessions and debt forgiveness.[a] The European Commission has proposed negotiating "mobility partnerships" with third countries, with a view to meeting labor shortages through short-term movements of low-skilled workers, as well as circular migration programs covering the highly skilled to mitigate the problem of brain drain and foster skills transfers.

The Africa–EU Migration, Mobility and Employment (MME) partnership was launched in 2007 to improve the prospects for employment in Africa and the management of migration flows between Africa and the European Union (Africa–EU MME Partnership 2010). The first action plan under the joint strategy, covering 2008–10, was adopted in 2007. A new action plan for managing migration during 2011–13 was endorsed at the Africa–EU Heads of States Summit in Libya in November 2010. Examples of initiatives under the partnership include the following:

- the African Remittances Institute, which aims to facilitate cheaper, faster, and more secure remittance flows from Europe to Africa
- the Human Trafficking Initiative, designed to strengthen the protection of migrants and enhance prosecution of human trafficking in line with the Ouagadougou Action Plan
- the Diaspora Outreach Initiative, which builds on existing work to transfer skills, capacity, and knowledge to Africa
- the Observatory on Migration, established to create a network of researchers and research centers to provide policy makers, civil society, and the public with reliable and harmonized data on migration
- the Pan-African University's Nyerere Program, which aims to contribute to high-level African human resource development and retention while supporting intra-African academic mobility
- the Centre for Migration Management and Information in Mali (with support from the Economic Community of West African States [ECOWAS], France, Spain, and the European Commission)
- work on an African Guarantee Fund (by the African Development Bank and Spain) to increase access to finance for small and medium enterprises.

a. The readmission agreement signed by Italy and Egypt in January 2007 allowed Egypt to benefit from a bilateral debt-swap agreement, as well as from trade concessions for its agricultural produce and larger entry quotas for Egyptian nationals in Italy (Cassarino 2009). The bilateral agreement on the circulation of persons and readmission concluded in July 2006 between Algeria and the United Kingdom was part of a round of negotiations that extended to issues such as energy security, the fight against terrorism, and police cooperation.

A few African countries have entered into bilateral agreements with European nations to gain acceptance of some legal migration and support for development in return for cooperation in the return of undocumented migrants. Italy negotiated readmission agreements with Egypt, Morocco, and Tunisia by offering cooperating partner countries increases in legal admissions. France, Greece, Italy, and Spain have entered into agreements that link readmission to various incentives (Cassarino 2009). Negotiations are underway between some West African governments and France, Italy, Portugal, and Spain to establish temporary migration programs as a means of discouraging undocumented migration. In general, Europe's policies toward reducing undocumented migration from North Africa through bilateral agreements have evolved significantly over the past few decades (box 1.4).

As return to one's nation of origin is a fundamental right recognized in UN declarations and few countries have limits on return, the leverage that origin countries gain by promising to facilitate return is minimal. Some of the agreements with North African countries go farther, however, by including commitments to strengthen immigration controls to limit undocumented migration from Sub-Saharan Africa (a large portion of which is assumed to be in transit to Europe). Morocco and Tunisia, for example, have passed laws with severe penalties for assisting undocumented migration (de Haas 2007). These efforts may have resulted in human rights violations, including the return of refugees to countries where they face persecution and the holding of refugees and undocumented migrants in detention camps (Adepoju, van Noorloos, and Zoomers 2009). Return from transit countries is a contentious issue between West African countries and countries in North Africa.

ANNEX 1A

Table 1A.1   Net Migration Rates in Africa per 1,000 People, 1975–2010

Region/country	1975–1980	1980–85	1985–1990	1990–95	1995–2000	2000–05	2005–10
Eastern Africa	−1.09	−0.65	0.39	−1.56	1.2	−0.9	−1.1
Burundi	−2.83	4.33	−0.11	−8.6	−13.02	5.5	8.1
Comoros	5.68	−2.14	−1.83	0	0	−3.4	−3.1
Djibouti	56.77	5.65	38.49	−10.95	6.57	0.0	—
Eritrea	0	0	0	−22.42	−0.23	11.3	2.3
Ethiopia	−11.77	3.21	3.54	3.35	−0.15	−1.0	−0.8
Kenya	−0.04	0.04	0.05	1.74	−0.15	0.2	−1
Madagascar	−0.71	−0.17	−0.13	−0.09	−0.04	−0.1	−0.1
Malawi	−0.35	−0.3	20.95	−17.13	−0.93	−0.5	−0.3
Mauritius	−4.41	−5.45	−5.77	−1.28	−0.35	0.0	—
Mozambique	1.54	−5.89	−19.46	9.79	1.01	−0.2	−0.2
Reunion	−9.54	0.72	−0.62	2.68	2.45	—	—
Rwanda	−2.18	−3.96	0.48	−57.56	61.49	0.1	0.3
Somalia	59.79	−25.37	−16.06	−21.86	1.71	−5.1	−5.6
Uganda	−2.7	−1.56	3.11	1.44	−0.6	0.0	−0.9
Tanzania	−0.25	0.36	0.57	4.16	−1.25	−1.9	−1.4
Zambia	0.19	1.51	0.85	−0.16	1.74	−1.5	−1.4
Zimbabwe	−3.08	3.74	2.71	−3.28	−0.25	−11.2	−11.1
Central Africa	0.2	−0.43	−0.09	3.71	−3.27	0.2	−0.2
Angola	0.58	6.12	−3.41	2.83	−2.07	2.3	0.9
Cameroon	1.45	−1.05	0.46	−0.08	0	−0.1	−0.2
Central African Republic	−0.09	3.25	−2.94	2.38	0.64	−2.3	0.2
Chad	−5.37	−3.14	1.53	0.63	2.73	4.8	−1.4
Congo, Rep.	0	0.11	0.18	1.05	2.6	0.2	−2.8
Congo, Dem. Rep.	0.77	−2.31	0.43	5.9	−6.4	−0.9	−0.3
Equatorial Guinea	−26.85	48.77	0	0	0	5.3	3.1
Gabon	6.17	5.31	4.53	3.88	2.43	1.5	0.7
São Tomé and Príncipe	−2.53	−10.68	−4.42	−3.24	−2.86	−9.6	−8.8
Southern Africa	−0.05	0.73	0.39	0.25	−0.26	2.4	2.4
Botswana	−2.05	−1.66	−1.54	−1.01	−0.86	2.2	1.6
Lesotho	−3.27	−2.27	−7.28	−7.37	−4.15	−3.7	−3.5
Namibia	−9.16	−5.39	11.78	0.46	2.27	−0.1	−0.1
South Africa	0.54	1.16	0.25	0.81	−0.16	3.0	2.8
Swaziland	−2.95	0.33	5.98	−8.37	−109	−8.4	−1

ANNEX 1A

Table 1A.1 Net Migration Rates in Africa per 1,000 People, 1975–2010 *(continued)*

Region/country	1975–1980	1980–85	1985–1990	1990–95	1995–2000	2000–05	2005–10
Western Africa	0.4	−0.8	−0.71	−0.71	−0.45	−0.4	−0.6
Benin	−4.85	−3.75	−3.23	1.84	−3.2	2.7	1.2
Burkina Faso	−6.73	−5.98	−3.07	−2.66	−2.3	1.6	−0.9
Cape Verde	−17.37	−11.11	−10.1	−4.65	−2.42	−5.5	−5.1
Côte d'Ivoire	11.07	9.11	4.35	2.98	0.8	−3.7	−1.4
Gambia, The	7.29	7.01	10.53	8.78	7.42	4.4	1.8
Ghana	−10.77	3.4	−0.42	0.49	−1.19	0.1	−0.4
Guinea	1.55	−1.52	2.45	10.41	−7.18	−9.7	−6.1
Guinea-Bissau	17.45	−0.04	0.35	3.63	−1.68	0.2	−1.6
Liberia	1.38	0	−34.17	−26.51	35.89	4.1	13.3
Mali	−5.25	−5.81	−5.65	−5.37	−5.1	−2.4	−3.2
Mauritania	−1.28	−1.88	−3.15	−1.36	0.8	2.1	0.6
Niger	−0.71	−0.81	−0.52	0.12	−0.12	−0.5	−0.4
Nigeria	2.87	−1.94	−0.23	−0.21	−0.18	−0.3	−0.4
Senegal	0.78	0.35	0	−1.79	−1.13	−1.9	−1.7
Sierra Leone	0	0	3.29	−18.68	−5.19	14.4	2.2
Togo	−8.36	3.64	0.06	−6.67	6.06	−0.1	−0.2
Northern Africa	−1	0.3	−2	−1.5	−1.7	−1.6	−0.7
Algeria	0.1	0.8	−0.6	−0.4	−1	−0.9	−0.8
Egypt, Arab Rep.	−4	−1.8	−2.1	−1.6	−1.6	−0.8	−0.8
Libya	8.6	10.7	0.5	0.4	0.4	0.5	0.6
Morocco	−1.9	−0.5	−2.1	−3.5	−3.6	−3.7	−2.7
Sudan	3.5	3.7	−3.6	−1.2	−1.4	−2.9	0.7
Tunisia	−0.6	−0.7	−0.6	−1	−1.2	−1.7	−0.4
Sub-Saharan Africa	−1.35	−2.72	−0.35	−1.53	−0.94	−0.4	0.125
Africa	−0.4	−0.4	−0.6	−0.5	−0.6	−0.6	−0.5

Source: United Nations Population Division.

NOTES

1. The main data set used was the bilateral migration matrix compiled by the World Bank (2011), which takes stock of migrants by origin as well as destination. The analysis also relied on data provided by the United Nations Population Division (UNPD 2009), the Ghana Living Standard Measurement Survey (Ghana Statistical Service 2008), and household migration surveys collected in 2009 through the Africa Migration Project.

2. Sub-Saharan Africa's working-age population is projected to increase by 699 million between 2005 and 2050. Over the same period, the working-age population of Europe and North America is projected to fall by a total of 100 million (Koettl 2010).

3. Hatton and Willamson (2003) estimate a regression model to capture the determinants of net migration for Africa. Their findings suggest that movements of refugees; labor market conditions, specifically the wage gap; and the supply of labor, particularly among the young, explain a significant part of the variation in net migration rates in Africa.

4. The data for net migration are based on residual estimates from demographic accounting exercises compiled by the UN Population Division using census data.

5. See also UNDP (2009), Ratha and Shaw (2007), and Page and Plaza (2006) for useful discussions of intra-African migration.

6. The purpose of the discussion of figures 1.5–1.7 is to compare migration patterns with income levels and colonial ties. There is no claim that these are causal relationships. Establishment of causality would require a model that takes into account the main determinants of migration.

7. Other determinants of migration were not controlled for; this association may be driven by other variables (such as distance). It is also possible that the relationship is biased because errors in measuring migration may be correlated with per capita income.

8. Earlier studies on Africa include Lucas (1985), Bigsten (1994), and Hoddinott (1994). Azam and Gubert (2006) studied internal as well as international migration in Mali in the Senegal River Valley.

9. See Azam and Gubert (2005) for discussion of the pattern of migration in rural Senegal.

10. In Burkina Faso, for example, 9.5 percent of children ages 6–17 do not live with their parents; 29 percent of these children live abroad, mostly in Côte d'Ivoire (Pizarro 2006).

11. Information on Ethiopia is based on an interview with Ato Abebe Haile, Director of the Employment Service Promotion Directorate, Ministry of Labour and Social Affairs, and a presentation by Minelik Alemuk, Director General for International Law and Consular Affairs of the Ministry of Foreign Affairs of Ethiopia.

12. For example, a married women requires her husband's permission to travel abroad in Algeria (applies only to women under age 18), the Democratic Republic of Congo, Gabon, and Uganda (when traveling with children). Unmarried women under the age of 21 require their father's permission to travel in

Egypt. Libya, Swaziland, Sudan, and Yemen impose restrictions on both married and unmarried women (McKenzie 2005).

13. The International Labour Organization (ILO 2002) estimates that the informal sector accounted for 72 percent of total employment in Sub-Saharan Africa (78 percent if South Africa is excluded).

14. Employers wishing to hire foreign workers through legal procedures need to obtain the services of a recruitment company, which will recruit in the country of origin after a "no-objection certificate" has been obtained from the Ministry of Home Affairs. Alternatively, employers may support the regularization of undocumented foreign workers whom they may already have employed for a few months, but the law requires that applicants return to their home countries before work permits are granted.

15. See UNDP (2009) on Côte d'Ivoire; Lassailly-Jacob, Boyer, and Brachet (2006) on Nigeria; and de Haas (2007) on Ghana.

BIBLIOGRAPHY

Adams, R. H., Jr. 2009. "An Overview of Data Contained in the 2005/06 Ghana Living Standards Survey (GLSSS 5) (Sub-sample) on Migration and Remittances." World Bank, Washington, DC.

Adepoju, Aderanti. 2005. *Creating a Borderless West Africa: Constraints and Prospects for Intra-Regional Migration*. United Nations Educational, Scientific and Cultural Organization (UNESCO), Paris.

Adepoju, Aderanti, Femke van Noorloos, and Annelies Zoomers. 2009. "Europe's Migration Agreements with Migrant-Sending Countries in the Global South: A Critical Review." *International Migration* 48 (3): 42–75.

Africa–EU Migration, Mobility and Employment (MME) Partnership. 2010. *Meeting Report*. Senior Officials Meeting, Brussels, September 15–17. http://www.africa-eu-partnership.org/.

Ammassari, Savina. 2005. *Gestion des migrations et politiques de développement: optimiser les benefices de la migration internationale en Afrique de l'ouest*. Geneva: International Labour Office.

Azam, J. P., and F. Gubert. 2006. "Migrants' Remittances and the Household in Africa: A Review of the Evidence." *Journal of African Economies* (Supplement 2): 426–62.

Barnett, Tony, and Alan Whiteside. 2002. *AIDS in the 21st Century: Disease and Globalisation*. London: Palgrave McMillan.

Beine, Michel, Frédéric Docquier, and Maurice Schiff. 2009. "International Migration, Transfers of Norms and Home Country Fertility." World Bank Policy Research Working Paper 4925, Washington, DC.

Bigsten, A. 1994. "The Circular Migration of Smallholders in Kenya." *Journal of African Economies* 5 (1): 1–20.

Black, Richard, Lyndsay McLean Hilker, and Claire Pooley. 2004. "Migration and Pro-Poor Policy in East Africa." Development Research Centre on Migration, Globalisation and Poverty, University of Sussex, United Kingdom.

Brummer, D. 2002. "Labor Migration and HIV/AIDS in Southern Africa." International Organization for Migration, Regional Office for Southern Africa, Pretoria, South Africa.

Cassarino, Jean-Pierre. 2009. "Dealing with Unbalanced Reciprocities: Cooperation on Readmission and Implications." In *Unbalanced Reciprocities: Readmission Agreements*, ed. Jean-Pierre Cassarino. Special Edition of Viewpoints, Middle East Institute, Washington, DC. http://ssrn.com/abstract=1730633.

Collyer, Michael. 2004. "The Development Impact of Temporary International Labour Migration on Southern Mediterranean Sending Countries." DRC Working Paper T6, Development Research Centre on Migration, Globalisation and Poverty, University of Sussex, United Kingdom.

Decosas, J., F. Kane, J. Anarfi, K. D. Sodji, and H. U. Wagner. 1995. "Migration and AIDS." *Lancet* 346 (8978): 826–28.

de Haas, Hein. 2007. "The Myth of Invasion: Irregular Migration from West Africa to the Mahgreb and the European Union." International Migration Institute, Oxford, United Kingdom.

Delap, Emily, Boureima Ouedraogo, and Bakary Sogoba. 2005. "Developing Alternatives to the Worst Forms of Child Labour in Mali and Burkina Faso." Save the Children, London.

D'Emilio, A. L., B. Cordero, B. Bainvel, C. Skoog, D. Comini, J. Gough, M. Dias, R. Saab, and T. Kilbane. 2007. "The Impact of International Migration: Children Left Behind in Selected Countries of Latin America and the Caribbean." United Nations Children's Fund (UNICEF), Division of Policy and Planning, New York.

Deshingkar, P., and S. Grimm. 2005. "International Migration and Development: A Global Perspective." Migration Research Series 19, International Organization for Migration, Geneva.

Docquier, Frédéric, and Abdeslam Marfouk. 2004. "Measuring the International Mobility of Skilled Workers (1990–2000). Release 1.0." World Bank Policy Research Working Paper 3381, Washington, DC.

Docquier, Frédéric, and Maurice Schiff. 2009. "Measuring Skilled Emigration Rates: The Case of Small States." IZA Discussion Paper 3388, Institute for the Study of Labor, Bonn.

ECA (Economic Commission for Africa). 2006. *International Migration and Development: Implications for Africa*. Addis Ababa: Economic Commission for Africa. http://www.uneca.org/eca_resources/Publications/MigrationReport2006.pdf.

Ek, R., and A. Karadawi. 1991. "Implications of Refugee Flows on Political Stability in the Sudan." *Ambio* 20 (5).

Gallego, J. M., and M. Mendola. 2010. "Labor Migration and Social Networks Participation: Evidence from Southern Mozambique." Working Paper 183, Department of Economics. University of Milano-Bicocca, Milan.

Ghana Statistical Service. 2008. *Ghana Living Standards Survey: Report of the Fifth Round*. Accra. http://www.statsghana.gov.gh/docfiles/glss5_report.pdf.

Ghosh, J. 2009. "Migration and Gender Empowerment: Recent Trends and Emerging Issues." Human Development Research Paper 4, United Nations Development Programme, New York.

Giesbert, L. 2007. "Seeking Opportunties: Migration as an Income Diversification Strategy of Households in Kakamega District in Kenya." GIGA Research Programme: Transformation in the Process of Globalization 58, German Institute of Global Area Studies, Hamburg.

Global Forum on Migration and Development. 2008. *Compendium of Good Practice Policy Elements in Bilateral Temporary Labour Arrangements*. Geneva.

Hatton, T. J., and J. G. Williamson. 2003. "Demographic and Economic Pressure on Emigration out of Africa." *Scandinavian Journal of Economics* 105 (3): 465–86.

———. 2009. "Emigration in the Long Run: Evidence from Two Global Centuries." *Asian Pacific Economic Literature* 23 (2): 7–28.

Hoddinott, J. 1994. " A Model of Migration and Remittances Applied to Western Africa."*Oxford Economic Papers* 46 (3): 459–76.

Hugo, Graeme. 2008. "Migration, Development and Environment." Draft paper for the research workshop "Migration and the Environment: Developing a Global Research Agenda," Munich, April 16–18. http://www.ciesin.columbia.edu/repository/pern/papers/hugo_statement.pdf.

ILO (International Labour Organization). 2002. "ILO Compendium of Official Statistics on Employment in the Informal Sector." STAT Working Paper 1, Geneva.

Kahn, K., M. Collison, S. Tollman, B. Wolff, M. Garenne, and S. Clark. 2003. "Health Consequences of Migration: Evidence from South Africa's Rural Northeast (Agincourt)." Paper prepared for conference "African Migration in Comparative Perspective," Johannesburg, June 4–7.

Kane, F., M. Alary, I. Ndoye, A. M. Coll, S. M'boup, A. Gueye, P. J. Kanki, and J. R. Joly. 1993. "Temporary Expatriation Is Related to HIV-1 Infection in Rural Senegal." *AIDS* 7 (9): 1261–65.

King, R., and J. Vullnetari. 2006. "Orphan Pensioners and Migrating Grandparents: The Impact of Mass Migration on Older People in Rural Albania." *Aging and Society* 26 (5): 783–816.

Koettl, J. 2010. "Prospects for Management of Migration between Europe and the Middle East and North Africa." World Bank, Middle East and North Africa Region, Poverty Reduction and Economic Management Network, Washington, DC.

Konseiga, A. 2005. "New Patterns of Migration in West Africa." Stichproben 8/2005, Vienna.

Kulu, H. 2005. "Migration and Fertility: Competing Hypothesis Re-examined." *European Journal of Population* 21 (1): 51–87.

Lassailly-Jacob, Veronique, Florence Boyer, and Julien Brachet. 2006. "South-South Migration: Example of Sub-Saharan Africa." European Parliament, Brussels.

Leger, J. P. 1992. "Occupational Disease in South African Mines: A Neglected Epidemic?" *South African Medical Journal* 81 (4): 197–201.

Lucas, R. E. B. 2005. *International Migration and Economic Development: Lessons from Low-Income Countries.* Expert Group on Development Issues. Northampton, MA: Edward Elgar Publishing.

———. 2006. "Migration and Economic Development in Africa: A Review of Evidence." *Journal of African Economies* (Supplement 2): 337–95.

Lurie, M., B. Williams, A. W. Sturm, G. Garnett, K. Zuma, J. Gittlesohn, and K. Abdool. 2000. "Migration and the Spread of HIV in Southern Africa: Prevalence and Risk Factors among Migrants and Their Partners and Non-migrants and Their Partners." Presented at the International Conference on AIDS, Durban, South Africa. July 9–14.

Manuh, Takyiwaa. 2001 "Ghanaian Migrants in Toronto, Canada: Care of Kin and Gender." *Institute of African Studies Research Review* 17 (2): 17–26, University of Ghana, Legon.

Martens, Jonathan, Maciej "Mac" Pieczkowski, and Bernadette van Vuuren-Smyth. 2003. "Seduction, Sale and Slavery: Trafficking in Women and Children for Sexual Exploitation in Southern Africa." International Organization of Migration, Regional Office for Southern Africa, Pretoria, South Africa.

Martin, Philip. 2010. "Africa: Regions South Africa." *Migration News* 17 (October): 4.

McKenzie, David J. 2005. "Paper Walls Are Easier to Tear Down: Passport Costs and Legal Barriers to Emigration." World Bank Policy Research Working Paper 3783, Washington, DC.

McKenzie, D., and H. Rapoport. 2006. "Can Migration Reduce Educational Attainment? Evidence from Mexico." Policy Research Paper 3952, World Bank, Washington, DC.

Musette, M. S. 2006. "Systems of Statistical Information on Migrant Workers in Central Maghreb." ILO International Migration Paper 76E, International Labour Office, Geneva.

Odotei, I. 2006. "Fat Money, Thin Body: Between Vulnerability and Survival in the Era of HIV/AIDS: The Case of Migrant Fishermen and Fish Mongers." In *Sex and Gender in an Era of AIDS: Ghana at the Turn of the Millennium*, ed. C. Oppong, M. Y. Oppong, and I. K. Odotei. Accra: Sub-Saharan Publishers.

OECD (Organisation for Economic Co-operation and Development). 2007. *Policy Coherence for Development 2007: Migration and Developing Countries*. Paris.

Packard, R. M. 1989. *White Plague, Black Labor: Tuberculosis and the Political Economy of Health and Disease in South Africa*. Berkeley: University of California Press.

Page, John, and Sonia Plaza. 2006. "Migration Remittances and Development: A Review of Global Evidence." *Journal of African Economies* 15 (Suppl 2): 245–336.

Perez-Armendariz, C., and D. Crow. 2010. "Do Migrants Remit Democracy? International Migration, Political Beliefs, and Behaviour in Mexico." *Comparative Political Studies* 43 (1): 119–48.

Pizarro, Gabriela Rodriguez. 2006. "Specific Groups and Individuals: Migrant Workers." E/CN.4/2006/73/Add.2, UN Economic and Social Council, Commission on Human Rights, New York.

Plaza, Sonia, Mario Navarette, and Dilip Ratha. 2011. "Migration and Remittances Household Surveys in Sub-Saharan Africa: Methodological Aspects and Main Findings." World Bank Development Economics Prospects Group, Washington, DC.

Puerto-Gomez, Margarita, and Asger Christensen. 2010. *The Impacts of Refugees on Neighboring Countries: A Development Challenge*. World Bank, Human Security Report Project, Washington, DC.

Ratha, Dilip. 2003. "Workers' Remittances: An External and Stable Source of External Development Finance." In *Global Development Finance*, 157–76. Washington, DC: World Bank.

Ratha, Dilip, and William Shaw. 2007. "South-South Migration and Remittances." World Bank Working Paper 102, Washington, DC.

Russell, S. S., K. Jacobsen, and W. D. Stanley. 1990. "International Migration and Development in Sub-Saharan Africa." Discussion Paper 101, World Bank, Washington, DC.

Shaw, W. 2007. "Migration in Africa: A Review of Economic Literature on International Migration in 10 Countries." World Bank, Development Economics Prospects Group, Washington, DC.

Shinn, D. 2008. "African Migration and the Brain Drain." Paper presented at the Institute for African Studies and Slovenia Global Action Ljubljana, June 20.

Todaro, M. 1969. "A Model of Labor Migration and Urban Unemployment in Developing Countries." *American Economic Review* 59 (1): 101–14.

UNAIDS (Joint United Nations Programme on HIV/AIDS). 2008. *2008 Report on the Global AIDS Epidemic*. Geneva: UNAIDS.

UNDP (United Nations Development Programme). 1994. "A Model of Migration and Remittances Applied to Western Africa." *Oxford Economic Papers* 46 (3): 459–76.

———. 2009. *Human Development Report. Overcoming Barriers: Human Mobility and Development*. New York: UNDP.

UNFPA (United Nations Population Fund). 2006. *State of the World Population*. New York: UNFPA.

UNHCR (United Nations High Commissioner for Refugees). 2010. "Global Trends." Division of Programme Support and Management, Geneva. http://www.unhcr.org/4c11f0be9.html.

Wongboonsin, Patcharawalai. 2003. "Comparative Migration Policies in the ESCAP Region." In *Migration Patterns and Polices in the Asia Pacific Region*. Asian Population Studies Series 160, United Nations, Economic and Social Commission for Asia and the Pacific, New York.

World Bank. 1993. "Mali: Assessment of Living Conditions." Report 11842-MLI, Washington, DC.

———. 2006. *Global Economic Prospects: Economic Implications of Remittances and Migration*. Washington, DC: World Bank.

———. 2008. *Migration and Remittances Fact Book 2008*. Washington, DC: World Bank.

———. 2009. *World Development Indicators*. Washington, DC: World Bank.

———. 2011. *Migration and Remittances Fact Book 2011*. Washington, DC: World Bank.

Wouterse, Fleur, and Marrit van den Berg. 2004. "Migration for Survival or Accumulation: Evidence from Burkina Faso." Wageningen University and Research Center, Mansholt Graduate School of Social Sciences, Wageningen, the Netherlands.

2

Migrant Remittances

Remittances are the central and most tangible link between migration and development (Russell 1992; Ratha 2007). Remittance inflows to Africa quadrupled between 1990 and 2010, reaching nearly $40 billion in 2010, equivalent to 2.6 percent of Africa's gross domestic product (GDP) in 2009 (see table 2.1). After foreign direct investment (FDI), remittances are the continent's largest source of foreign inflows. Migrant remittances contribute to international reserves, help finance imports, and improve the current account position of recipient countries. They are associated with reductions in poverty, improved health and education outcomes, and increased business investments. Although the limited reach of intermediaries in rural areas, lack of effective competition, and inadequate financial and regulatory infrastructure contribute to high remittance costs and the prevalence of informal channels (especially for intra-African remittances), the rapid adoption of innovative money transfer and branchless banking technologies are increasing access to remittances and broader financial services for the poor.

This chapter draws on extensive literature and new surveys of households, central banks, and remittance service providers conducted in select African countries and key migrant-destination countries as part of the Africa Migration Project.[1] It discusses the economic implications of migrant remittances for African countries and recipient households, examines the challenges and opportunities for remittance markets in Africa, and makes policy recommendations for better leveraging remittances and thus promoting development in Africa.

The chapter presents three main findings.

- At the macro level, remittances are a large and stable source of external finance for African countries that improves their creditworthiness and access to capital. In many African countries, these flows exceed

FDI, portfolio equity, and debt flows; in some countries they are equal in size to official aid. Remittances tend to be more stable than other sources of foreign exchange, and they are often countercyclical, helping sustain consumption and investment during downturns and performing the role of a shock absorber. These beneficial effects of remittances improve sovereign creditworthiness and the external debt sustainability of African countries. Securitization of future remittance flows can increase the access of African banks and firms to international capital markets; it can also be used to fund longer-term development projects, such as infrastructure and low-income housing. Using remittances for such purposes should be accompanied by prudential debt management and efforts to ensure medium-term sustainability of external debt.

- Remittance receipts are associated with reductions in poverty, increased household resources devoted to investment, and improved health and education outcomes. Migrant remittances help smooth household consumption and act as a form of insurance for households facing shocks to their income and livelihood caused by drought, famine, and other natural disasters. Household surveys in Africa show that remittance-receiving households have greater access to secondary and tertiary education, health services, information and communication technology, and banking than households that do not receive remittances. The surveys also reveal that the average amount of remittances received by households from outside Africa is larger than that of intraregional and domestic remittances. A significant part of all remittances is spent on human and physical capital investments, such as education, health, land, housing, starting a business, improving farms, and purchasing agricultural equipment.

- Remittance markets in Africa remain relatively underdeveloped in terms of their financial infrastructure and the regulatory environment, but the rapid adoption of innovative money transfer technologies is transforming the landscape for remittances and broader financial services. Sub-Saharan Africa has the highest remittance costs among developing regions and the largest share of informal and unrecorded remittances among developing regions. These costs represent an unnecessary burden on African migrants, reducing the amounts sent and their development impact. In a survey conducted for this study, almost 70 percent of central banks in Sub-Saharan Africa cited high costs as the most important factor inhibiting the use of formal remittance channels. A large share of international remittances to Africa is channeled through a few large international money transfer agencies, which often work in exclusive partnership with African banks and post offices. At the same time, the remittance landscape in Africa is rapidly changing with the introduction of innovative, mobile money transfer and branchless banking technologies. Although adoption of these technologies has been limited largely to domestic money transfers (in part because of concerns about money laundering and terrorist financing related to cross-border remittances), these technologies have the potential to vastly improve access to both remittances and broader financial services, including low-cost savings and credit products, for African migrants and remittance recipients in African countries.

This chapter is organized as follows. The first section discussed the trends and prospects for remittance flows to Africa. The second section examines the implications of remittances for growth and access to external finance. The third section considers the implications of remittances for the welfare of African households, drawing on the global evidence and literature on Africa. The fourth section reviews the nature of remittance markets in Africa, including issues of cost, competition, legal and regulatory environments, and technological innovations. The last section provides policy recommendations.

RECENT REMITTANCE TRENDS AND THE IMPACT OF THE GLOBAL FINANCIAL CRISIS

Remittances have become one of the most significant sources of foreign exchange for African countries. They are likely to remain so despite a slowdown in their growth as a result of the global financial crisis.

SIZE AND IMPORTANCE OF REMITTANCES TO AFRICA

Officially recorded remittance flows to Africa are estimated to have reached $40 billion in 2010 (divided roughly equally between North Africa and Sub-Saharan Africa), almost twice the amount received in 2005 and more than four times the $9.1 billion received in 1990 (table 2.1 and figure 2.1). Although part of the recorded growth of remittances reflects improvements in measurement, the main reasons for the extraordinary level of growth are the increase in emigration from Africa and the rising incomes of African migrants, on the back of a booming global economy before the financial crisis in 2008–10. Remittances to Africa equaled 2.6 percent of GDP in 2009, somewhat more than the 1.9 percent average for all developing countries.

Table 2.1 **Remittances and Other Resource Flows to Africa, 1990–2010**
($ billions, except where otherwise indicated)

Region/resource flow	1990	1995	2000	2005	2007	2008	2009	2010e	Percent of GDP, 2009
Sub-Saharan Africa									
Migrant remittances	1.9	3.2	4.6	9.4	18.6	21.4	20.6	21.5	2.2
Official aid	16.9	17.8	12.1	30.8	32.6	36.0	..	..	3.7
Foreign direct investment	1.2	4.4	6.7	18.1	28.7	37.0	30.2	..	3.2
Private debt and portfolio equity flows	0.6	2.5	4.9	10.6	15.6	−6.5	12.3	..	1.3
North Africa									
Migrant remittances	7.2	7.0	6.6	13.1	18.3	19.8	17.5	18.2	3.3
Official aid	7.2	3.0	2.2	2.5	3.0	3.5	..	..	0.6
Foreign direct investment	1.1	0.9	2.8	9.9	22.5	21.6	14.9	..	2.9
Private debt and portfolio equity flows	−0.1	0.0	1.2	1.7	−3.6	−0.4	−0.5	..	−0.1
All Africa									
Migrant remittances	9.1	10.2	11.3	22.5	36.9	41.2	38.1	39.7	2.6
Official aid	24.1	20.7	14.3	33.2	35.6	39.5	..	..	2.6
Foreign direct investment	2.4	5.3	9.5	28.0	51.1	58.6	45.1	..	3.1
Private debt and portfolio equity flows	0.5	2.5	6.2	12.3	12.0	−6.8	11.8	..	0.8

Source: Authors' calculations based on data from World Development Indicators (December 2010) database.
Note: .. = negligible. e = estimated. Data for official aid as percentage of GDP are for 2008.

Figure 2.1 **Remittances and Other Resource Flows to Africa, 1990–2010**

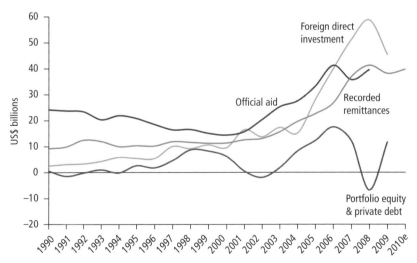

Source: Authors' calculations based on data from World Development Indicators (December 2010) database.
Note: e = estimated.

Recorded remittance flows to the African continent are similar in size to official aid flows. They are several times larger than official aid to North Africa (3.3 percent of GDP versus 0.6 percent of GDP) and two-thirds the size of official aid flows to Sub-Saharan Africa (2.2 percent of GDP versus 3.7 percent of GDP). Remittance flows in many African countries are larger than private capital flows, such as FDI and portfolio debt and equity flows. Private capital flows are more important for South Africa, the largest economy in Sub-Saharan Africa, and for oil and mineral producers (for example, Angola, Gabon, and Sudan) that receive substantial FDI flows. But for many low-income African countries, remittances exceed private investment flows and represent a lifeline to the poor.

A few countries account for a substantial share of remittances to Sub-Saharan Africa and North Africa (see annex table 2A.1). Nigeria's $10 billion equaled about half of all officially recorded remittances to Sub-Saharan Africa in 2010. Other large remittance recipients in dollar terms include Sudan, Kenya, Senegal, South Africa, and Uganda. However, as a share of GDP, the largest recipients are Lesotho (28.5 percent), Togo (10.7 percent), Cape Verde (9.4 percent), Senegal (9.3 percent), and The Gambia (8.2 percent). Egypt and Morocco, the two largest recipients in North Africa in terms of both absolute flows and share of GDP, account for three-quarters of flows to North Africa, followed by Algeria and Tunisia.

These estimates of remittance inflows, based on data officially reported in the International Monetary Fund (IMF) balance of payments statistics, are likely well below the actual volume of remittance flows to Africa. The remittance inflows data reported by country authorities themselves are often higher than the IMF figures. For example, Ghana's central bank reported $1.6 billion in remittance inflows in 2009—more than 10 times the $114 million reported in the IMF balance of payments statistics. Ethiopia reported more than $700 million—about twice the $353 million reported by the IMF. These discrepancies are in part related to the misreporting of migrant remittances with other types of current transfers, such as transfers to nongovernmental organizations and embassies and payments related to small-value-trade transactions.

In addition, only about half of Sub-Saharan African countries report remittance data with any regularity (Irving, Mohapatra, and Ratha 2010); some countries—such as the Central African Republic, the Democratic Republic of Congo, Somalia, and Zimbabwe, all of which are believed to receive significant remittance flows—report no remittance data at all. Even fewer Sub-Saharan African countries report monthly or quarterly data on remittances.[2] Remittance flows through money transfer companies are often captured indirectly, in the reporting of partner banks, for example, but the independent operations of such firms may not be fully captured. Cross-border flows through other institutions, such as post offices, savings cooperatives, microfinance institutions, and emerging channels, such as mobile money transfer services, are not captured in most Sub-Saharan African countries.

Surveys of migrants and remittance recipients and other secondary sources suggest that informal remittance flows, which are not included in the IMF estimates, could be equal to or exceed official figures for Sub-Saharan Africa (Page and Plaza 2006; IFAD 2009). Central banks in some African countries, such as Uganda, are making efforts to estimate these informal flows—through, for example, foreign exchange transactions data and surveys of remittance-receiving households—but these efforts appear to be limited to a few countries.

Data on the sources of remittance flows to Sub-Saharan Africa are not available. However, estimates based on bilateral migration stocks, incomes in destination countries, and incomes in countries of origin indicate that the top sources of remittances for Sub-Saharan Africa are the EU15 countries (41 percent of inflows) and the United States (28 percent) (Ratha and Shaw 2007; World Bank 2011) (figure 2.2). The remaining sources are other developing countries, primarily in Africa (13 percent); the Gulf Cooperation Council (GCC) countries (9 percent), and other high-income countries (8 percent). North African countries are even more dependent on remittances from Western Europe (54 percent) and the GCC countries (27 percent), receiving only 5 percent of remittances from the United States.

Although intraregional migration is more important in Sub-Saharan Africa than in any other developing region (two-thirds of international emigrants from Sub-Saharan African countries are within the region [see chapter 1]), intraregional remittances are estimated to be much smaller than remittances from outside the region. These remittances are smaller primarily because the incomes of cross-border migrants within Africa are lower than the incomes of African migrants in Europe, the United States, and the Gulf.

EFFECT OF THE GLOBAL FINANCIAL CRISIS

Analysis of the impact of the global financial crisis on remittance flows is difficult because of the lack of timely and reliable data in most Afri-

Figure 2.2 Source of Remittances to Africa and to All Developing Regions, 2010

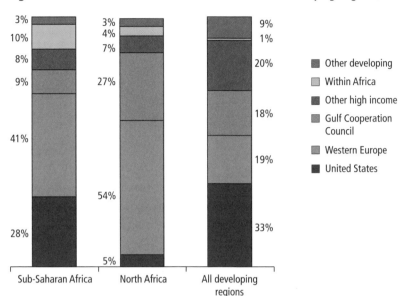

Source: Authors' calculations updating the methodology of Ratha and Shaw 2007 using bilateral migration data from World Bank 2011 and economic data from the World Development Indicators (December 2010).

can countries. Model-based estimates of remittance inflows suggest that remittance flows to Sub-Saharan Africa declined by a modest 3.7 percent in 2009 (Ratha, Mohapatra, and Silwal 2010; see table 2.1). The decline in North African countries was more severe, in part because most North African migrants live in Europe, where GDP fell sharply in 2009.[3] Flows to North Africa are estimated to have fallen 11.1 percent in 2009.

Remittance flows to Sub-Saharan Africa appear to have been less affected than those to North Africa because the remittance sources are more diversified (see figure 2.2). Remittance flows to Egypt, the largest recipient in the North African region, declined 18 percent in 2009; flows to Morocco, the second-largest recipient, declined 9 percent. In Sub-Saharan Africa, flows to Kenya remained flat in 2009 and declined by 6 percent in Cape Verde and 9 percent in Ethiopia.

Some African countries experienced recovery in remittance flows in the first half of 2010. For the year as whole, remittance flows to Africa are estimated to have risen 4 percent. The uncertain economic recovery, persistently high unemployment rates, and tighter immigration restrictions in destination countries, however, could restrain the growth of remittance inflows to Africa in the medium term.

IMPLICATIONS OF REMITTANCES AT THE MACROECONOMIC LEVEL

A review of the macroeconomic impact of remittances, focusing on Sub-Saharan Africa, underlines their positive impact on access to finance and growth.

STABILITY AND COUNTERCYCLICALITY OF REMITTANCES

Remittances tend to behave countercyclically. They thus act as a form of insurance against macroeconomic shocks for origin countries (Chami, Hakura, and Montiel 2009). Remittances rose during the financial crises in Mexico in 1995 and in Indonesia and Thailand in 1998 (Ratha 2007). They have increased with natural disasters and political conflicts (Clarke and Wallsten 2004; Yang and Choi 2007; Yang 2008a; Mohapatra, Joseph, and Ratha 2009).

Remittances thus behave very differently from most other private flows, which tend to be procyclical (Ratha 2003; Frankel 2010), largely because most remittances involve transactions among members of the same household and are thus less driven by profit-seeking motives than private resource flows. Remittances are also less at the mercy of changes in the priorities of official aid donors and their fiscal situation (World Bank 2006). Remittances can be procyclical when they are sent for investment purposes, as they sometimes are in middle-income countries (Sayan 2006; Lueth and Ruiz-Arranz 2008).[4] In Sub-Saharan Africa, where private capital flows have fluctuated considerably from year to year, remittances have been more stable than both FDI and private debt and equity flows (Gupta, Pattillo, and Wagh 2009; Singh, Haacker, and Lee 2009) (figure 2.3).

SOVEREIGN CREDITWORTHINESS AND EXTERNAL FINANCING

Remittance inflows can improve sovereign creditworthiness by increasing the level and stability of foreign exchange receipts (Ratha 2007; Avendaño, Gaillard, and Nieto-Parra 2009). Given their size, in the absence of remittance receipts, several African countries would have had access to a much lower level of imports or would have run much larger current account deficits. Remittances also help stabilize the current account by reducing the volatility of overall capital flows (Chami and others 2008). Remittances can reduce the probability of current account reversals, especially when they exceed 3 percent of GDP (Bugamelli and Paterno 2009).

Appropriately accounting for remittances can improve evaluations of African countries' external debt sustainability and creditworthiness. The

Figure 2.3 Stability of Various Sources of Resource Flows to Africa, 1990–2008

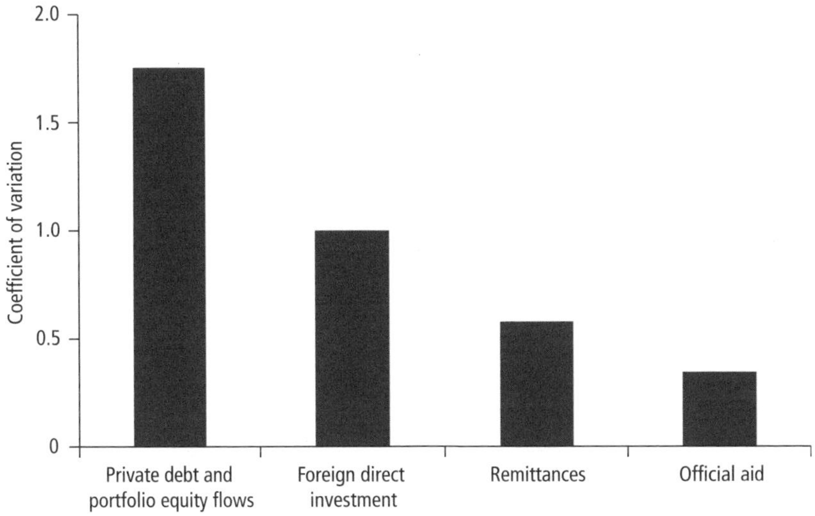

Source: Authors' calculations based on World Bank Global Development Finance database 2010.

ratio of external debt to exports would be significantly lower in many African countries if remittances were included in the denominator (figure 2.4). Remittances are now being factored into sovereign ratings in middle-income countries and debt sustainability analysis in low-income countries (IMF 2010). In several remittance-recipient countries, country creditworthiness analysis by the major rating agencies often cite remittances as a factor in their rating decisions (Avendaño, Gaillard, and Nieto-Parra 2009).[5] But less than half of African countries have a sovereign rating from one of the three major rating agencies (Ratha, Mohapatra, and Plaza 2009). Obtaining a sovereign rating—and improving the sovereign rating in those African countries that have one (after appropriately accounting for remittances)—will translate into improved market access for subsovereign entities, such as African banks and firms, whose foreign currency borrowing is typically subject to the country's "sovereign ceiling" (Borensztein, Cowan, and Valenzuela 2007; Ratha, De, and Mohapatra 2011).

Including remittances in the calculation of the debt-to-exports ratio can provide a more accurate evaluation of debt sustainability and the amount of fiscal adjustment that may be needed to place debt on a sustainable path (Abdih and others 2009; IMF and World Bank 2009). The joint World Bank–IMF Low-Income Country Debt Sustainability Framework now allows for more explicit consideration of remittances in evaluating the ability of countries to repay external obligations and take on nonconcessional borrowing from private creditors (IMF 2010). Including

Figure 2.4 **External Debt as a Share of Exports from and Remittances to Selected Countries in Sub-Saharan Africa**

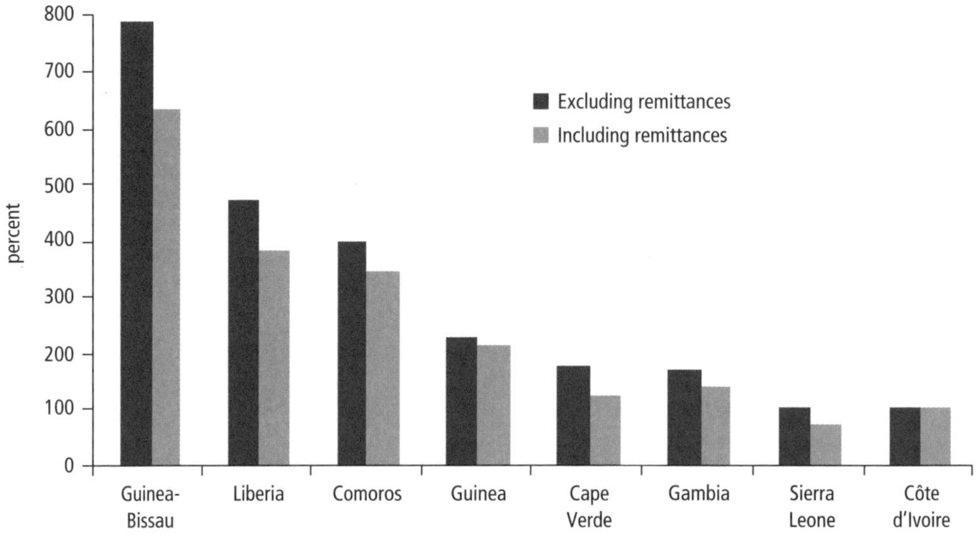

Source: Authors' calculations based on World Bank World Development Indicators database, December 2010.

remittances in creditworthiness analysis using the shadow ratings model of Ratha, De, and Mohapatra (2011) suggests that the creditworthiness of remittance-recipient countries would improve by one to three notches. The poor quality of national remittance data in many African countries makes it difficult to assess the extent of improvement in sovereign creditworthiness that would result from the inclusion of remittances in the Africa region, however.

SECURITIZATION OF FUTURE REMITTANCES

African countries can potentially use future remittances (and other future receivables) as collateral to raise financing from international capital markets for financing development projects (Ratha 2005; Ketkar and Ratha 2009a). Banks in several developing countries—including Brazil, Egypt, El Salvador, Guatemala, Kazakhstan, Mexico, and Turkey—have been able to raise cheaper and longer-term financing (more than $15 billion since 2000) from international capital markets by securitizing future remittance flows. A reputable bank in a remittance-receiving country can use remittances (which represent a hard-currency asset for the bank) as collateral as long as it is able to pay out local currency remittances to beneficiaries. The use of an offshore special-purpose vehicle helps mitigate several key elements of the sovereign risk (including expropriation and convertibility risks). The future flow securitization structure allows securities to be rated higher than the sovereign credit rating and to reach out to a wider group of potential investors.[6]

Banks in several African countries, aided by the African Export-Import Bank, have used remittance securitization to raise international financing at lower cost and longer maturities. In 1996, the African Export-Import Bank coarranged the first ever future-flow securitization by a Sub-Saharan African country, a $40 million medium-term loan to a development bank in Ghana, backed by its Western Union remittance receivables (Afreximbank 2005; Rutten and Oramah 2006). Afreximbank launched its Financial Future-Flow Prefinancing Programme in 2001 to expand the use of migrant remittances and other future flows—credit cards and checks, royalties arising from bilateral service agreements on air flight fees, and so forth—as collateral to leverage external financing to fund agricultural and other projects in Sub-Saharan Africa. In 2001, it arranged a $50 million remittance-backed syndicated note issuance facility for a Nigerian entity using Moneygram receivables; in 2004 it coarranged a $40 million remittance-backed syndicated term loan facility to an Ethiopian bank using its Western Union receivables (Afreximbank 2005).

Many African countries can potentially issue bonds backed by future remittances, with amounts ranging from a tenth to a fifth of their annual remittance flows, depending on the level of overcollateralization required to implement these transactions. Updated estimates using the methodology used by Ratha, Mohapatra, and Plaza (2009) suggest that the potential for securitization of remittances and other future receivables is $35 billion annually for Sub-Saharan Africa (table 2.2).

A low level of domestic financial development, a lack of banking relationships with banks abroad, and the high fixed costs of legal, investment

Table 2.2 Securitization Potential for Sub-Saharan Africa, 2009 *($ billions)*

Type of collateral	Receivables	Securitization potential
Fuel exports	91.1	18.2
Agricultural raw materials exports	6.7	1.3
Ores and metals exports	37.7	7.5
Travel services	19.0	3.8
Remittances	20.6	4.1
Total	175.0	35.0

Source: Authors' estimates of securitization potential, based on the methodology of Ratha, Mohapatra, and Plaza 2009 and data from World Development Indicators, December 2010.

banking, and credit-rating services—especially in poor African countries with few large entities—make the use of securitization instruments difficult for Sub-Saharan countries (Ketkar and Ratha 2009a). The viability of securitization of future remittance flows can be facilitated by introducing a securitization law and improving flows through formal channels.

Bilateral and multilateral donors can play a significant role in facilitating remittance securitization and mitigating the risks to African countries of issuing these remittance-backed bonds. Efforts can include providing seed money for hiring investment banking services; providing legal help, financial guarantees, and technical assistance in project design and creditworthiness analysis; and advising on prudential debt management to ensure fiscal and debt sustainability. The international community can also help African countries obtain sovereign ratings, which act as a ceiling for private sector borrowings.[7]

Potential issuers of remittance-backed bonds should be reminded of the risks of currency mismatch associated with foreign currency debt. Considerations must be given to prudential risk management before taking on additional debt. Potential volatility in remittance flows and disruption in relationship with the diaspora can occur quickly in countries where political risks are high. Large foreign currency inflows after a bond issuance can also cause currency appreciation, which requires careful macroeconomic management.

ECONOMIC GROWTH, FINANCIAL DEVELOPMENT, AND COMPETITIVENESS

Remittances can affect economic growth directly, by raising consumption and investment expenditures; by increasing expenditures on health, education, and nutrition that contribute to long-term productivity (see next section); and by improving the stability of consumption and output at both the household and macroeconomic level (Chami, Hakura, and Montiel 2009; Mohapatra, Joseph, and Ratha 2009). These benefits in turn increase the supply of investment from both domestic and foreign sources by increasing financial intermediation (Aggarwal, Demirgüç-Kunt, and Martinez Peria 2006; see Gupta, Pattillo, and Wagh 2009 for evidence for Sub-Saharan Africa), which can ultimately contribute to higher growth (Rajan and Zingales 1998; see Ghirmay 2004 and Akinlo and Egbetunde 2010 for Sub-Saharan Africa).[8]

Remittances also may reduce growth, for several reasons. First, large inflows of remittances can cause the real exchange rate to appreciate ("Dutch disease"), which can impair growth if tradable production imparts external benefits, such as economies of scale and learning effects (see World Bank 2006; Acosta, Lartey, and Mandelman 2009; Gupta, Pattillo, and Wagh 2009). But remittances do not appear to have had a significant impact on competitiveness for developing countries on average (Rajan and Subramanian 2005).[9] And there is little evidence of this effect for Africa, apart from some small countries, such as Cape Verde, where remittance inflows are nearly 10 percent of GDP (Bourdet and Falck 2006).

Second, in principle, large remittance receipts may reduce the supply of labor (Lucas 1987; Azam and Gubert 2006; Bussolo and Medvedev 2007; Chami and others 2008). There is little evidence of this phenomenon, however, and choices by some individuals to work less would be unlikely to have a significant impact on output in African countries with high levels of underemployment.

Third, some experts argue that the additional income from remittances can reduce pressure to improve the quality of policies and institutions by making recipients less dependent on government benefits (Abdih and others 2008) or by providing sufficient foreign exchange to ease governments' concerns over structural rigidities. Others, however, find that remittances have a positive impact on growth in countries with higher-quality political and economic policies and institutions (Catrinescu and others 2009).

The complexity of the growth process and the well-known problems of cross-country growth regressions make it difficult to determine whether remittances increase growth rates. Empirical specifications that include remittances in cross-country growth regressions provide mixed results (Barajas and others 2009; Catrinescu and others 2009; Singh, Haacker, and Lee 2009). The lack of significance of remittances in some growth equations may reflect the fact their effects on human and physical capital are realized only over a very long time period; that the effects are endogenous (that is, they rise with declines in output); or that official data on remittances are of poor quality.[10]

In economies in which the financial system is underdeveloped, remittances may alleviate liquidity and credit constraints and help finance small business investments, thereby effectively acting as a substitute for financial development (Giuliano and Ruiz-Arranz 2009). The authors find evidence that the impact of remittances on growth is stronger when the level of financial development is weaker. Regression analysis suggests that remittances have the greatest impact on growth when the share of the broad money supply (M2) in GDP (an indicator of financial development) is below 28 percent, as it is in most African economies.

DEVELOPMENT IMPACT OF REMITTANCES AT THE MICROECONOMIC LEVEL

Remittances can help reduce poverty, raise household investment, and increase access to health and education services. This section reviews the literature on the development implications of remittances from several developing regions, including Africa. It also looks at recent evidence collected through the Africa Migration Project surveys of the characteristics of households that receive remittances from outside Africa, within Africa, and within the same country (see Plaza, Navarrete, and Ratha 2011 for the survey methodology). Although it can be difficult to separate the effects of remittances from the overall effect of migration in empirical studies (McKenzie and Sasin 2007), it is well established that the primary economic benefit of migration to recipient households is the receipt of remittances (World Bank 2006; see chapter 4 of this book for other benefits, such as the transmission of knowledge, trade and investment linkages, fertility norms, and so on). The findings regarding households receiving remittances in origin countries complement information about the characteristics of remittance senders in destination countries (see World Bank 2006; Bollard, McKenzie, and Morten 2010).

IMPACT OF REMITTANCES ON POVERTY AND INEQUALITY

Remittances can reduce the level of poverty by directly augmenting the incomes of poor recipient households and increasing aggregate demand, thereby increasing employment and wages of the poor. Cross-country regressions generally find that remittances have reduced the share of poor people in the population (Adams and Page 2003, 2005).

Econometric analyses suggest that remittances have reduced poverty in Africa. Anyanwu and Erhijakpor (2010) find that a 10 percent increase in official international remittances as a share of GDP led to a 2.9 percent decline in the share of people living in poverty in a sample of 33 African countries for 1990–2005, with declines also observed for the depth and severity of poverty (see also Ajayi and others 2009). Gupta, Pattillo, and Wagh (2009) find that the impact of remittances on poverty in Africa, although positive, was smaller than for other developing countries, a result they attribute to the possibility that poverty can itself cause increased migration and hence larger remittances. Studies of Burkina Faso (Lachaud 1999; Wouterse 2010); Ghana (Quartey and Blankson 2004; Adams 2006; Adams, Cuecuecha, and Page 2008a); Lesotho (Gustafsson and Makonnen 1993); Morocco (Sorensen 2004); and Nigeria (Odozia, Awoyemia, and Omonona 2010) conclude that remittances are associ-

Figure 2.5 **Percentage of Remittance Recipients in Top Two Consumption Quintiles in Selected African Countries, by Source of Remittances**

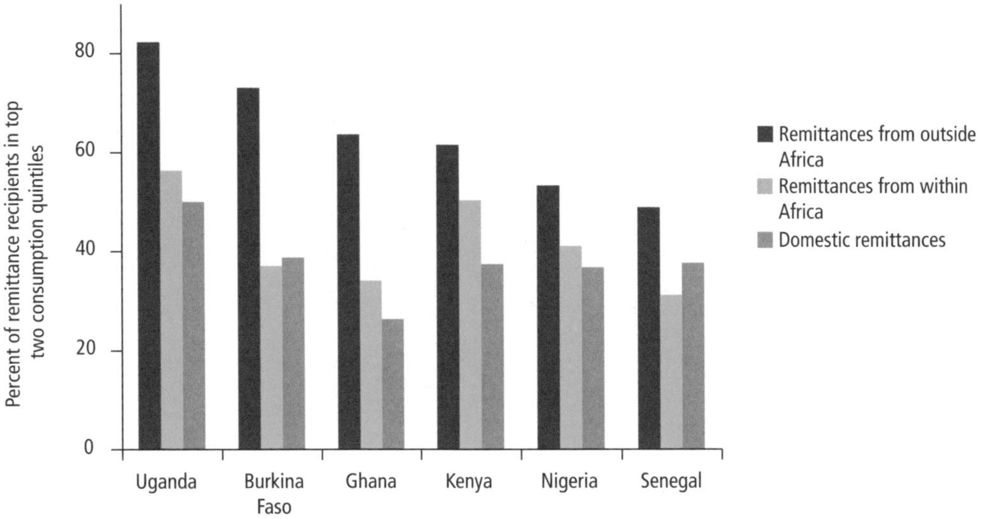

Source: Authors' calculations based on results household surveys conducted in Burkina Faso, Kenya, Nigeria, Senegal, and Uganda in 2009 as part of the Africa Migration Project and Ghana Living Standards Survey 2005–06.

ated with a reduction in the share of people in poverty—and in some cases the depth and severity of poverty as well. A substantial part of remittances in Mali is saved for unexpected events, thus serving as insurance for entire households (Ponsot and Obegi 2010). Food security in rural areas of Nigeria improved considerably with an increase in remittances (Babatunde and Martinetti 2010).

The evidence on the implications of remittances for inequality is less clear, because it is not possible to observe counterfactual incomes in the absence of migration (World Bank 2006; Ratha 2007). Households that receive remittances, especially from outside Africa, may have been richer to begin with (allowing a family member to migrate in the first place); they may also have higher incomes because of migration and the receipt of remittances. Recent household surveys conducted as a part of the Africa Migration Project and an earlier survey in Ghana find that more than half of households in Burkina Faso, Ghana, and Nigeria and 30 percent of households in Senegal receiving remittances from outside Africa are in the top two consumption quintiles (figure 2.5). Remittances from outside Africa tend to be much larger on average than remittances from other African countries or domestic sources (Bollard, McKenzie, and Morten 2010; figure 2.6).

In contrast to remittances from outside Africa, remittances from African countries may reduce inequality (see Wouterse 2010 for this effect in Burkina Faso).[11] Households receiving remittances from other African

Figure 2.6 Average Annual Remittances in Selected African Countries, by Source of Remittances

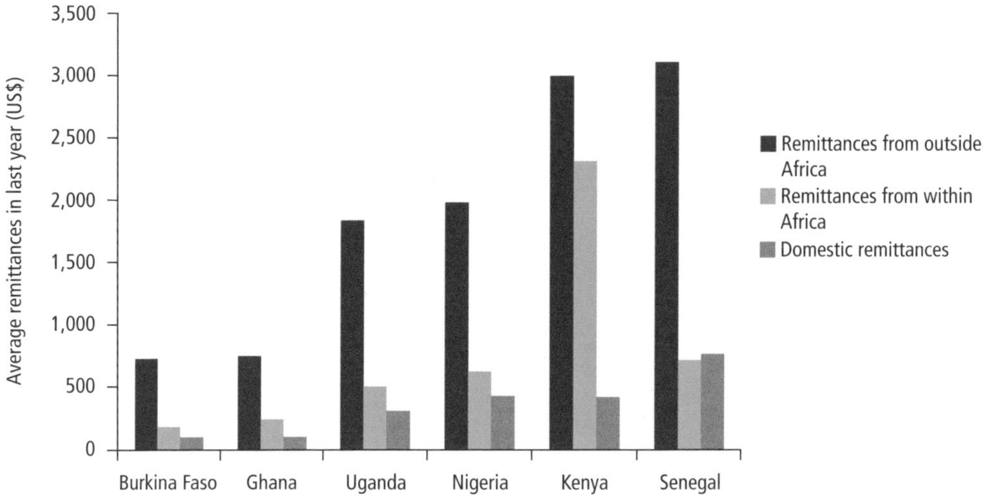

Source: Authors' calculations based on household surveys conducted in Burkina Faso, Kenya, Nigeria, Senegal, and Uganda in 2009 as part of the Africa Migration Project and Ghana Living Standards Survey 2005–06.

countries or domestic sources tend to be more evenly distributed across consumption expenditure quintiles. Similar analysis for the distribution of wealth using an asset index broadly mirrors these findings.[12]

A recent study on the characteristics of African remittance senders based on microdata of more than 12,000 African migrants in nine Organisation for Economic Co-operation and Development (OECD) countries (Bollard, McKenzie, and Morten 2010) complements the findings from surveys of remittance-recipient households. The destination country data suggest that Africans remit twice as much on average as migrants from other developing countries. The average annual remittance sent by an African emigrant household is $1,263—more than the average annual per capita income of Sub-Saharan African countries. Africans also tend to remit more often, and African migrants from poorer African countries are more likely to remit than those from richer African countries.[13] Male African migrants in the OECD send larger amounts on average than females ($1,446 compared with $878 for females) partly because of their higher earnings, but also because they are more likely to have spouses back home.

USES OF REMITTANCES

Some observers claim that remittances are spent mostly on consumption rather than investment, on ceremonies and luxuries rather than essentials. This section reviews the substantial literature and data indicating that remittances are often spent on essential consumption, investment in physical and human capital, and expenditures that improve welfare and productivity, including health, education, and information and communication technology, and that these expenditures serve as insurance against adverse shocks.

Comparison of the uses of remittances by source (outside Africa, cross-border remittances within Africa, and domestic remittances) suggests that the average amount of remittances received by households from outside Africa is larger than that of intraregional and domestic remittances and that a significant part of it tends to be spent on human and physical capital investments, such as education, health, land, building a house, starting a business, improving the farm, or purchasing agricultural equipment (table 2.3). There are also gender-specific differences in the uses of remittances: evidence from previous studies suggest that remittance-receiving households headed by women tend to spend more on health and education expenditures than do similar households headed by men.

Investment in physical capital and entrepreneurship

It is difficult to identify the share of remittances devoted to specific uses, as money is fungible, and reports from remittance recipients on how they use remittances may be biased.[14] Evidence from other regions suggests that a significant part of remittances is spent on housing investment and the purchase of land, particularly where few other assets are reliable stores of value. Taylor and Wyatt (1996) argue that the shadow value of remittances for overcoming risk and liquidity constraints is particularly important to households in the low- to middle-income range, which otherwise tend to be credit constrained. Guatemalan households receiving remittances spend more at the margin on housing, even after controlling for the endogeneity of remittance-receiving status (Adams and Cuecuecha 2010). About one-fifth of the capital invested in 6,000 microenterprises in urban Mexico was financed by remittances (Woodruff and Zenteno 2001; see also Massey and Parrado 1998).[15] In rural Pakistan, international remittances raise the propensity to invest in agricultural land (Adams 1998). Remittance-receiving households that benefited from an exchange rate shock spent more hours in self-employment and were more likely to start relatively capital-intensive entrepreneurial enterprises in the Philippines (Yang 2008b). Some recent studies (for example, Ashraf and others 2010) find that giving migrants more control over the uses of remittances can increase savings rates among both migrants and remittance recipients.

Table 2.3 Use of Remittances by Recipient Households in Selected African Countries, by Source of Remittances *(percent of total remittances)*

Use	Burkina Faso			Kenya			Nigeria			Senegal			Uganda		
	Outside Africa	Within Africa	Domestic	Outside Africa	Within Africa	Domestic	Outside Africa	Within Africa	Domestic	Outside Africa	Within Africa	Domestic	Outside Africa	Within Africa	Domestic
Food	23.5	34.9	48.7	12.8	14.5	29.7	10.1	20.1	1.0	52.6	72.6	81.9	7.6	9.7	12.4
Education	12.4	5.9	9.4	9.6	22.9	20.5	22.1	19.6	4.5	3.6	2.3	4.6	12.7	14.5	20.2
Health	11.3	10.1	12.5	7.3	5.8	7.0	5.1	12.0	10.6	10.7	7.3	2.9	6.3	14.5	24.8
Clothing	5.0	0.7	0.7	..	..	..	..	..	..	..	..	..	..	..	..
Rent (house, land)	1.4	0.6	1.7	5.7	0.4	7.4	4.4	4.9	0.8	1.0	0.0	2.2	5.1	8.1	4.5
Cars/trucks	0.1	0.0	0.1	1.3	1.0	0.4	0.0	0.0	0.5	0.2	0.0	0.0	2.5	0.0	0.0
Marriage/funeral	2.1	3.9	3.1	0.9	1.7	2.0	0.4	1.0	0.7	2.9	2.4	1.1	7.6	6.5	1.7
Construction of new house	25.7	10.1	2.6	11.2	27.5	1.3	5.8	0.0	0.1	7.0	0.7	0.0	2.5	1.6	0.4
Rebuilding of house	0.3	1.0	1.2	5.3	3.1	1.3	4.7	3.2	7.0	4.2	0.7	0.1	6.3	3.2	2.1
Purchase of land	0.0	1.4	0.1	8.4	7.0	1.3	24.8	16.6	18.2	3.0	0.0	0.0	3.8	4.8	2.1
Improvement of farm[a]	0.0	3.9	1.1	2.3	0.4	4.4	..	..	..	..	..	..	..	..	..
Business	10.4	2.6	2.4	3.9	8.4	13.0	21.7	20.1	11.1	1.3	5.7	0.2	7.6	9.7	2.1
Investment	..	..	..	24.2	0.6	4.7	..	..	..	..	..	..	..	..	..
Other	7.7	24.9	16.3	7.2	6.6	6.9	0.8	2.6	3.5	13.5	8.3	6.9	38.0	27.4	29.8

Source: Authors' calculations based on results of household surveys conducted in Burkina Faso, Kenya, Nigeria, Senegal, and Uganda in 2009 as part of the Africa Migration Project.
Note: .. = negligible or missing.
a. Includes agricultural equipment.

The evidence for Africa on the uses of remittances for investment and entrepreneurship is somewhat limited. In Egypt, overseas savings are associated with a higher likelihood of entrepreneurship (and thus investment) among return migrants (McCormick and Wahba 2001, 2003). In 1997, Osili (2004) conducted a survey of 112 Nigerian migrant households in Chicago and a matched sample of 61 families in Nigeria. She found that a third of remittances were spent on housing investment the preceding year and that migrants' housing investment was responsive to changes in macroeconomic conditions such as inflation, the real exchange rate, and political stability.

The household surveys conducted as part of the Africa Migration Project find that a significant portion of international remittances are spent on land purchases, building a house, business, improving a farm, agricultural equipment, and other investments (as a share of total remittances, investment in these items represented 36.4 percent in Burkina Faso, 55.3 percent in Kenya, 57.0 percent in Nigeria, 15.5 percent in Senegal, and 20.2 percent in Uganda [see table 2.3]). A substantial share of within-Africa remittances was also used for these purposes in Burkina Faso, Kenya, Nigeria, and Uganda. The share of domestic remittances devoted to these purposes was much lower in all of the countries surveyed, with the exception of Nigeria and Kenya (see figure 4.3 in chapter 4).

Education

Remittances may increase expenditure on education by helping finance schooling and reducing the need for child labor. But the absence of an adult household member may put pressure on children to perform additional household chores or work on the family farm, reducing time for education. Evidence from other regions suggests that remittances can contribute to better school attendance, higher school enrollment rates, and additional years in school (box 2.1).

The paucity of household survey data means that the evidence on the impact of remittances on educational outcomes in Africa is relatively weak. In Egypt children of remittance-receiving households were more likely to enroll in university than other children, and girls ages 15–17 in remittance-receiving households performed less domestic work and were more likely to be in school than other girls the same age (Elbadawi and Roushdy 2009). Remittance-receiving households in Ghana invested more in education than other households (Adams, Cuecuecha, and Page 2008b).

Evidence from household surveys referenced above show that education was the second-highest use of remittances from outside Africa in

Box 2.1 How Do Remittances Affect Education Outcomes?

Numerous studies (particularly in Latin America) find a positive impact of remittances on education. Using cross-country data for 82 countries, Ebeke (2010) finds that remittances reduce the prevalence of child labor in developing countries characterized by weak financial systems and income instability. Remittances in Ecuador increased school enrollment for the poor and decreased the incidence of child labor, especially for girls and people in rural areas (Calero, Bedi, and Sparrow 2009). In El Salvador, the impact of remittances on the likelihood of children remaining in school was 10 times that of other sources of income in urban areas and 3 times that of other sources in rural areas (Cox-Edwards and Ureta 2003). Guatemalan households receiving international remittances spent twice as much at the margin on education as they would have spent had they not received remittances (Adams and Cuecuecha 2010). In Haiti, remittance-receiving households reported higher school attendance than households that did not receive remittances (Amuedo-Dorantes, Georges, and Pozo 2010; Bredl 2011). Girls in migrant-sending households in Mexico in which the mother had a low level of education completed 0.2–0.9 years more schooling than girls from households without a migrating relative (Hanson and Woodruff 2003). In Mexico, remittances had a positive effect on literacy and school attendance for children ages 6–14 (Lopez-Cordova 2005) .

Results are similar in Asia. Bansak and Chezum (2009) find a net positive impact of migration and remittances on schooling in Nepal. School enrollment rates for girls in migrant-sending households in rural Pakistan were 54 percent higher than those of other households (Mansuri 2007). Remittance-receiving households in the Philippines had a higher level of schooling and educational expenditure and lower rates of child labor for children ages 10–17 (Yang 2008b). In Sri Lanka remittances were used to finance private education, which can improve educational outcomes (De and Ratha 2006).

Other studies have found a negative impact of migration on educational outcomes. McKenzie and Rapoport (2010) find that living in a migrant-sending household in Mexico reduced the likelihood of children completing high school by 13–15 percent. This result may reflect the fact that a large share of Mexican migration to the United States is for unskilled work and the opportunity cost of gaining an additional year of schooling is small when there are few domestic employment options after school. Using micro-level data, Acosta, Fajnzylber, and López (2007) and Acosta and others (2008) find that remittances were associated with increased educational attainment in only 6 of 11 Latin American countries.

Nigeria and Uganda, the third highest in Burkina Faso, and the fourth highest in Kenya (see table 2.3). Households that receive international remittances have substantially more household members who have completed secondary and tertiary education than other households (figure 2.7). In Kenya and Uganda, households devote 15 percent or more of domestic and intraregional remittances to education; Nigerian households devote 20 percent of intra-Africa remittances to education. Although the amounts spent were much smaller than those from remittances from outside Africa, these figures indicate that a significant share of all sources of remittances goes to education. Although these findings do not control for the possible endogeneity of remittance-receiving sta-

Figure 2.7 Secondary and Tertiary Education Attainment of Remittance Recipient and Nonrecipient Households in Selected Countries in Africa

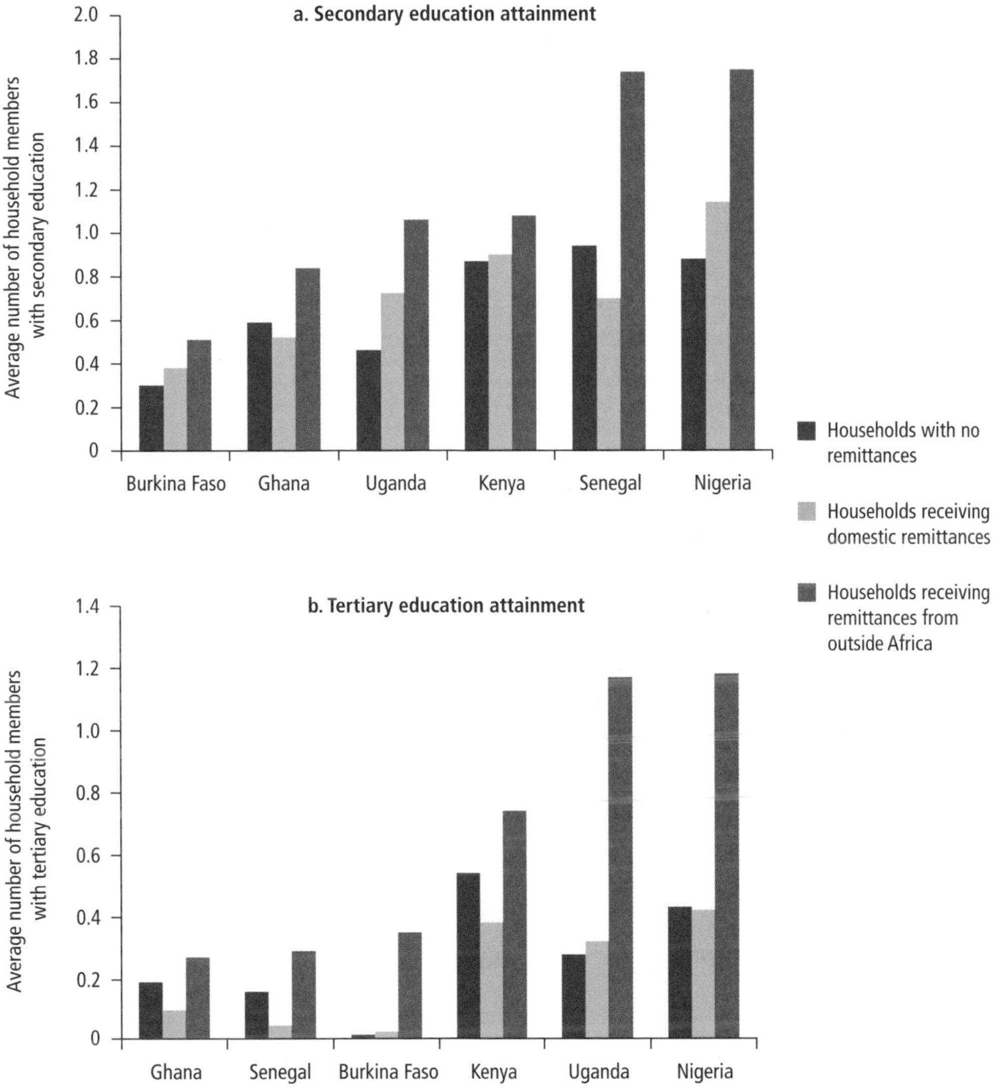

Legend:
- Households with no remittances
- Households receiving domestic remittances
- Households receiving remittances from outside Africa

Source: Authors' calculations based on Africa Migration Project household surveys in Burkina Faso, Kenya, Nigeria, Senegal, and Uganda in 2009 and Ghana Living Standards Survey 2005–06.

tus, they nevertheless suggest that remittances may help raise the level of resources devoted to education.

Health

Remittances can contribute to better health outcomes by enabling household members to purchase more food and healthcare services and perhaps by increasing information on health practices. In a cross-country analysis of 56 developing countries, Drabo and Ebeke (2010) find that higher remittances per capita were associated with greater access to private treatment for fever and diarrhea and that remittances complemented foreign health aid in poor countries. In a cross-country analysis of 84 countries (46 countries with quintile-level data), Chauvet, Gubert, and Mesplé-Somps (2009) find that remittances reduced overall child mortality but tended to be more effective in reducing mortality among children from the richest households than the poorest households.[16]

The evidence on the impact of remittances on health outcomes is rather sparse for Africa. Evidence from the household surveys referenced above indicates that households dedicate 5–12 percent of remittances from outside Africa to healthcare (see table 2.3). A similar share of within-Africa and domestic remittances is devoted to health expenditures, but the amounts spent are much lower because of the smaller average size of these remittances. Among households in Ghana that receive remittances from outside and within Africa, households headed by women spend more on healthcare than households headed by men (Guzmán, Morrison, and Sjöblom 2007). In rural Mali, households receiving remittances increased demand for health services and were more likely to seek modern care (Birdsall and Chuhan 1986). In a recent study using panel data for 1993–2004 for the KwaZulu-Natal province in South Africa, Nagarajan (2009) finds that remittance-receiving households spent a larger budget share on food and health expenditures and that remittances enabled poorer households to access better-quality medical care.

Insurance against adverse shocks

Migration enables households to diversify their sources of income and thus reduce their vulnerability to risks such as drought, famine, and other natural disasters. In Ecuador, remittances helped keep children of remittance-receiving households in school when faced with adverse shocks (Calero, Bedi, and Sparrow 2009). Increased remittances helped smooth household consumption and compensate for the loss of assets after an earthquake in El Salvador in 2001 (Halliday 2006). Transfers from friends and relatives in the United States played an important role in reducing the distress caused in Haiti by Cyclone Jeane in 2004 (Weiss-Fagan 2006) and after the devastating earthquake in 2010 (Ratha 2010). Remittance-receiving households in the Aceh region of Indonesia recovered more quickly than other households after the 2004 tsunami (Wu 2006). Migrant remittances were important factors in disaster recovery and reconstruction after a devastating earthquake in Pakistan in 2005

Table 2.4 Food Security Strategies and Remittance Receipts among Ethiopian Households
(percent of households relying on strategy to cope with food shortages)

Strategy	Households not receiving remittances	Households receiving domestic remittances	Households receiving remittances from outside Africa
Food aid	42.3	55.9	0.0
Sale of livestock and livestock products	40.5	3.9	0.0
Sale of other agricultural products	18.2	3.7	0.0
Own cash	10.3	5.3	31.3
Sale of household assets	4.1	4.6	11.5
Other	15.6	33	48.9

Source: Mohapatra, Joseph, and Ratha 2009.
Note: Columns sum to more than 100 percent because households reported more than one response.

(Suleri and Savage 2006). In the Philippines, remittances helped compensate for the loss in income caused by adverse rainfall shocks (Yang and Choi 2007). In Thailand, domestic remittances increased in response to below-average rainfall in the recipients' region and to increases in medical expenses in recipient households (Miller and Paulson 2007).

Migration and remittances have been a part of coping mechanisms adopted by African households facing shocks to incomes and livelihoods (Block and Webb 2001). During droughts in Botswana, families at risk of losing cattle and those relying on crops for their sustenance tended to receive more remittances than other families (Lucas and Stark 1985). Ethiopian households that receive international remittances were less likely than other households to sell their productive assets, such as livestock, to cope with food shortages (Mohapatra, Joseph, and Ratha 2009 (table 2.4). Remittances in Ghana helped smooth the household consumption of rural farmers (Quartey and Blankson 2004; Quartey 2006).

In rural Mali, remittances responded positively to shocks suffered by recipient households (Gubert 2002, 2007). Surveys in the Senegal River Valley in Mali and in Senegal suggest that migration acts as an intrahousehold risk-diversification strategy, with remittances a contingent flow that supports family consumption in case of an adverse shock (Azam and Gubert 2005, 2006). Similar mechanisms for sharing risk through interhousehold transfers of cattle have been observed for East African pastoralists (Huysentruyt, Barrett, and McPeak 2009).

Remittances can also enable recipient households to build stronger and more resilient housing. Mohapatra, Joseph, and Ratha (2009) find that remittance-receiving households in Burkina Faso and Ghana were more likely to have a concrete house, after controlling for the possible endogeneity of the remittance-receiving status by using propensity score-matching methods (figure 2.8).

Figure 2.8 **Share of Population in Burkina Faso and Ghana with Concrete Houses, by Remittance Status**

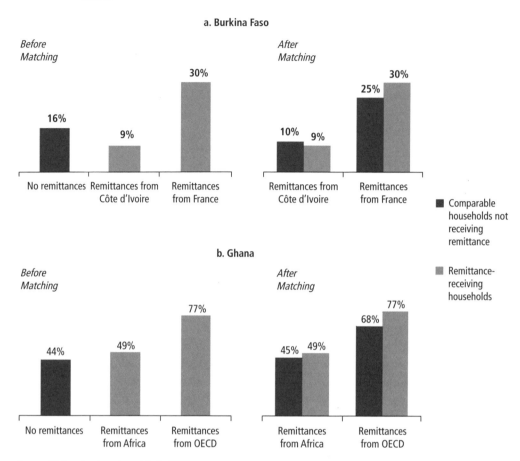

Source: Mohapatra, Joseph, and Ratha 2009.
Note: Matching refers to the technique of constructing a sample of households that do not receive remittances but are similar in other aspects to households that receive remittances (see Mohapatra, Joseph, and Ratha 2009 for details).

Information and communication technology

Remittances can play an important role in improving access to information and communication technology. In Burkina Faso, 66 percent of international remittance recipients have access to a mobile phone compared with 41 percent of nonrecipients (table 2.5).[17] These households also have significantly higher ownership of radios (66 percent versus 39 percent), televisions (41 percent versus 9 percent), and computers (14 percent versus 2 percent). Households in Ghana, Nigeria, Senegal, and Uganda receiving international remittances also have higher rates of access to mobile phones, radios, televisions, and computers.

Table 2.5 Household Access to Information and Communication Technology in Selected African Countries, by Remittance Status *(percent of households with selected devices)*

Country/device	Households receiving domestic remittances	Households receiving remittances from within Africa	Households receiving remittances from outside Africa	Households receiving no remittances
Burkina Faso				
Mobile phone	40.1	40.6	65.5	39.3
Radio	65.4	64.1	69.0	61.5
Television	7.8	6.9	41.4	8.7
Computer access	1.0	1.6	13.8	1.8
Number of observations	422	507	29	1,145
Ghana				
Mobile phone	9.1	14.6	45.4	19.6
Radio	48.2	31.4	47.3	49.9
Television	18.7	16.9	52.7	33.6
Computer access	0.5	0.0	3.3	2.4
Number of observations	367	33	133	8,105
Kenya				
Mobile phone	79.5	82.3	87.0	77.3
Radio	84.8	86.7	88.9	82.7
Television	50.4	56.6	76.2	52.2
Computer access	7.1	17.7	30.4	20.6
Number of observations	395	113	369	1,065
Nigeria				
Mobile phone	70.4	87.3	95.5	57.3
Radio	86.9	94.3	93.8	82.5
Television	54.2	75.8	93.8	48.8
Computer access	7.2	15.1	22.6	10.7
Number of observations	573	77	328	1,272
Senegal				
Mobile phone	72.8	82.3	97.5	75.2
Radio	76.3	66.9	95.1	75.9
Television	40.3	37.9	79.7	49.1
Internet access	1.6	0.9	9.6	6.6
Number of observations	320	163	460	1,010
Uganda				
Mobile phone	58.3	76.2	85.4	50.4
Radio	78.1	81.0	90.2	73.4
Television	19.4	28.6	59.8	25.7
Internet access	4.1	3.2	28.1	7.1
Number of observations	242	63	82	1,528

Source: Authors' calculations based on results household surveys conducted in Burkina Faso, Kenya, Nigeria, Senegal, and Uganda in 2009 as part of the Africa Migration Project and Ghana Living Standards Survey 2005–06.

FINANCIAL ACCESS

Remittances are often the only relationship that many poor people have with the formal financial system. If remittances are received through banks or other financial intermediaries (such as microfinance institutions or savings cooperatives), there is a high likelihood that some part of the remittance will be saved (Aggarwal, Demirgüç-Kunt, and Martinez Peria 2006; Gupta, Pattillo, and Wagh 2009). Even if remittances are received through money transfer companies or informal providers, recipients may save the remittance in some type of financial institution rather than put it under the mattress. The steady stream of remittance receipts can also be used as a factor in evaluating the creditworthiness of recipients for microloans, consumer loans, and small business loans (sought, for example, to purchase agricultural equipment) (Ratha 2007). Remittances also play a role in smoothing the income stream of poor households that face high income volatility and shocks. This reduced income volatility can make them more attractive borrowers.

Data from recent household surveys referenced above reveal that households that receive international remittances typically have better access to financial services, such as bank accounts (figure 2.9). Households receiving domestic remittances tend to be worse off in terms of financial access than households receiving international remittances, in

Figure 2.9 Percent of Households with Bank Accounts in Selected African Countries, by Remittance Status

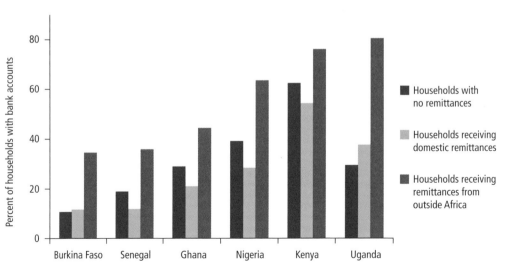

Source: Authors' calculations based on results household surveys conducted in Burkina Faso, Kenya, Nigeria, Senegal, and Uganda in 2009 as part of the Africa Migration Project and Ghana Living Standards Survey 2005–06.

part because households that send out domestic migrants tend to be poorer. There are some notable exceptions, such as Kenya, where the widespread use of mobile money transfers and the ability to save using mobile phones has effectively substituted for formal banking services (see next section for a detailed discussion).

REMITTANCE MARKETS IN AFRICA

Remittance markets in Africa remain relatively underdeveloped in terms of their financial infrastructure and the regulatory environment, but the rapid adoption of innovative money transfer technologies is transforming the landscape for remittances and broader financial services. Surveys of African households and remittance service providers conducted in the context of the Africa Migration Project indicate three broad patterns. First, intraregional (South-South) and domestic remittances are sent overwhelmingly through informal channels. They are hand carried during visits home, sent through transport companies, and delivered through other informal channels, in part because of limited access to and the high cost of formal financial (banking) services relative to average per capita incomes in African countries (Pendleton and others 2006; Bracking and Sachikonye 2008; Tevera and Chikanda 2009).

Second, a large share of remittances from outside Africa is channeled through a few large international money transfer agencies, which often work de facto or de jure in exclusive partnership with African banks and post offices (IFAD 2009). In a recent survey, almost 70 percent of central banks in Sub-Saharan Africa cited high costs as the most important factor inhibiting the use of formal remittance channels (Irving, Mohapatra, and Ratha 2010) (figure 2.10).

Finally, Africa (especially Kenya) has seen the introduction of innovative, mobile money transfer (Morawczynski and Pickens 2009; Aker and Mbiti 2010). Although the adoption of these innovative technologies has been limited mostly to domestic money transfers, largely because of concerns about money laundering and terrorist financing, the technologies have the potential to vastly improve access to both remittances and broader financial services, including low-cost savings and credit products, for African migrants and remittance recipients.

HIGH REMITTANCE COSTS

The cost of sending remittances to Sub-Saharan Africa is the highest among developing regions (figure 2.11). In mature corridors such as

Figure 2.10 Factors Inhibiting the Use of Formal Remittance Channels in Sub-Saharan Africa and All Developing Countries

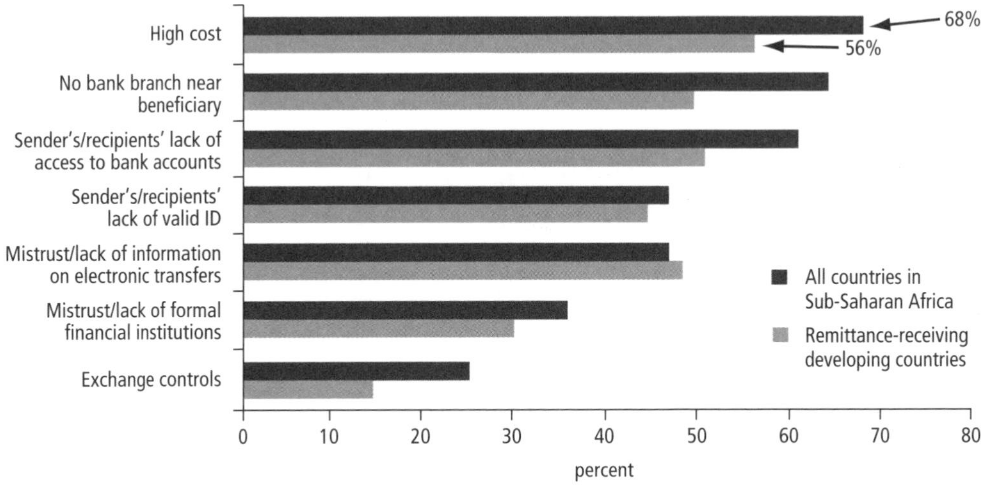

Source: Irving, Mohapatra, and Ratha 2010.

those between the United States and Mexico, remittance costs can be as low as $5; between the Gulf Cooperation Council countries and South Asia, remittance costs can be as low as $1 per transaction.[18] Data for select intra-African remittance corridors suggest that the cost of sending remittances within Africa ranges from 5 percent to 15 percent of the amount sent (figure 2.12). Large parallel market premiums between official and parallel market exchange rates in many African countries imply that the true cost is likely to be larger. Evidence based on surveys and field experiments suggests that remittance flows respond to reductions in costs (Gibson, McKenzie, and Rohorua 2006; Martinez, Aycinena, and Yang 2010). Reducing remittance costs can lead to increases in the remittances sent by migrants, increasing the resources available to recipient households.

High remittance costs represent an unnecessary burden on African migrants and likely reduce the amounts sent and their development impact (Ratha and Riedberg 2005; World Bank 2006). These high remittance costs are related to the low level of financial development in Africa (Aggarwal, Demirgüç-Kunt, and Martinez Peria 2006; Beck and Martinez Peria 2009) and the small number of firms handling remittance transfers (IFAD 2009; Orozco 2009).[19] The cost of banking services tends to be high relative to income levels in African countries, and the reach of banks outside of urban areas is limited (Demirgüç-Kunt, Beck, and Honohan 2008).[20] For example, the average fee to open a savings account is 28

Figure 2.11 Cost of Sending Remittances to and from Developing Regions

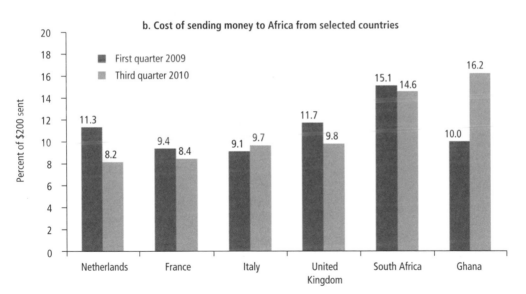

Source: Authors' calculations based on data from the World Bank Remittance Prices database, October 2010.
Note: Remittance cost includes fees and foreign exchange commissions.
a. Excludes the Pacific Islands.

percent of the average African's annual income—compared with less than 1 percent in countries in Latin America and the Caribbean (figure 2.13). The number of bank branches and automatic teller machines (ATMs) per square kilometer is lower in Sub-Saharan Africa than in any other developing region.

Figure 2.12   Cost of Sending $200 within Sub-Saharan Africa[a]

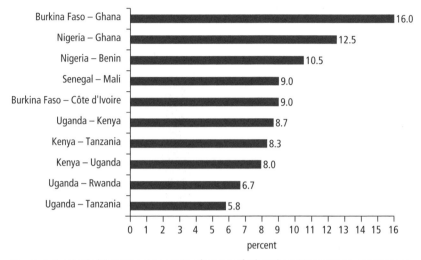

Source: Authors' calculations based on results of surveys of selected remittance service providers conducted at end of 2008.
a. Figure shows percentage cost of sending $200 or local currency equivalent.

Surveys of remittance service providers in Africa suggest that the high costs of remittances in Africa is in part caused by exclusivity agreements between banks and international money transfer companies (IFAD 2009; Irving, Mohapatra, and Ratha 2010). Other studies show that such exclusive partnerships keep costs high for migrants and reduce the amounts sent, thereby limiting the development impact of remittances (Ratha and Riedberg 2005; World Bank 2006). Several African countries, including Ethiopia, Nigeria, and Rwanda, have taken steps to eliminate these partnerships in recent years.

Surveys and interviews of remittance service providers in key destination countries (France, the United Kingdom, and the United States) reveal that African migrants' lack of access to formal financial services and required identification, exclusive partnerships, and regulations related to anti–money laundering and combating the financing of terrorism (AML-CFT) also raise the costs of transferring money to Africa.[21] Because remittance senders lack access to banking facilities, most transfers from destination countries outside Africa are sent as cash through money transfer companies or through banks acting as agents of money transfer companies rather than through potentially less expensive account-to-account and cash-to-account transfers.

Some West African banks have representative offices in France and operate through partnerships with French banks (Ponsot 2011), but

Figure 2.13   Measures of Retail Banking Accessibility in Developing Regions

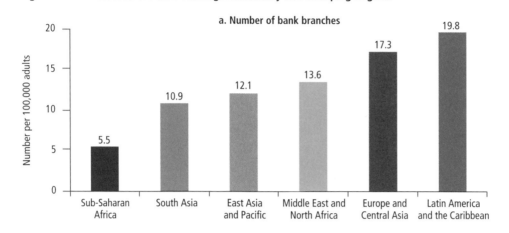

a. Number of bank branches

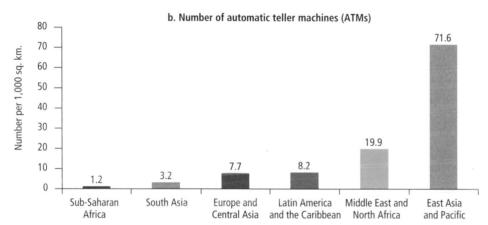

b. Number of automatic teller machines (ATMs)

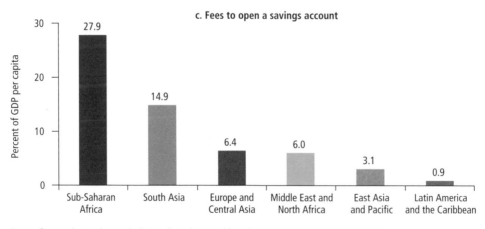

c. Fees to open a savings account

Source for panel a: Authors' calculations based on World Bank FinStats database, February 2011.
Source for panels b and c: Authors' calculations based on data from World Bank's Finance for All database 2007; Demirgüç-Kunt, Beck, and Honohan 2008.

the range of services provided appears to be small.[22] Many West African migrants in France appear to prefer to send money through friends, relatives, or even community groups.

Exclusivity partnerships are also found in some remittance-sending countries. The French postal service has an exclusive partnership with Western Union (Ponsot 2011). Although documented remittance costs are among the lowest for France–Africa corridors, such partnerships can limit competition and the access of migrants to alternative remittance service providers. U.S. regulations aimed at AML–CFT implemented after September 11, 2001, have made it more difficult for smaller remittance service providers to access banking and settlement facilities for the transfer of remittances to Africa (Mohapatra and Ratha 2011). Mainstream U.S. banks appear to be wary of having money transfer operators—particularly from East Africa and other African subregions—as clients.

REMITTANCE CHANNELS IN AFRICA

As a result of the high cost and limited reach of formal channels—as well as the informal and seasonal character of African migration—informal channels play a large role in remittance transfers within Africa (see annex table 2A.2). Some estimates suggest that the prevalence of informal transfers in Africa is the highest among all developing regions (Page and Plaza 2006; Ratha and Shaw 2007). Surveys conducted in Southern Africa in 2004–05 found that carrying remittances by hand during visits home accounted for about half of remittance transfers in southern Africa: remittances carried by hand and sent through friends and relatives accounted for 88 percent in Lesotho, 73 percent in Swaziland, 68 percent of remittances in Botswana, and 46 percent in Zimbabwe (Pendleton and others 2006; Tevera and Chikanda 2009; see Bracking and Sachikonye 2008 for evidence from Zimbabwe on the increasing reliance on informal channels during a period of hyperinflation).[23]

Recent household surveys conducted in the context of the Africa Migration Project in 2009 and an earlier survey conducted in Ghana in 2005–06 (Ghana Living Standards Survey 2005–06) show some country variation in the importance of informal channels. The share of households receiving within-Africa remittances that used informal channels was 60 percent or more in Burkina Faso, Ghana, and Senegal (figure 2.14 and annex table 2A.2). Among migrants in South Africa sending remittances to other African countries, mostly within the Southern African region, the share of emigrants using informal channels was almost 80 percent.

Informal channels were even more prevalent for domestic money transfers (95 percent in Burkina Faso and Senegal, 94 percent in Ghana, and 78 percent in Uganda). In relatively prosperous South Africa, informal

Figure 2.14   **Formal and Informal Remittance Channels in Africa**

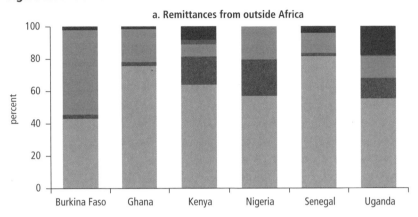

a. Remittances from outside Africa

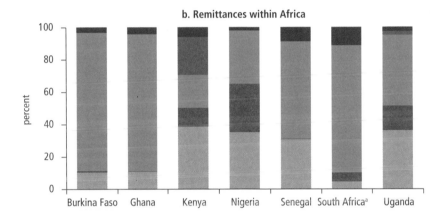

b. Remittances within Africa

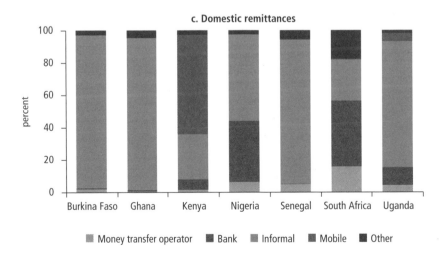

c. Domestic remittances

■ Money transfer operator   ■ Bank   ■ Informal   ■ Mobile   ■ Other

Source: Authors' calculations based on results of household surveys conducted in Burkina Faso, Kenya, Nigeria, Senegal, South Africa, and Uganda in 2009 as part of the Africa Migration Project and Ghana Living Standards Survey 2005–06.
a. Channels used to send remittances from South Africa to other African countries. For other countries, the figure indicates channels for inward remittances.

remittance channels account for only a quarter of domestic remittances, in part because of a well-developed financial system and recent efforts to improve financial inclusion, such as the introduction of the Mzansi scheme, through which South African banks provide basic, low-cost bank accounts to the poor (Bankable Frontier Associates 2009). Banks in South Africa account for 41 percent of domestic remittances, about three times the volume money transfer companies handle (16 percent). In Nigeria, which has a better banking infrastructure than most other African countries, banks account for 37 percent of the volume of remittances and money transfer companies 6 percent). In contrast, 62 percent of domestic transfers in Kenya were remitted through mobile phones as of late 2009.

During the second half of 2009, the share of households receiving within-Africa remittances that used informal channels was 24 percent in Kenya (the only country of the five with extensive reliance on transfers through mobile phones, which account for 24 percent of within-Africa remittances); 33 percent in Nigeria, where banks are more widely used than in the other countries; and 44 percent in Uganda, where money transfer operators and banks account for about half and 5 percent of domestic remittances were sent using mobile phones (this share is likely to have increased since the survey). By contrast, the share of households using informal channels for remittances from outside Africa was less than 21 percent in five of the six countries surveyed (the exception was 52 percent in Burkina Faso).

Formal channels for remittances from outside Africa and within the region are heavily dominated by money transfer companies, particularly Western Union). For the Sub-Saharan African countries in figure 2.14, only about 2 percent of households receiving remittances from outside Africa use banks; the share is slightly higher in Uganda (12.5 percent), Kenya (16.2 percent) and Nigeria (22.3 percent). The role of other intermediaries—including post offices, microfinance institutions, savings and credit cooperatives, and new technologies such as Internet transfers and mobile money transfers—is even more limited for remittances from outside Africa.

MOBILE MONEY SERVICES

Mobile money transfer services have transformed the landscape for domestic remittances in several African countries. Box 2.2 describes the transformation of the domestic remittance landscape in Kenya since the introduction of the M-Pesa mobile money service in early 2007. Mobile money transfer services are now increasingly being used for savings. More than a fifth (21 percent) of respondents in the 2008 Financial Sector

Box 2.2 Moving Money through M-Pesa in Kenya

Vodafone, through its subsidiary Safaricom, launched a mobile banking service called M-Pesa in 2007, which rapidly expanded to reach more than 12 million clients in Kenya (Joseph 2010).[a] M-Pesa operates an electronic float, or e-float. Agents of M-Pesa buy a certain amount of e-float when they join the network. For example, the minimum per branch may be K Sh 50,000 (about $620). M-Pesa agents are given a "till" for each branch—a special phone on which to transact business and manage the float. The M-Pesa agent centrally monitors the float in its branches to determine whether people are buying e-money or withdrawing cash, and transfers the e-float between branches as necessary. The e-money purchased by a registered user can be sent to other registered and nonregistered users, and withdrawn at any M-Pesa agent. The M-Pesa e-money can also be used to pay electricity bill (under an agreement with the Kenya Power Company) and school fees; it is being expanded to other types of bill payments. M-Pesa has now partnered with Equity Bank to offer M-Kesho savings accounts, by which the M-Pesa account is linked to a bank account.[24]

The availability of the M-Pesa mobile money service has wrought a profound change in the types of domestic remittance channels used by Kenyans (Pulver, Jack, and Suri 2009). Surveys by Kenya's Financial Sector Deepening found that the most commonly used means of sending money within Kenya in 2006 were by hand (58 percent), bus (27 percent), post office and money order (24 percent), direct deposit (11 percent), and money transfer service (9 percent). By 2008 M-Pesa had come to dominate domestic remittances, with 47 percent of Kenyans using M-Pesa. As a result, the share of remittances sent by hand decreased to 32 percent and the share of remittances sent by transport companies fell to just 9 percent.

The use of mobile phones to transfer money has also enabled recipients to send smaller amounts of money more often (and collectively more), because of the greater accessibility of M-Pesa agents. Average transaction size decreased by 30 percent between March 2007 and March 2009, from K Sh 3,300 (about $41 at prevailing exchange rates) to K Sh 2,300 (about $29) (Pulver, Jack, and Suri 2009) (box figure 2.2.1).

Box figure 2.2.1 Average Size of Transactions through M-Pesa, March 2007–March 2009

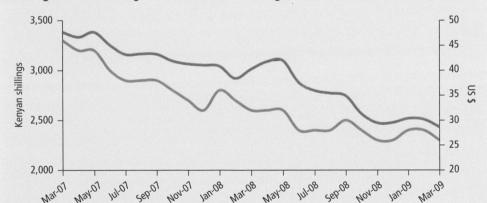

Source: Authors' calculations based on Pulver, Jack, and Suri 2009.

Source: www.safaricom.co.ke; Mas and Radcliffe 2010; meetings with Safaricom officials.
a. In the Philippines, G-Cash and S MART provide deposit, credit, and money transfers through mobile phones (World Bank 2006).

Deepening survey reported using electronic money (e-money) on their mobile phones for storing or saving money for everyday use and emergencies. Safaricom, in partnership with Kenya's Equity Bank, recently launched a mobile savings account called M-Kesho, which provides access to interest-bearing savings accounts and access to Equity Bank's network of ATMs. Other firms, such as the mobile operator Zain, are now competing with M-Pesa in Kenya to provide similar services. In neighboring Uganda, Zain and MTN's mobile money services have more than 1 million users (Business Daily Africa 2010).

Similar mobile money transfer and mobile banking services have expanded to other countries and subregions in Africa. Zain, recently acquired by Bharti Airtel, with 42 million subscribers in 15 African countries, offers Zain Zap, a mobile remittance service that offers money transfers and services such as payments for bills and groceries (Economist 2010).[25] Orange Money offers mobile money transfers in a number of West African countries, including Côte d'Ivoire, Mali, Senegal, and Madagascar.[26] In Benin, mobile operator MTN and Ecobank have launched a service that allows users to open accounts and to transfer, deposit, and withdraw money. In Sierra Leone, Splash introduced a mobile money service in September 2009, gaining more than 150,000 clients within a year (Awareness Times 2010). In South Africa, Wizzit offers person-to-person mobile money transfer services and works in partnership with ABSA Bank and the South African post office to provide banking facilities, including access to point-of-sale devices and debit cards that can be used at ATMs.[27]

Mobile money technologies are being used largely for domestic money transfers in Africa and other regions; their use for cross-border remittances is still nascent (see CGAP and Dalberg 2010 for some examples). The limited use partly reflects concerns related to money laundering using cross-border transfers, as discussed earlier. It also reflects the lack of maturity of branchless banking infrastructure on the receiving end and lack of customer awareness and trust in new services (Bold 2010).

Some telecommunications firms that operate across countries are starting to offer cross-border remittances in certain subregions. In East Africa, for example, Zain Zap (in partnership with CitiBank and Standard Chartered Bank) allows its customers to send money to any bank in Kenya, Tanzania, and Uganda and to receive money from any bank account in the world. However, in West Africa, even though members of the West African Economic and Monetary Union have a common central bank and similar monetary regulations, cross-border mobile money transfer services do not appear to be functional. Mobile money transfers being piloted in partnership with international money transfer companies (for example, from the United Kingdom and the United States to M-Pesa mobile money accounts in Kenya and in various other remittance corridors) are almost identical to cash-based remittances for the remittance sender and have a similar cost structure, with the difference that the remittance is deposited into the mobile money account of the recipient.

Even within this limited scope, the deposit of cross-border remittances directly into the mobile money account of the recipient has potentially significant advantages over traditional cash-based money transfer services. It increases the reach of remittance services, as the recipient can withdraw the remittance at domestic money transfer outlets. In Kenya, for example, the international remittance service provider can piggyback on the vast network of M-Pesa agents, greatly reducing, if not eliminating, the need to build a costly network for distribution of international remittances or to form alliances with banks or post offices. For the recipient, receiving remittances directly into a mobile money account obviates the need to travel to the nearest town or outlet of the money transfer operator to receive cash.

Money transfers through mobile phones raise the issue of whether telecommunications or banking regulators should regulate these services. Kenya's M-Pesa was allowed to operate with very little regulatory oversight or reporting requirements in its initial years. Regulators appear to be learning how to deal with this innovation. There is considerable variation in the experience of countries with mobile money services in Africa and other regions.[28] Regulatory "forbearance" may allow new technologies to scale up rapidly, but it can expose the financial system to systemic risk if the volume of transactions flowing through the mobile money transfer system is large and the deposits are stored in one or two financial institutions. The issue of how to regulate and create a level playing field between mobile network operators and banks is becoming more important as banks enter the mobile money space. Another issue is how to replicate the Kenyan example in other African countries where telecommunications infrastructure is less developed and operators are state monopolies.

Maimbo, Saranga, and Strychacz (2010) identify some issues relevant to the introduction of cross-border mobile money transfers within the Southern African Development Community. They include developing a robust and efficient regulatory framework that provides clear guidelines, expands permitted points of service (such as retail agents), reduces reporting requirements for small-value cross-border transactions, eliminates requirements for proof of legal residence to set up a bank account, and enables small-value money transfers. The authors caution that developing such regulatory frameworks can be difficult and time consuming. They therefore suggest launching pilot programs and learning from the experiences of countries such as Brazil and the Philippines to come up with innovative regulatory solutions.[29] Some pilot projects are attempting to bridge the divide between community-based pooled remittances and the use of Internet and mobile technologies. Some service providers are attempting to use Internet-based technologies to transfer remittances from France to villages in Mali (Ponsot 2011).

ROLE OF POST OFFICES

Post offices typically have very strong networks in both urban and rural areas, with significant potential to reach poor populations. They also have the right business model for serving the poor. Clotteau and Anson (2011) of the Universal Postal Union estimate that more than 80 percent of post offices in Sub-Saharan Africa are located outside the three largest cities, in areas where more than 80 percent of people in the country live. This distribution of outlets stands in sharp contrast to that of mainstream commercial banks, which are concentrated in the largest cities in Africa. Postal networks thus have a unique opportunity to become key players in both international and domestic remittances and to bring the unbanked into the formal financial system (box 2.3).

Post offices are also integrating new technologies into their operations. Some mobile money transfer operators, such as M-Pesa in Kenya and Wizzit in South Africa, are actively working with post offices and postal savings banks as their agents.[30]

TOWARD LESS COSTLY AND MORE TRANSPARENT REMITTANCES: POLICY CHANGES

This section outlines policies to improve the quality of data on remittances, reduce remittance costs, and improve transparency in remittance markets; encourage innovative money transfer technologies; use remittances to improve access to capital markets; and cope with large remittance inflows. Several policy initiatives have been undertaken on these issues in recent years (box 2.4).

IMPROVING REMITTANCE DATA

A majority of central banks in remittance-receiving countries in Sub-Saharan Africa cite better statistics on migration and remittances and improved delivery to remote areas as the top issues in need of attention to promote more efficient and secure transfer and delivery of migrant

Box 2.3 Post Offices and Remittances in Africa: A Pilot Project in West Africa

A pilot project for cross-border remittances by post offices called Mandat Express International has been implemented in six West African countries by the Universal Postal Union in collaboration with IFAD. The project provides remittance services from France to West Africa and within West Africa. An analysis of transaction data for the project in Burkina Faso shows that almost half of international remittances are received outside the two largest cities, in semi-urban or rural areas; only 8–12 percent is sent from rural areas. This pattern suggests that post offices with large networks in rural areas can play a potentially valuable role in expanding access to money transfers, basic financial services, and trade-related payments. In Mali, for example, the volume of transactions is higher for both small and large transaction than for intermediate transactions, possibly indicating that both migrants and small traders are benefiting from the post offices' international money order system.

This project addresses the issues that post offices in West Africa face in providing remittance services. Their staffs lack adequate training, and their information technology systems are outdated. In 2008, for example, only 17 percent of post offices in Sub-Saharan Africa were equipped with computers and had Internet access. Only 2 of 43 African countries that responded to a questionnaire had developed a cost accounting system. Furthermore, most postal operators are public corporations or government departments. As a result, post office workers are not always customer oriented, which has a negative impact on the quality of service. Perhaps most important, exclusivity arrangements between post offices and international money transfer companies prevent effective competition in the remittances market. These agreements can include offices that are not providing any remittance service and offices in which the partner of the post will never deploy the service.

For very small remittances, the application of anti–money laundering regulations is not proportional to the risk raised by such transactions and hinders the reduction of remittance fees. Most post offices are not connected to national clearing and settlement systems, considerably limiting their efficiency. Furthermore, a number of posts are prevented from collecting savings, a natural complement to remittance services. There is also a problem coordinating regulation. In some instances, the post is regulated by the postal regulator for international money orders and by the financial regulator for account-based services. Better coordination among the various regulating entities should be promoted to ensure better consumer protection.

Source: Clotteau and Anson 2011.

remittances (Irving, Mohapatra, and Ratha 2010 (figure 2.15). Improving data collection on remittances is also receiving attention from the international community: the G-8 Global Remittances Working Group lists improving remittance data collection as one of its four thematic areas (World Bank 2009).

African central banks and statistical agencies can improve data collection by expanding the reporting of remittances from banks to nonbank providers of remittance services (such as money transfer companies, post offices, savings cooperatives, and microfinance institutions); using surveys of migrants and recipient households to estimate remittance flows

---

Box 2.4 Policy Initiatives on Remittances in Africa

The World Bank, in partnership with the European Commission, the African Development Bank, and the International Organization for Migration, is helping the African Union Commission create the African Remittances Institute (ARI). Funded by €1.7 million contributed by the European Commission and administered by the World Bank under the guidance of the African Union Commission and the European Commission, ARI aims to strengthen the capacities of all actors (African governments, banks, remittance senders and recipients, and so on) to better use remittances as development tools for poverty reduction and to achieve less expensive, faster, and more secure remittance flows to Africa. Activities will include technical assistance, training, education, and dissemination of data. The preparatory phase project (both technical and consultative) started in 2010.

In June 2010, the World Bank launched the Future of African Remittances (FAR) program to reduce the cost of remittances, increase the availability of financial products linked to remittances, and increase the flow of remittances through formal channels. The program aims to promote the development of nontraditional remittance channels through microfinance institutions and mobile and nonbank correspondent agency networks (branchless banking) to reach rural areas. As the program matures, its focus will shift toward facilitating best practices in supervising and regulating remittance markets, developing and deploying financial products for households receiving remittances, and designing outreach strategies for engaging migrant communities. Small-scale surveys estimating the volume of remittances, the uses of remittance funds, channels used, transfer costs, and profiles of remittance-receiving households have been completed in Ethiopia, Kenya, and Uganda.

A multilateral trust fund was established in October 2009 to improve African migrant remittances by the African Development Bank group and the French government, together with International Fund for Agricultural Development (IFAD). The fund, which will be managed by the African Development Bank, has an initial capital of more than €6 million. It aims to provide finance to enhance knowledge on African migrant remittances through thematic and sectoral studies; improve regulatory frameworks and transfer conditions, with a view to reducing transfer costs; provide financial products that meet the needs of migrants and their families; and encourage the African diaspora to invest in individual productive initiatives and in the development of their countries of origin.

Source: Authors, based on information from the African Development Bank, the International Fund for Agricultural Development, and the World Bank Africa Region.

---

through formal and informal channels; and asking labor ministries and embassies in destination countries to provide estimates of remittance flows and the associated costs paid by migrants (see IMF 2009 for additional recommendations).

REDUCING COSTS AND INCREASING TRANSPARENCY IN THE PROVISION OF REMITTANCE SERVICES

Policies designed to increase financial sector development—by, for example, encouraging greater competition among banks and promoting alternative providers, such as microfinance institutions, credit cooperatives,

Figure 2.15 Most Important Areas Related to Migrants and Remittances Needing Attention, According to Central Banks in Sub-Saharan Africa

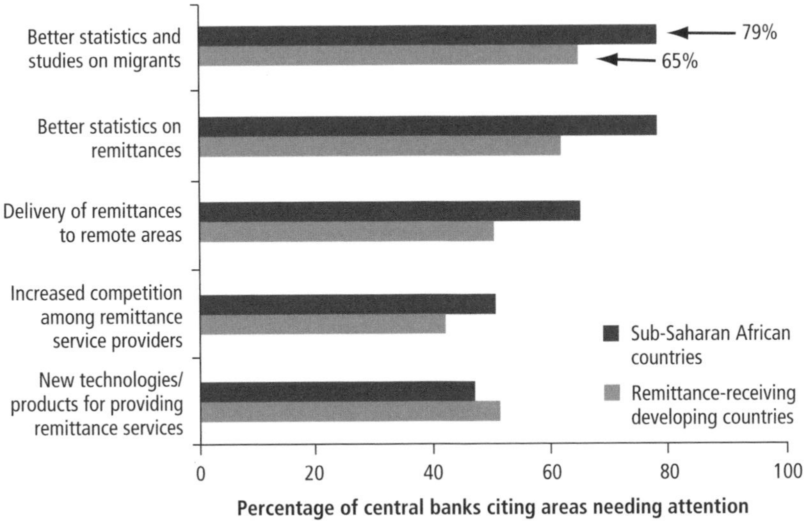

Source: Irving, Mohapatra, and Ratha 2010.

and postal savings banks—are likely to have a beneficial impact on the market for remittances. Increasing the role of postal savings banks deserves emphasis, given their strong networks in both urban and rural areas, with significant coverage of poor populations.

This section focuses on policies directed specifically at the remittance market. Discouraging exclusive partnerships—for example, between banks and international money transfer agencies—would reduce remittance costs, benefitting both migrants and remittance recipients. The General Principles for International Remittance Services, compiled by the World Bank and the Bank for International Settlements, discourage such partnerships; this recommendation has already led to policy changes in some African countries and has been implemented by the Central Bank of Nigeria and by Rwandan authorities (World Bank and BIS–CPSS 2007).

Disseminating information on remittance channels and the costs of sending money to Africa would increase transparency and competition in the remittance industry, encouraging lower prices and new entrants while fostering the increased use of formal channels. Following the success of a U.K. remittance price database, France, Germany, Italy, the Netherlands, New Zealand, and Norway have commissioned websites that provide information on available channels. The World Bank has launched a Remittance Prices Worldwide database, which covers more than 150 remittance corridors.

The World Bank is helping several countries control the quality of national price databases and integrate their information into the global database. The information on remittance channels and costs should also be provided in pamphlet form to emigrants at airports before departure, during predeparture orientation/training, and at embassies and associations in destination countries to reach migrants without access to the Internet. It could also be made available through central banks, labor ministries, foreign employment bureaus, and recruitment associations in origin countries.

Regulations in destination countries could encourage greater transparency in remittance markets. The United States has introduced regulations requiring remittance service providers to disclose prices and exchange rate commissions and establish error resolution mechanisms for consumers. A similar initiative to improve transparency, competition, and consumer protection in remittance markets is under way in Europe (box 2.5).

Box 2.5 Increasing Transparency and Competition in Remittance Markets: Wall Street Reforms and the European Union's Payment Services Directive

The Wall Street Reform and Consumer Protection Act, signed into law by President Obama on July 21, 2010, aims to increase transparency in the pricing of remittance services. Providers of remittance services in the United States will be required to disclose to remitters the equivalent amount that will be received in local currency by the beneficiary, the fees for the transaction, access to error-resolution mechanisms, and contact details of the relevant regulatory authority. Remittance issues will be integrated into the strategy for financial literacy for low-income communities as part of the U.S. government's Strategy for Assuring Financial Empowerment (SAFE). The Federal Reserve and the Treasury will work to extend automatic clearinghouse systems and other payment systems for remittances to foreign countries, with a focus on countries that receive significant remittance transfers from the United States. Studies will be conducted on the feasibility of using remittance history to improve credit scores and the legal and business model barriers to such credit scoring.

Concurrently, the European Payment Services Directive implemented in the European Union (EU) will increase transparency and improve consumer protection for remittance services. A new type of institution, called a *payment institution*, has been created that is subject to less stringent licensing, capital, and reporting requirements than conventional banks and financial institutions (previously, money transfer operators had to register as financial institutions in some EU countries). In the United Kingdom, remittance transactions will come under an independent financial ombudsman service for the first time. Although the Payment Services Directive applies only for transactions from one EU country to another, some remittance-sending countries, such as Italy, have extended these rules to transfers to countries outside the EU.

Source: www.appleseednetwork.org; Isaacs 2011.

FOSTERING THE USE OF INNOVATIVE MOBILE MONEY TRANSFER TECHNOLOGIES

M-Pesa in Kenya is a striking example of the ability of African countries to "leapfrog" even developed countries in the use of innovative mobile money services. Measures that would encourage the expansion of mobile phones to cross-border remittances include the following:

- harmonizing banking and telecommunications regulations to enable mainstream African banks to participate in mobile money transfers and telecommunications firms to offer microdeposit and savings accounts
- simplifying AML-CFT regulations for low-value transfers
- ensuring that mobile distribution networks are open to multiple international remittance service providers, instead of becoming exclusive partnerships between an international money transfer operator and a country-based mobile money services.

The price structure of mobile money services should also be examined; the price of mobile money services appear to be similar to that charged for sending cash remittances in the U.K.–Kenya and U.S.–Philippines corridors, despite the fact that reliance on mobile phone transfers reduces the need to build costly distribution networks.

INCREASING THE ROLE OF POST OFFICES AND MICROFINANCE INSTITUTIONS IN REMITTANCES

Increasing the role of African post offices in remittance transmissions can leverage their strong networks in both urban and rural areas and better reach poor populations. African post offices can partner with destination-country post offices, banks, and money transfer companies to extend existing domestic money order facilities to international remittances. Some measures suggested by Clotteau and Anson (2011) include the following:

- *Providing universal service.* Many African governments are in the process of defining their universal service. Some, like Benin, have included money orders and basic savings accounts in the definition. The inclusion of financial services in the definition of universal service should be encouraged to foster financial inclusion by leveraging postal networks.
- *Developing infrastructure.* Connecting post offices to high-speed Internet and creating integrated management information systems are necessary to ensure adequate quality of service. Burkina Faso, Botswana,

Gabon, Morocco, South Africa, Togo, and Tunisia have already completed or are in the process of completing these steps. At the opposite end of the spectrum are countries such as Chad and the Democratic Republic of Congo, where funds and technical assistance are needed to strengthen infrastructure.

- *Developing new products.* Basic savings accounts into which remittances can be paid, small savings deposited, and payments processed should be offered in connection with remittances. Countries such as Côte d'Ivoire, Lesotho, and Mali, where postal banking services have been separated from the rest of post office services, might explore other models, such as the agent banking model, in which the post office acts as an agent of a bank, which could also be good alternatives for countries in which the regulatory framework does not allow post offices to develop financial services.

- *Creating new models.* New technologies are changing the way financial services are being delivered. In Kenya, for example, where the success of M-Pesa has been well documented, the post office is acting as a "super-agent," providing e-float (working capital) for smaller agents. In Tunisia the post office has partnered with the national telecommunications company to develop mobile payment services. Each post office has to take advantage of its own key strengths (the size and reach of its physical network, its know-how in cash logistics, the number of postal banking clients) to make better use of new technologies.

A clear policy recommendation is to eliminate exclusive partnerships and encourage African post offices to partner with more money transfer companies (and even banks), in order to put downward pressure on costs. The revenue losses in the short term will most likely be offset by larger volumes, benefiting postal networks, migrants, and remittance recipients. Rural banks, savings cooperatives, and microfinance institutions in Africa can play a similar role in improving access to formal remittance (and financial) services. Measures to encourage the participation of savings and credit cooperatives, rural banks, and microfinance institutions in providing remittance services will help improve financial access. Money transfers can act as an entry point for providing remittance senders and unbanked recipients in rural areas with other financial products and services, such as deposits, savings, and credit facilities. Policies should also promote multiple partnerships for sending and delivering remittances among rural banks and microfinance institutions.

DEALING WITH THE EXCHANGE RATE EFFECTS OF LARGE REMITTANCE INFLOWS

Policy makers in Sub-Saharan Africa should be particularly alert to Dutch disease in countries in which remittances inflows are large compared with the size of the economy, supply constraints are a significant hindrance to the expansion of the nontradable sector, and a significant portion of remittances is spent on domestic goods, especially nontradables (Gupta, Pattillo, and Wagh 2009). Countries should adjust to large remittance inflows that are likely to be permanent by maintaining market-based exchange rate policies; supporting the production of tradables that might be harmed by overvaluation of the exchange rate (through infrastructure investments, for example); and reducing labor and product market rigidities that impair competitiveness. Large inflows that are likely to be temporary can be sterilized, although the cost of sterilization can be high. Meanwhile, the resulting rise in domestic interest rates can attract more capital inflows, placing further pressure on the exchange rate (Fajnzylber and Lopez 2007). It can be difficult to distinguish between temporary and permanent levels of remittance inflows, although as remittances tend to be relatively stable, the risk of Dutch disease effects is lower than it is for natural resource windfalls and other cyclical flows.

ANNEX 2A

Table 2A.1   Remittance Flows to African Countries, 2006–10
($ millions, except where otherwise indicated)

Region/country	2006	2007	2008	2009	2010e	Growth (percent) 2008–09	Growth (percent) 2009–10e	Share of GDP (percent) 2009
Sub-Saharan Africa	12,668	18,584	21,359	20,575	21,490	−3.7	4.4	2.6
Nigeria	5,435	9,221	9,980	9,585	9,975	−4.0	4.1	5.5
Sudan	1,179	1,769	3,100	2,993	3,178	−3.5	6.2	5.5
Kenya	1,128	1,588	1,692	1,686	1,758	−0.3	4.3	5.7
Senegal	925	1,192	1,288	1,191	1,164	−7.5	−2.3	9.3
South Africa	734	834	823	902	1,008	9.7	11.8	0.3
Uganda	411	452	724	694	773	−4.1	11.3	4.3
Lesotho	361	451	439	450	525	2.6	16.7	28.5
Mali	212	344	431	405	385	−6.1	−4.8	4.5
Ethiopia	172	358	387	353	387	−8.8	9.7	1.2
Togo	232	284	337	307	302	−9.0	−1.7	10.7
North Africa	13,945	18,267	19,815	17,489	18,163	−11.7	3.9	3.3
Egypt, Arab Rep.	5,330	7,656	8,694	7,150	7,681	−17.8	7.4	3.8
Morocco	5,451	6,730	6,895	6,271	6,447	−9.0	2.8	6.9
Algeria	1,610	2,120	2,202	2,059	2,031	−6.5	−1.3	1.5
Tunisia	1,510	1,716	1,977	1,966	1,960	−0.5	−0.3	5.0
Djibouti	28	29	30	28	28	−6.8	−0.3	2.7
Libya	16	16	16	14	16	−10.1	9.3	0.0
All Africa	26,613	36,851	41,174	38,063	39,652	−7.6	4.2	2.6
All developing countries	226,707	278,456	324,832	307,088	325,466	−5.5	6.0	1.9

Source: World Bank migration and remittances unit, based on IMF balance of payment statistics.
Note: e = estimated.

Table 2A.2   Formal and Informal Remittance Channels in Selected African Countries, 2009
(percent of recipients)

Country/channel	Remittances from outside Africa	Remittances from within Africa	Domestic remittances
Burkina Faso			
Money transfer operator	43.2	10.5	2.0
Brought home by migrant during visit	34.1	15.2	49.5
Friend or relative	18.2	64.7	37.4
Bank	2.3	0.7	0.4
Postal money order	0	3.2	1.4
Courier, bus, transport, or travel agency	0	3.0	5.8
Informal individual agent	0	2.5	1.9
ATM card or Internet money transfer	0	0	0.2
Other	2.3	0.2	1.3
Total	100.0	100.0	100.0
Ghana (for 2005–06)			
Money transfer operator	67.8	10.9	0.6
Friend or relative	16.1	52.2	45.1
Fast money transfer	7.8	0	0
Brought home by migrant during visit	4.4	32.6	49.0
Bank	2.2	0	0.6
Other	1.7	4.3	4.7
Total	100.0	100.0	100.0
Kenya			
Money transfer operator	64.0	38.6	1.5
Bank	17.2	11.4	6.3
Foreign exchange bureau, credit union	6.3	1.5	0.6
Friend or relative	3.8	9.1	6.5
Brought home by migrant during visit	2.0	7.6	20.0
Postal money order	1.4	1.5	1.1
Informal individual agent	1.4	0	0
Courier, bus, other transport, or travel agency	0.5	3.8	1.5
Mobile phone	2.9	23.5	61.5
ATM card or Internet money transfer	0.5	0	0
Other	0	0	0.8
Total	100.0	100.0	100.0

Table 2A.2   Formal and Informal Remittance Channels in Selected African Countries, 2009 *(continued)*
(percent of recipients)

Country/channel	Remittances from outside Africa	Remittances from within Africa	Domestic remittances
Nigeria			
Money transfer operator	57.1	35.2	6.3
Friend or relative	12.8	15.4	21.2
Direct transfer to bank account	11.8	12.1	35.0
Bank as paying agent for money transfer operator	10.5	17.6	2.6
Brought home by migrant during visit	5.4	13.2	27.7
Informal individual agent	2.5	4.4	4.1
Postal money order	0	1.1	0
Foreign exchange bureau	0	1.1	0.1
Credit union	0	0	0.2
Travel agency	0	0	0.4
Courier, bus, or other transport	0	0	0.5
Mobile phone or telecom service provider	0	0	0.4
Prepaid card or ATM card	0	0	0.2
Internet money transfer	0	0	0.1
Other	0	0	1.2
Total	100.0	100.0	100.0
Senegal			
Money transfer operator	81.5	30.8	4.9
Friend or relative	10.1	41.1	37.3
Postal money order	2.5	6.3	3.4
Informal individual agent	1.9	4.3	3.4
Bank as paying agent for money transfer operator	1.5	0	0.1
Credit union	0.7	0	0
Foreign exchange bureau	0.4	0.4	0
Direct transfer to bank account	0.3	0	0
Brought home by migrant during visit	0.5	14.2	36.7
Courier, bus, or other transport	0	0.6	11.8
Mobile phone or telecom service provider	0	0	0.6
Travel agency	0	0	0
Prepaid card or ATM card	0	0	0
Internet money transfer	0	0	0
Other	0.4	2.2	1.9
Total	100.0	100.0	100.0

Table 2A.2 **Formal and Informal Remittance Channels in Selected African Countries, 2009** *(continued)*
(percent of recipients)

Country/channel	Remittances from outside Africa	Remittances from within Africa	Domestic remittances
Uganda			
Money transfer operator	55.4	36.3	4.2
Foreign exchange bureau, credit union	13.4	1.3	0.9
Bank	12.5	15.0	10.8
Friend or relative	8.9	21.3	27.4
Brought back by migrant during visit	4.5	20.0	47.6
Postal money order	2.7	0	0.2
Mobile phone	0.9	2.5	5.2
ATM card or Internet money transfer	0.9	0	0
Courier, bus, other transport, or travel agency	0	2.5	3.1
Informal individual agent	0	0	0
Other	0	1.3	0
Total	100.0	100.0	100.0

South Africa (outward remittances)	Remittances sent to other countries in Africa	Domestic remittances
Friend or relative	58.0	18.8
Money transfer operator	4.6	15.8
Courier, bus, or other transport	18.3	1.2
Direct transfer to bank account	5.3	40.6
Foreign exchange bureau	0	0.6
Mobile phone or telecom service provider	0	0.6
Postal money order	6.1	6.7
Travel agency	0	0.6
Credit union	0	0.6
Brought back by migrant during visit	2.3	5.5
Prepaid card or ATM card	2.3	2.4
Internet money transfer	0	1.8
Other nonfinancial institution that provides remittance services	0	1.2
Other	1.5	3.6
Total	100.0	100.0

Source: Authors, based on results household surveys conducted in Burkina Faso, Kenya, Nigeria, Senegal, South Africa, and Uganda in 2009 as part of the Africa Migration Project and Ghana Living Standards Survey 2005–06.
Note: For all countries except South Africa, figures show remittance channels for receipt of remittances by households. For South Africa, the first column shows channels for remittances sent by immigrants from other African countries living in South Africa. Money transfer operators include Western Union, Moneygram, and others. Data for Ghana are from 2005 to 2006.

NOTES

1. The Africa Migration Project household surveys were conducted in the second half of 2009 in Burkina Faso, Kenya, Nigeria, Senegal, South Africa, and Uganda. This chapter also draws on an earlier survey conducted in Ghana in 2007–08.

2. There are some notable exceptions in Sub-Saharan Africa. For example, Cape Verde, Ethiopia, Kenya, and Nigeria collect and publish monthly data on remittances. Several North African countries, such as Egypt and Morocco, publish quarterly data.

3. Remittances do not appear to have been affected by economic cycles in migrants' destination countries in the past. Roache and Gradzka (2007) find that remittance flows to Latin America were relatively insensitive to business cycle fluctuations in the United States over the 1990–2007 period. Given the magnitude of the financial crisis that began in 2008, there is a strong possibility that it has affected the incomes of migrants and their ability to send money home.

4. Sayan (2006) finds that remittances are strongly countercyclical in poor countries, such as Bangladesh and India, but procyclical in middle-income countries, such as Jordan and Morocco. Lueth and Ruiz-Arranz (2008) find that remittances to Sri Lanka are positively correlated with oil prices—perhaps reflecting the economic situation of Sri Lankan migrants in destination countries in the Gulf—but tend to decline when the Sri Lankan currency weakens.

5. The stability of remittances to the Philippines was an important factor in its ability to issue a $750 million bond despite the global financial crisis. Bangladesh was rated for the first time in April 2010, receiving a BB–rating from Standard & Poor's Investor Service and a Ba3 from Moody's Investor Service, similar to the ratings of many emerging markets. The rating agencies cited the high share of remittance flows in GDP and the high growth rate as important factors in their rating decisions.

6. An investment-grade rating makes these transactions attractive to a wider range of "buy-and-hold" investors, such as pension funds and institutional investors, which have institutional limitations on buying subinvestment-grade assets. As a result, the issuer can access a wider pool of international investors, allowing it to reduce the cost of capital and lengthen maturities. Moreover, by establishing a credit history for the borrower, these deals enhance the ability to access capital markets and reduce the costs of doing so in the future.

7. The United Nations Development Programme (UNDP), in partnership with Standard and Poors, helped 11 African countries obtain sovereign ratings. The United States, in partnership with the Inter-American Development Bank, launched the BRIDGE (Building Remittance Investments for Development, Growth and Entrepreneurship) initiative, which aims to securitize remittances for infrastructure projects in developing countries, starting with pilots in El Salvador and Honduras.

8. An empirical study of 109 countries for 1990–2003 shows that a well-developed financial sector can more effectively intermediate remittances with investment and that the impact of remittance inflows on exchange rate appreciation is smaller when the level of financial development is higher (Acosta, Baerg,

and Mandelman 2009). Increased receipt of remittances is also associated with higher market capitalization, a key indicator of financial market development (Billmeier and Massa 2009). A higher sovereign rating as a result of remittances can translate into greater access of subsovereign entities to international capital markets, thereby increasing the level of investment in the economy.

9. Latin American countries receiving remittances have experienced some exchange rate appreciation (Amuedo-Dorantes and Pozo 2004; Fajnzylber and Lopez 2007), but Fajnzylber and Lopez (2007) find little or no impact of remittance flows on the exchange rate outside Latin America.

10. Another factor accounting for the lack of significance may be omitted variables, such as policies and institutions (Catrinescu and others 2009), the level of financial development (Giuliano and Ruiz-Arranz 2009), and other indirect channels through which remittances can influence economic growth (Rao and Hassan 2009).

11. Acosta, Fajnzylber, and López (2007) find that remittances to Latin America reduce inequality on average, but the extent of the reduction in inequality is relatively small, with variation across countries.

12. An asset index composed of land, quality of housing, access to electricity, and household amenities was used as a proxy for consumption expenditure (Filmer and Pritchett 2001).

13. The evidence on whether skilled or unskilled migrants send larger remittances is mixed. Some studies suggest that skilled migrants remit less, because they are more likely to settle down in their host countries and eventually bring their families (Niimi and Ozden 2006; Faini 2007). Other studies, based on microdata, find a positive relationship between education and the amounts remitted (Bollard and others 2009; Clemens 2009). Some authors suggest that remittances sent by skilled migrants may exceed the cost of their training (Clemens 2009; Easterly and Nyarko 2009).

14. Self-reported uses of remittances should be treated with caution, for several reasons. Recipients may recall more recent expenses, especially on infrequent "big ticket" purchases and underestimate the amounts spent on day-to-day expenses. They may also be reluctant to divulge details of remittances on purposes that the remitter may not have intended or approved of. The absence of detailed bookkeeping that separates remittances from other sources of income implies that few recipients are in a position to provide an accurate picture of the uses of remittances. Despite these caveats, it is still useful to examine the uses of remittances reported by recipient households.

15. Woodruff and Zenteno (2007) find that migration is associated with higher investment and higher profits for a set of firms and looser capital constraints for a subsample of firms in capital-intensive sectors.

16. Fajnzylber and Lopez (2007) find that in Guatemala and Nicaragua, children 1–5 in remittance-receiving households were more likely to be of above average height and weight and to have had a doctor-assisted delivery. Studies of Mexico find that remittances were associated with lower infant mortality rates (Hildebrandt and McKenzie 2005; Lopez-Cordova 2005) and higher healthcare expenditures (Amuedo-Dorantes, Pozo, and Sainz 2007; Valero-Gill 2009). Kanaiaupuni and Donato (1999) find that infant mortality rates initially rose in

Mexican villages with very high rates of migration to the United States but that remittances eventually reduced infant mortality rates.

17. Mohapatra, Joseph, and Ratha (2009) find that remittance-receiving households in Ghana are likely to have better access to communication equipment and mobile phones than households that do not receive any remittances, even after controlling for the possibility of self-selection of remittance-receiving households.

18. The World Bank's remittance price database provides average remittance costs through banks and nonbank intermediaries for more than 150 migration corridors.

19. Transfer costs tend to be lower when financial systems are more developed and exchange rates less volatile (Freund and Spatafora 2008). Beck and Martinez Peria (2009) find that remittance corridors with larger stocks of migrants, a larger number of remittance service providers, and greater banking competition have lower costs.

20. Access to "bank-like" institutions, such as microfinance institutions and savings and credit cooperatives, is also limited outside of urban areas.

21. Surveys of remittance markets in France and the United Kingdom were conducted as part of the *Remittance Markets in Africa* report (Mohapatra and Ratha 2011), and qualitative information was collected for the United States. Conducting a survey in the United States proved infeasible, because there is no national-level institutional focal point; each state has a different legal and regulatory framework, compliance requirements, and institutions governing remittances (Andreassen 2006).

22. Mainstream banks in France are starting to target African migrants for remittances and other financial services, such as burial insurance and transnational mortgages; they continue to play a limited role in remittances (Ponsot 2011). Several French banks have branches and subsidiaries in North Africa and West Africa. They are more established in North African countries, where they provide a range of services to current and former migrants, such as low-cost banking accounts for North African migrants, distribution of pension benefits of former migrants who have retired in their countries of origin, and even transnational mortgages for current migrants who wish to purchase property. French banks appear to provide a smaller range of services to migrants from North Africa; some banks cite inadequate property rights as their reason for not issuing transnational loans.

23. The Southern African Migration Project conducted national-level representative surveys on remittance flows and usage at the household level for five countries belonging to the Southern African Development Community: Botswana, Lesotho, Mozambique, Swaziland, and Zimbabwe, with a focus on intraregional transfers from South Africa and Botswana (Pendleton and others 2006). The use of informal channels is predominant in remittances sent from South Africa to neighboring countries. Among formal channels used, TEBA Bank provides bank transfers for migrant mining workers in South Africa, accounting for about 16 percent of transfers to Botswana and 8 percent to Swaziland.

24. http://mobile-financial.com/node/8174/M-PESA-meets-microsavings-with-Equity-Bank-deal-in-Kenya.

25. The concept of mobile money transfers is being transferred from Africa to other developing regions. India's Bharti Telecom, which recently acquired Zain, has received approval from India's central bank to start mobile payments services in India. This "mobile wallet" will allow Bharti Airtel's customers in India to exchange physical cash for virtual money, which they can use to pay for goods and services up to Rs. 5,000 (about $108) per transaction. It does not, however, allow cash withdrawals (Economic Times 2010).

26. http://allafrica.com/stories/201006071332.html.

27. http://www.wizzit.co.za.

28. In the Philippines, for example, regulators have imposed the same reporting requirements on bank and nonbank mobile money providers (Dolan 2009).

29. Brazil has considerable experience with branchless banking, using retail payment networks and point-of-sale devices deployed at agents such as grocery stores (Pickens, Porteous, and Rotman 2009). The Philippines has been at the forefront of mobile money transfer services (World Bank 2006).

30. http://www.postbank.co.ke/.

BIBLIOGRAPHY

Abdih, Yasser, Ralph Chami, Jihad Dagher, and Peter Montiel. 2008. "Remittances and Institutions: Are Remittances a Curse?" IMF Working Paper 08/29, International Monetary Fund, Washington, DC.

Abdih, Yasser, Michael Gapen, Amine Mati, and Ralph Chami. 2009. "Fiscal Sustainability in Remittance-Dependent Economies. IMF Working Paper 09/190, International Monetary Fund, Washington, DC.

Acosta, Pablo, Nicole Baerg, and Federico Mandelman. 2009. "Financial Development, Remittances, and Real Exchange Rate Appreciation." *Economic Review* 94 (1), Federal Reserve Bank of Atlanta.

Acosta, Pablo A., Cesar Calderon, Humberto Lopez, and Pablo Fajnzylber. 2008. "What Is the Impact of International Remittances on Poverty and Inequality in Latin America?" *World Development* 36 (1): 89–114.

Acosta, Pablo, Pablo Fajnzylber, and Humberto López. 2007. "The Impact of Remittances on Poverty and Human Capital: Evidence from Latin American Household Surveys." In *International Migration, Economic Development and Policy*, ed. Caglar Özden and Maurice Schiff, 59–98. New York: World Bank and Palgrave Macmillan.

Acosta, Pablo, Emmanuel Lartey, and Federico Mandelman. 2009. "Remittances and the Dutch Disease." *Journal of International Economics* 79 (1): 102–16.

Adams, Richard H. 1998. "Remittances, Investment and Rural Asset Accumulation in Pakistan." *Economic Development and Cultural Change* 47: 155–73.

———. 2006. "Remittances and Poverty in Ghana." Policy Research Working Paper 3838, World Bank, Washington, DC.

Adams, Richard H., and Alfredo Cuecuecha. 2010. "Remittances, Household Expenditure and Investment in Guatemala." *World Development*. http://class.povertylectures.com/AdamsCuecuechaRemittancesinGuatemala.pdf.

Adams, Richard H., Alfredo Cuecuecha, and John Page. 2008a. "The Impact of Remittances on Poverty and Inequality in Ghana." Policy Research Working Paper 4732, World Bank, Washington, DC.

———. 2008b "Remittances, Consumption and Investment in Ghana." Policy Research Working Paper 4515, World Bank, Washington, DC.

Adams, Richard H., and John Page. 2003. "International Migration, Remittances and Poverty in Developing Countries." Policy Research Working Paper 3179, World Bank, Washington, DC.

———. 2005. "Do International Migration and Remittances Reduce Poverty in Developing Countries?" *World Development* 33 (10): 1645–69.

Afreximbank (African Export-Import Bank). 2005. *Annual Report.* http://www.afreximbank.com.

Aggarwal, Reena, Asli Demirgüç-Kunt, and Maria Soledad Martinez Peria. 2006. "Do Workers' Remittances Promote Financial Development?" Policy Research Working Paper 3957, World Bank, Washington, DC.

Ajayi, M. A., M. A. Ijaiya, G. T. Ijaiya, R. A. Bello, M. A. Ijaiya, and S. L Adeyemi. 2009. "International Remittances and Well-Being in Sub-Saharan Africa." *Journal of Economics and International Finance* 1 (3): 078–084.

Aker, Jenny C., and Isaac M. Mbiti. 2010. "Mobile Phones and Economic Development in Africa." *Journal of Economic Perspectives* 24 (3): 207–32 .

Akinlo, Anthony E., and Tajudeen Egbetunde. 2010. "Financial Development and Economic Growth: The Experience of 10 Sub-Saharan African Countries Revisited." *Review of Finance and Banking* 2 (1): 17–28.

Amuedo-Dorantes, Catalina, and Susan Pozo. 2004. "Workers' Remittances and the Real Exchange Rate: A Paradox of Gifts." *World Development* 32 (8): 1407–17.

———. 2010. "New Evidence on the Role of Remittances on Health Care Expenditures by Mexican Households." *Review of Economics of the Household* DOI 10.1007/s11150-009-9080-7.

Amuedo-Dorantes, Catalina, Annie Georges, and Susan Pozo. 2010. "Migration, Remittances, and Children's Schooling in Haiti." In *The Annals of the American Academy of Political and Social Science*, issue: "Continental Divides: International Migration in the Americas," ed. Katharine M. Donato, Jonathan Hiskey, Jorge Durand, and Douglas S. Massey. Thousand Oaks, CA: Sage.

Amuedo-Dorantes, Catalina, Susan Pozo, and Tania Sainz. 2007. "Remittances and Healthcare Expenditure Patterns of Populations in Origin Communities: Evidence from Mexico." *Integration and Trade Journal* 27: 159–84.

Andreassen, Ole. 2006. "Remittance Service Providers in the United States: How Remittance Firms Operate and How They Perceive Their Business Environment." Financial Sector Discussion Series, Payments Systems and Remittances, June. World Bank, Washington, DC.

Anyanwu, John C., and Andrew E. O. Erhijakpor. 2010. "Do International Remittances Affect Poverty in Africa?" *African Development Review* 22 (1): 51–91.

Ashraf, Nava, Diego Aycinena, Claudia Martinez, and Dean Yang. 2010. "Remittances and the Problem of Control: A Field Experiment among Migrants from El Salvador." University of Michigan, Ann Arbor.

Avendaño, Rolando, Norbert Gaillard, and Sebastián Nieto-Parra. 2009. "Are Workers' Remittances Relevant for Credit Rating Agencies?" OECD Development Centre Working Paper 282, Organisation for Economic Co-operation and Development, Paris.

Awareness Times (Sierra Leone). 2010. "In Sierra Leone, over 150,000 Clients Registered with Splash Mobile Money." September 16. http://news.sl/drweb site/publish/article_200516307.shtml.

Azam, Jean-Paul, and Flore Gubert. 2005. "Those in Kayes. The Impact of Remittances on their Recipients in Africa." *Revue économique* 56 (6): 1331–58.

———. 2006. "Migrants' Remittances and the Household in Africa: A Review of Evidence." *Journal of African Economies* 15 (AERC Supplement): 426–62.

Babatunde, Raphael O., and Enrica C. Martinetti. 2010. "Impact of Remittances on Food Security and Nutrition in Rural Nigeria." Centre for International Cooperation and Development, University of Pavia, Italy.

Bankable Frontier Associates. 2009. *The Mzansi Bank Account Initiative in South Africa*. Report commissioned by FinMark Trust, Somerville, MA. http://www.finmark.org.za/documents/R_Mzansi_BFA.pdf.

Bansak, Cynthia, and Brian Chezum. 2009. "How Do Remittances Affect Human Capital Formation of School-Age Boys and Girls?" *American Economic Review* 99 (2): 145–48.

Barajas, Adolfo, Ralph Chami, Connel Fullenkamp, Michael Gapen, and Peter J. Montiel. 2009. "Do Workers' Remittances Promote Economic Growth?" IMF Working Paper 09/153, International Monetary Fund, Washington, DC.

Barro, Robert. 1997. *Determinants of Economic Growth: A Cross-Country Empirical Study*. Cambridge, MA: MIT Press.

Beck, Thorsten, and Maria Soledad Martinez Peria. 2009. "What Explains the Cost of Remittances? An Examination across 119 Country Corridors." Policy Research Working Paper 5072, World Bank, Washington, DC.

Billmeier, Andreas, and Isabella Massa. 2009. "What Drives Stock Market Development in Emerging Markets—Institutions, Remittances, or Natural Resources?" *Emerging Markets Review* 10 (2): 23–35.

Birdsall, Nancy, and Punam Chuhan. 1986. "Client Choice of Health Care Treatment in Rural Mali." World Bank, Health, Nutrition and Population Department, Washington, DC.

Block, S., and P. Webb. 2001. "The Dynamics of Livelihood Diversification in Post Famine Ethiopia." *Food Policy* 26 (4): 333–50.

Bold, Chris. 2010. "Borderless Branchless Banking." December 14, CGAP Technology Blog, Consultative Group to Assist the Poor, Washington DC.

Bollard, Albert, David McKenzie, and Melanie Morten. 2010. "The Remitting Patterns of African Migrants in the OECD." *Journal of African Economies* 19 (5): 605–34.

Bollard, Albert, David McKenzie, Melanie Morten, and Hillel Rapoport. 2009. "Remittances and the Brain Drain Revisited: The Microdata Show That More Educated Migrants Remit More." Policy Research Working Paper 5113, World Bank, Washington, DC.

Borensztein, Eduardo, Kevin Cowan, and Patricio Valenzuela. 2007. "Sovereign Ceilings 'Lite'? The Impact of Sovereign Ratings on Corporate Ratings in Emerging Market Economies." IMF Working Paper 07/75, International Monetary Fund, Washington, DC.

Bourdet, Yves, and Hans Falck. 2006. "Emigrants' Remittances and Dutch Disease in Cape Verde." *International Economic Journal* 20 (3): 267–84.

Bracking, Sarah, and Lloyd Sachikonye. 2008 "Remittances, Poverty Reduction and Informalization in Zimbabwe 2005-6: A Political Economy of Dispossession?" Brooks World Poverty Institute Working Paper 28, University of Manchester, United Kingdom.

Bredl, Sebastian. 2011. "Migration, Remittances and Educational Outcomes: The Case of Haiti." *International Journal of Educational Development* 31(2): 162–68.

Bugamelli, Matteo, and Francesco Paterno. 2009. "Do Workers' Remittances Reduce the Probability of Current Account Reversals?" *World Development* 37 (12): 1821–38.

Business Daily Africa. 2010. "Mobile Money Transforms Uganda." September 7. http://www.businessdailyafrica.com/Mobile%20money%20transforms%20Uganda/-/539546/1004934/-/dhr8ubz.

Bussolo, Maurizio, and Dennis Medvedev. 2007. "Do Remittances Have a Flip Side? A General Equilibrium Analysis of Remittances, Labor Supply Responses, and Policy Options for Jamaica." Policy Research Working Paper 4143, World Bank, Washington, DC.

Calero, Carla, Arjun S. Bedi, and Robert Sparrow. 2009 "Remittances, Liquidity Constraints and Human Capital Investments in Ecuador." *World Development* 37 (6): 1143–54.

Catrinescu, Natalia, Miguel Leon-Ledesma, Matloob Piracha, and Bryce Quillin. 2009. "Remittances, Institutions, and Economic Growth." *World Development* 37 (1): 81–92.

CGAP (Consultative Group to Assist the Poor), and Dalberg Global Development Advisers. 2010. "Improving Access and Reducing Costs of International Remittances through Branchless Banking Solutions." http://www.cgap.org/gm/document-1.9.49049/Dalberg-CGAP_Intl_Remit_Branchless_Banking_Findings.pdf.

Chami, Ralph, Adolfo Barajas, Thomas Cosimano, Connel Fullenkamp, Michael Gapen, and Peter Montiel. 2008. "Macroeconomic Consequences of Remittances." IMF Occasional Paper 259, International Monetary Fund, Washington, DC.

Chami, Ralph, Dalia Hakura, and Peter Montiel. 2009. "Remittances: An Automatic Stabilizer?" IMF Working Paper 09/91, International Monetary Fund, Washington, DC.

Chauvet, Lisa, Flore Gubert, and Sandrine Mesplé-Somps. 2009. "Are Remittances More Effective than Aid to Reduce Child Mortality? An Empirical Assessment Using Inter- and Intra-Country Data." DIAL Working Paper DT/2009-11, Développement, Institutions et Analyses de Long terme (DIAL), Paris.

Clarke, George, and Scott Wallsten. 2004. "Do Remittances Protect Household in Developing Countries against Shocks? Evidence from a Natural Disaster in Jamaica." World Bank, Development Research Group, Washington, DC.

Clemens, Michael. 2009. "The Financial Effects of High-Skilled Emigration: New Data on African Doctors Abroad." Paper presented at the International Conference on Diaspora for Development, Washington, DC, July 13–14. http://siteresources.worldbank.org/INTPROSPECTS/Resources/334934-1110315015165/Clemens.pdf.

Clotteau Nils, and Jose Anson. 2011. "Role of Posts in Remittances and Financial Inclusion." Background note prepared for the Africa Migration Project, Universal Postal Union, Berne, Switzerland. Migration and Development Brief 15, World Bank, Washington, DC.

Cox-Edwards, Alejandra, and Manuelita Ureta. 2003. "International Migration, Remittances and Schooling: Evidence from El Salvador." *Journal of Development Economics* 72 (2): 429–61.

De, Prabal, and Dilip Ratha. 2006. "Migration and Remittances in Sri Lanka." World Bank, Development Prospects Group, Washington, DC.

De Haas, H. 2005. "International Migration, Remittances and Development: Myths and Facts." *Third World Quarterly* 26 (8): 1269–84.

Demirgüç-Kunt, Asli, Thorsten Beck, and Patrick Honohan. 2008. "Finance for All? Policies and Pitfalls in Expanding Access." Policy Research Report, World Bank, Washington, DC.

Dolan, Jonathan. 2009. *Accelerating the Development of Mobile Money Ecosystems.* Report on the Mobile Money Summit 2009, International Finance Corporation and Kennedy School of Government, Harvard University, Cambridge, MA. http://www.hks.harvard.edu/m-rcbg/CSRI/publications/report_39_mobile_money_january_09.pdf.

Drabo, Alassane, and Christian Ebeke. 2010. "Remittances, Public Health Spending and Foreign Aid in the Access to Health Care Services in Developing Countries." Working Paper E 2010.04, Centre d'Etudes et de Recherche sur le Développement International (CERDI), Clermont-Ferrand, France.

Easterly, William, and Yaw Nyarko. 2009. "Is the Brain Drain Good for Africa?" In *Skilled Immigration Today: Prospects, Problems, and Policies*, ed. Jagdish Bhagwati and Gordon Hanson, 316–60. New York: Oxford University Press.

Ebeke, Christian H. 2010. "The Effect of Remittances on Child Labor: Cross-Country Evidence." *Economics Bulletin* 30 (1): 351–64.

Economic Times. 2010. "Bharti Gets RBI Nod for Mobile Money Services." September 17. http://economictimes.indiatimes.com/articleshow/6559841. cms?prtpage=1.

Economist. 2010. "Low-Cost Bundle." February 18. http://www.economist.com/ business-finance/displaystory.cfm?story_id=15546456.

Elbadawi, Asmaa, and Rania Roushdy. 2009. "Impact of International Migration and Remittances on Child Schooling and Child Work: The Case of Egypt." Paper prepared for the World Bank's MENA International Migration Program, Funded by the European Commission, Washington, DC.

Faini, Riccardo. 2007. "Remittances and the Brain Drain: Do More Skilled Migrants Remit More?" *World Bank Economic Review* 21 (2): 177–91.

Fajnzylber, Pablo, and Humberto Lopez. 2007. *Close to Home: The Development Impact of Remittances in Latin America*. Washington, DC: World Bank.

Fargues, Philippe. 2006. "The Demographic Benefit of International Migration: A Hypothesis and Its Application to Middle Eastern and North African Contexts." In *International Migration, Economic Development and Policy*, ed. Caglar Özden and Maurice Schiff, 59–98. Washington, DC: World Bank, and New York: Palgrave Macmillan.

Filmer, Deon, and Lant Pritchett. 2001. "Estimating Wealth Effects without Expenditure Data—or Tears: An Application to Educational Enrollments in States of India." *Demography* 38 (1): 115–32.

Frankel, Jeffrey. 2010. "Are Bilateral Remittances Countercyclical." *Open Economies Review* DOI: 10.1007/s11079-010-9184-y.

Freund, Caroline, and Nikola Spatafora. 2008. "Remittances, Transaction Costs, and Informality." *Journal of Development Economics* 86 (2): 356–66.

Ghirmay, Teame. 2004. "Financial Development and Economic Growth in Sub-Saharan African Countries: Evidence from Time Series Analysis." *African Development Review* 16 (3): 415–32.

Gibson, John, David McKenzie, and Halahingano Rohorua. 2006. "How Cost Elastic Are Remittances? Evidence from Tongan Migrants in New Zealand." *Pacific Economic Bulletin* 21 (1): 112–28.

Giuliano, Paola, and Marta Ruiz-Arranz. 2009. "Remittances, Financial Development and Growth." *Journal of Development Economics* 90 (1): 144–52.

Gubert, Flore. 2002. "Do Migrants Insure Those Who Stay Behind? Evidence from the Kayes Area (Western Mali)." *Oxford Development Studies* 30 (3): 267–87.

———. 2007. "Migration and Development: Mixed Evidence from Western Mali." *Development* 50 (4): 94–100.

Gupta, Sanjeev, Catherine A. Pattillo, and Smita Wagh. 2009. "Impact of Remittances on Poverty and Financial Development in Sub-Saharan Africa." *World Development* 37 (1): 104–15.

Gustafsson, Bjorn, and Negatu Makonnen. 1993. "Poverty and Remittances in Lesotho." *Journal of African Economies* 2 (1): 49–73.

Guzmán, Juan Carlos, Andrew R. Morrison, and Mirja Sjöblom. 2007. "The Impact of Remittances and Gender on Household Expenditure Patterns." In *The International Migration of Women*, ed. Maurice Schiff, Andrew R. Morrison, and Mirja Sjöblom, 125–52. Washington, DC: World Bank.

Halliday, Timothy. 2006. "Migration, Risk and Liquidity Constraints in El Salvador." *Economic Development and Cultural Change* 54 (4): 893–925.

Hanson, Gordon, and Christopher Woodruff. 2003. "Emigration and Educational Attainment in Mexico." Department of Economics, University of California San Diego.

Hildebrandt, Nicole, and David McKenzie. 2005. "The Effects of Migration on Child Health in Mexico." *Economia* 6 (1): 257–89.

Huysentruyt, Marieke, Christopher B. Barrett, and John G. McPeak. 2009. "Understanding Declining Mobility and Interhousehold Transfers among East African Pastoralists." *Economica* 76: 315–36.

IFAD (International Fund for Agriculture and Development). 2009. *Sending Money Home to Africa.* Rome.

IMF (International Monetary Fund). 2009. *International Transactions in Remittances: Guide for Compilers and Users*, Statistics Department, Washington, DC.

———. 2010. "Staff Guidance Note on the Application of the Joint Bank-Fund Debt Sustainability Framework for Low-Income Countries." Prepared by the staffs of the IMF and the World Bank, January 22.

IMF, and World Bank. 2009. *A Review of Some Aspects of the Low-Income Country Debt Sustainability Framework.* International Monetary Fund and the World Bank, Washington, DC. http://www.imf.org/external/np/pp/eng/2009/080509a.pdf.

Irving, Jacqueline, Sanket Mohapatra, and Dilip Ratha. 2010. "Migrant Remittance Flows: Findings from a Global Survey of Central Banks." Working Paper 194, World Bank, Washington, DC.

Isaacs, Leon. 2011. "Remittance Market in the United Kingdom." In *Remittance Markets in Africa*, ed. Sanket Mohapatra and Dilip Ratha. Washington, DC: World Bank.

Joseph, Michael. 2010. "Kenya's Telecom Revolution and Invention of Mobile Money." Paper presented at the World Bank, Washington, DC, November 12.

Kanaiaupuni, Shawn M., and Katharine M. Donato. 1999. "Migradollars and Mortality: The Effects of Migration on Infant Survival in Mexico." *Demography* 36 (3): 339–53.

Ketkar, Suhas, and Dilip Ratha, ed. 2009a. *Innovative Financing for Development.* Washington, DC: World Bank.

———. 2009b. "New Paths to Funding." *Finance and Development.* Washington, DC: International Monetary Fund.

Lachaud, Jean-Pierre. 1999. "Envoi de fonds, inégalité et pauvreté au Burkina Faso." Document de travail 40, Groupe d'Economie du Développement de l'Université Montesquieu Bordeaux IV.

Lopez-Cordova, E. 2005. "Globalization, Migration and Development: The Role of Mexican Migrant Remittances." *Economia* 6 (1): 217–56.

Lucas, Robert, E. B. 1987. "Emigration to South Africa's Mines." *American Economic Review* 77 (3): 313–30.

Lucas, Robert E. B. and Oded Stark. 1985. "Motivations to Remit: Evidence from Botswana." *Journal of Political Economy* 93 (5): 901–18.

Lueth, Erik, and Marta Ruiz-Arranz. 2008. "Determinants of Bilateral Remittance Flows." *B.E Journal of Macroeconomics* 8 (1), Article 26.

Maimbo, Samuel, Tania Saranga, and Nicholas Strychacz. 2010. "Facilitating Cross-Border Mobile Banking in Southern Africa." *Economic Premise* 26, World Bank, Washington, DC.

Mansuri, Ghazala. 2007. "Does Work Migration Spur Investment in Origin Communities? Entrepreneurship, Schooling, and Child Health in Rural Pakistan."

In *International Migration, Economic Development, and Policy*, ed. Çaglar Özden and Maurice Schiff, 99–140. Basingstoke: Palgrave Macmillan.

Martinez, Claudia, Diego Aycinena, and Dean Yang. 2010. "The Impact of Remittance Fees on Remittance Flows: Evidence from a Field Experiment among Salvadoran Migrants." Department of Economics, University of Michigan, Ann Arbor.

Mas, Ignacio, and Dan Radcliffe. 2010. "Mobile Payments Go Viral: M-PESA in Kenya." Working Paper, Bill and Melinda Gates Foundation, Seattle, WA.

Massey, Douglas, and Emilio A. Parrado. 1998. "International Migration and Business Formation in Mexico." *Social Science Quarterly* 79 (1): 1–20.

McCormick, Barry, and Jackline Wahba. 2001. "Overseas Work Experience, Savings and Entrepreneurship amongst Return Migrants to LDCs." *Scottish Journal of Political Economy* 48 (2): 164–78.

———. 2003 "Return International Migration and Geographical Inequality: The Case of Egypt." *Journal of African Economies* 12 (4): 500–32.

McKenzie, David, and Hillel Rapoport. 2010. "Can Migration Reduce Educational Attainment? Evidence from Mexico." *Journal of Population Economics* DOI: 10.1007/s00148-010-0316-x.

McKenzie, David, and Marcin J. Sasin. 2007. "Migration, Remittances, Poverty, and Human Capital: Conceptual and Empirical Findings." Policy Research Working Paper 4272, World Bank, Washington, DC.

Miller, Douglas L., and Anna L. Paulson. 2007. "Risk Taking and the Quality of Informal Insurance: Gambling and Remittances in Thailand." Working Paper 2007-01, Federal Reserve Bank of Chicago.

Mohapatra, Sanket, George Joseph, and Dilip Ratha. 2009. "Remittances and Natural Disasters: Ex-Post Response and Contribution to Ex-Ante Preparedness." Policy Research Working Paper 4972, World Bank, Washington, DC.

Mohapatra, Sanket, and Dilip Ratha. 2011. *Remittance Markets in Africa.* Washington, DC: World Bank.

Morawczynski, Olga, and Mark Pickens. 2009. "Poor People Using Mobile Financial Services: Observations on Customer Usage and Impact from M-PESA." CGAP Brief, Consultative Group to Assist the Poor, Washington, DC.

Nagarajan, Subha. 2009. "Migration, Remittances, and Household Health: Evidence from South Africa." Ph.D. diss., Department of Economics, George Washington University, Washington, DC.

Niimi, Yoko, and Caglar Ozden. 2006. "Migration and Remittances: Causes and Linkages." Policy Research Working Paper 4087, World Bank, Washington, DC.

Odozia, John C., Timothy T. Awoyemia, and Bolarin T. Omonona. 2010. "Household Poverty and Inequality: The Implication of Migrants' Remittances in Nigeria." *Journal of Economic Policy Reform* 13 (2): 191–99.

Orozco, Manuel. 2009. "Emerging Markets for Rwanda: Remittance Transfers, Its Marketplace and Financial Intermediation." Inter-American Dialogue, Washington, DC.

Osili, Una Okonkwo. 2004. "Migrants and Housing Investments: Theory and Evidence from Nigeria." *Economic Development and Cultural Change* 52 (4): 821–49.

Page, John, and Sonia Plaza. 2006. "Migration Remittances and Development: A Review of Global Evidence." *Journal of African Economies* 15 (Suppl. 2): 245–336.

Pendleton, Wade, Jonathan Crush, Eugene Campbell, Thuso Green, Hamilton Simelane, Daniel Tevera, and Fion de Vletter. 2006. "Migration, Remittances and Development in Southern Africa." Migration Policy Series 44, Southern African Migration Project, Cape Town, South Africa.

Pickens, Mark, David Porteous, and Sarah Rotman. 2009. "Scenarios for Branchless Banking in 2020." CGAP Focus Note 57, Consultative Group to Assist the Poor, Washington, DC. http://www.cgap.org/gm/document-1.9.40599/FN57.pdf.

Plaza, Sonia, Mario Navarrete, and Dilip Ratha. 2011. "Migration and Remittances Household Surveys in Africa: Methodological Aspects and Main Findings." World Bank, Washington, DC.

Ponsot, Frédéric. 2011. "Remittance Market in France." In *Remittance Markets in Africa*, ed. Sanket Mohapatra and Dilip Ratha. Washington, DC: World Bank.

Ponsot, Frédéric, and Bruno Obegi. 2010. "Etude de capitalisation des initiatives et mécanismes en matière de transferts de fonds au Mali." Study conducted for the Centre d'Information et de Gestion des Migrations (CIGEM), Mali.

Pulver, Caroline, William Jack, and Tavneed Suri. 2009. "The Performance and Impact of M-PESA: Preliminary Evidence from a Household Survey." FSD Kenya Trust. http://technology.cgap.org/technologyblog/wp-content/uploads/2009/10/fsd_june2009_caroline_pulver.pdf.

Quartey, Peter. 2006. "The Impact of Migrant Remittances on Household Welfare in Ghana." Research Paper 158, African Economic Research Consortium, Nairobi.

Quartey, Peter, and Theresa Blankson. 2004. "Do Migrant Remittances Minimize the Impact of Macro-volatility on the Poor in Ghana." Report prepared for the Global Development Network, University of Ghana, Legon.

Rajan, Raghuram G., and Arvind Subramanian. 2005. "What Undermines Aid's Impact on Growth?" IMF Working Paper 05/127, International Monetary Fund, Washington, DC.

Rajan, Raghuram G., and Luigi Zingales. 1998. "Financial Dependence and Growth." *American Economic Review* 88 (3): 559–86.

Rao, Bhaskara, and Gazi Hassan. 2009. "A Panel Data Analysis of the Growth Effects of Remittances." MPRA Working Paper 18021, Munich. http://mpra.ub.uni-muenchen.de/18021/1/MPRA_paper_18021.pdf.

Ratha, Dilip. 2003. "Workers' Remittances: An Important and Stable Source of External Finance for Developing Countries." In *Global Development Finance 2003*. Washington, DC: World Bank.

———. 2005. "Leveraging Remittances for Capital Market Access." World Bank, Development Prospects Group, Migration and Remittances team, Washington, DC.

———. 2007. "Leveraging Remittances for Development." *Policy Brief*, Migration Policy Institute, Washington, DC.

———. 2010. "Mobilize the Diaspora for the Reconstruction of Haiti." *SSRC Feature: Haiti, Now and Next*, Social Science Research Council, New York. http://www.ssrc.org/features/pages/haiti-now-and-next/1338/1438/.

Ratha, Dilip, Prabal De, and Sanket Mohapatra. 2011. "Shadow Sovereign Ratings for Unrated Developing Countries." *World Development* 39 (3): 295–307.

Ratha, Dilip, and Jan Riedberg. 2005. "On Reducing Remittance Costs." World Bank, Development Research Group, Washington, DC.

Ratha, Dilip, and Sanket Mohapatra. 2007. "Increasing the Macroeconomic Impact of Remittances." Paper prepared for the G8 Outreach Event on Remittances, Berlin, November 28–30. http://dilipratha.com/index_files/G8Berlin.pdf.

Ratha, Dilip, Sanket Mohapatra, and Sonia Plaza. 2009. "Beyond Aid: New Sources and Innovative Mechanisms for Financing Development in Sub-Saharan Africa." In *Innovative Financing for Development*, ed. Suhas Ketkar and Dilip Ratha, 143–83. Washington, DC: World Bank.

Ratha, Dilip, Sanket Mohapatra, and Ani Silwal. 2010. "Outlook for Remittance Flows 2010–11: Remittance Flows to Developing Countries Remained Resilient in 2009, Expected to Recover in 2010–11." Migration and Development Brief 12, World Bank, Development Prospects Group. http://www.worldbank.org/prospects/migrationandremittances.

Ratha, Dilip, and William Shaw. 2007. "South-South Migration and Remittances." Development Prospects Group Working Paper 102, World Bank, Washington, DC.

Roache, Shaun K., and Ewa Gradzka. 2007. "Do Remittances to Latin America Depend on the U.S. Business Cycle?" IMF Working Paper 07/273, International Monetary Fund, Washington, DC.

Russell, Sharon S. 1992. "Remittances from International Migration: A Review in Perspective." *World Development* 14 (6): 677–96.

Rutten, Lamon, and Okey Oramah. 2006. "Using Commoditized Revenue Flows to Leverage Access to International Finance; with a Special Focus on Migrant Remittances and Payment Flows." Study prepared for the Secretariat of the United Nations Conference on Trade and Development (UNCTAD), Geneva.

Sayan, Serdar. 2006. "Business Cycles and Workers' Remittances: How Do Migrant Workers Respond to Cyclical Movements of GDP at Home?" IMF Working Paper 06/52, International Monetary Fund, Washington, DC.

Singh, Raju J., Markus Haacker, and Kyung-woo Lee. 2009. "Determinants and Macroeconomic Impact of Remittances to Sub-Saharan Africa." IMF Working Paper 09/216, International Monetary Fund, Washington, DC.

Skeldon, Ronald. 2002. "Migration and Poverty." *Asia-Pacific Population Journal* 17 (4): 67–82.

Sorensen, Ninna Nyberg. 2004. "Migrant Remittances as a Development Tool: The Case of Morocco." IOM Working Paper 2, International Organization for Migration, Geneva. http://www.belgium.iom.int/pan-europeandialogue/documents/remittances_morocco.pdf.

Suleri, Abid Qaiyum, and Kevin Savage. 2006. "Remittances in Crisis: A Case Study of Pakistan." Overseas Development Institute, London. http://www.odi.org.uk/hpg/papers/BGPaper_RemittancesPakistan.pdf.

Taylor, J. Edward, and T. J. Wyatt. 1996. "The Shadow Value of Migrant Remittances, Income and Inequality in a Household-Farm Economy." *Journal of Development Studies* 32 (6): 899–912.

Tevera, Daniel, and Abel Chikanda. 2009. "Migrant Remittances and Household Survival in Zimbabwe." Working Paper, Southern African Migration Project, Cape Town.

Toxopeus, Helen S., and Robert Lensink. 2007. "Remittances and Financial Inclusion in Development." UNU-WIDER Research Paper 2007/49, United Nations University–World Institute for Development Economics Research, Helsinki.

Valero-Gil, Jorge N. 2009. "Remittances and the Household's Expenditures on Health." *Journal of Business Strategies* (Spring), Huntsville, TX.

Weiss-Fagan, Patricia. 2006. "Remittances in Crisis: A Haiti Case Study." Overseas Development Institute, London. http://www.odi.org.uk/hpg/papers/BG_Haiti_remittances.pdf.

Woodruff, Christopher, and Rene Zenteno. 2001. "Remittances and Microenterprises in Mexico." UCSD Graduate School of International Relations and Pacific Studies Working Paper, University of California San Diego.

———. 2007. "Migration Networks and Microenterprises in Mexico." *Journal of Development Economics* 82 (2): 509–28.

World Bank. 2006. *Global Economic Prospects 2006: Economic Implications of Remittances and Migration.* Washington, DC: World Bank.

———. 2009. *Issue Brief on Migration and Remittances.* Washington, DC: World Bank..

———. 2011. *Migration and Remittances Factbook 2011.* Washington, DC: World Bank.

World Bank, and BIS-CPSS (Bank for International Settlements–Committee on Payment and Settlement Systems). 2007. *Report on General Principles for International Remittances.* Washington DC: World Bank.

Wouterse, F. 2010. "Remittances, Poverty, Inequality and Welfare: Evidence from the Central Plateau of Burkina Faso" *Journal of Development Studies* 46 (4): 771–89.

Wu, Treena. 2006. "The Role of Remittances in Crisis. An Aceh Research Study." Overseas Development Institute, London. http://www.odi.org.uk/hpg/papers/BG_Remittances_Aceh.pdf.

Yang, Dean. 2008a. "Coping With Disaster: The Impact of Hurricanes on International Financial Flows, 1970–2002." *B.E. Journal of Economic Analysis and Policy* 8 (1), Article 13.

———. 2008b. "International Migration, Remittances and Household Investment: Evidence from Philippine Migrants' Exchange Rate Shocks." *Economic Journal* 118 (528): 591–630.

Yang, Dean, and HwaJung Choi. 2007. "Are Remittances Insurance? Evidence from Rainfall Shocks in the Philippines." *World Bank Economic Review* 21 (2): 219–48.

CHAPTER 3

Migration of the Highly Skilled

The migration of highly educated or skilled people is a critical, controversial, and difficult subject.[1] It is critical because it involves the transfer of human capital, which is a key to economic growth and poverty reduction. It is controversial because, in many cases, the transfer takes place from countries suffering from scarcity of such resources to countries enjoying relative abundance. It is difficult to analyze because the general lack of data means that neither the causes nor the impacts of the phenomenon are well understood.

A high level of skilled migration is rarely the root problem but rather a symptom of myriad other development problems. Without properly addressing various policy challenges—in education, labor and financial markets, healthcare, and public finance—efforts to design mechanisms to harness the benefits and minimize the costs of skilled migration will not be fully effective. Indeed, they may be futile. The discussion yields the following main conclusions:

- Although the emigration rate for tertiary-educated workers is high in many African countries, rates vary considerably across countries. High-skilled migration rates are particularly high in small, low-income, and conflict-affected countries. The low levels of human capital in many African countries amplify the impact of high-skilled migration. Rather than trying to stem migration, African governments and policy makers should focus on increasing education and skill levels and establishing an environment in which high-skilled workers have productive opportunities at home.
- Tertiary-educated migrants from different African countries exhibit vast differences in terms of their performance in the destination countries' labor markets. These differences reflect language ability, the quality of education in origin countries, and the speed of integration

in destination-country labor markets. The performance of tertiary-educated migrants is important for the overall development impact of skilled migration, because it affects their potential to send remittances and generate other positive diaspora externalities.

- The data and analysis have important implications for policies to limit the costs and maximize the benefits of tertiary-educated migration. Education should be a major focus. Shifting educational resources to less-sophisticated degree programs (for example, training physicians' assistants rather than doctors) could increase the supply of workers trained to provide services that are in short supply in underserved areas while also reducing the ability of trainees to find employment in destination countries. However, such policies should be implemented based on the country's need for the right mix of specialists and lower skilled workers, not the implications for high-skilled emigration. Requiring students to perform public service for a moderate period of time (since more onerous requirements are likely to encourage emigration and discourage return) and to pay for a portion of the cost of their education while providing performance-based subsidies to some students could increase the benefits of higher education while limiting the fiscal losses from high-skilled migration.

- Restrictions on the emigration of high-skilled professionals infringe on civil liberties; may not deter emigration, given the strength of incentives to emigrate; and discourage return. Incentives to return may be ineffective, may be provided to migrants who would have returned in any event, and may engender resentment from workers who never migrated. Removing restrictions on the recognition of foreign qualifications and experience could encourage return.

- Taxation of potential emigrants may prove difficult to enforce, as it would require the cooperation of destination-country governments that derive great benefits from high-skilled emigration. Destination countries might consider providing financial and technical assistance to origin countries' educational programs, provided that such aid does not replace existing programs. An option worth considering involves getting hiring institutions (whether public or private) to open training facilities in Africa.

This chapter is organized as follows. The first section reviews available data on high-skilled migration from Africa and compares high-skilled migration patterns across African countries.[2] The second section reviews the performance of tertiary-educated migrants in destination labor markets, focusing on the migration of healthcare professionals and the impact their migration has on Africa. The third section analyzes various policy options.

BENEFITS AND PATTERNS OF HIGH-SKILLED MIGRATION

Highly educated workers generate positive externalities that are critical to economic growth and development. These externalities are lost for high-skilled migrants' home countries upon their departure. Among such externalities are productivity spillovers to both high- and low-skilled workers; public services—such as healthcare and education—that have both immediate and future social spillovers; innovative and creative activities that are at the core of long-term growth; and contributions to the health of social, political, and economic institutions. In addition, in most countries, tertiary education is publicly financed, and the highly educated are net fiscal contributors once they enter the labor force. Their migration therefore implies a fiscal loss for their countries.

On the positive side, the migration of highly skilled people generates numerous benefits for their home countries. Migrants send remittances to their families and forge economic and social linkages between their home countries and the rest of the world. A wide range of other positive diaspora externalities, such as the return of professionals with enhanced skills, are addressed in chapter 4 (see also Wahba 2007; Dustmann, Fadlon, and Weiss 2010). An influential body of recent work claims that the migration of highly educated workers can have a net positive impact on the demand for education in a country (box 3.1).

Easterly and Nyarko (2009) argue that in Africa, the gains to migrants and their families are large enough to offset the general losses to the country associated with high-skilled migration and that migration increases overall human capital accumulation. They fail to find evidence of any negative growth effect of skilled migration, concluding that such migration is, on balance, good for Africa. They note that any loss to the origin country is minimal if the emigrating professionals are not able to use their skills efficiently in the origin country, because of a poor investment climate, inadequate complementary inputs (such as poor medical facilities), or lack of scale economies. The voluminous literature on this subject (see Docquier and Rapoport 2009) attests to the difficulty of measuring the costs and benefits and fails to reach a conclusion on the net benefits from high-skilled migration.

HIGH-SKILLED MIGRATION BY WORLD REGION

Migration levels from developing countries, especially from those in Africa, to OECD countries are low. This fact is surprising given the vast wage and income differentials between developing and developed coun-

Box 3.1   The Brain Gain

Individuals generally need to make their education decisions before migration opportunities materialize. In many instances, education increases the likelihood of emigration to a high-income country, since immigration policies in many countries favor highly educated people. Because of such policies, many people invest in more education than they otherwise would have in order to increase their chances of immigrating (Stark, Helmenstein, and Prskawetz 1997; Beine, Docquier, and Rapoport 2001). However, some individuals who acquire higher education, with the hope of immigration, may end up staying at home. This can result in an increase in the stock of human capital ("brain gain") if the number of people who acquire extra education but stay at home exceeds the number of people who migrate. A reduction in the stock of human capital ("brain drain") occurs otherwise (Mountford 1997; Stark 2004; World Bank 2006). In one of the few country-level analyses, Chand and Clemens (2008) argue that high rates of emigration by tertiary-educated Fiji Islanders raised investment in tertiary education in Fiji as well as the stock of tertiary-educated people, net of departures.

The empirical evidence is mixed for the relative importance of brain drain versus brain gain effects. Beine, Docquier, and Rapoport (2001) find that for a subgroup of developing countries whose per capita gross domestic product (GDP) is less than 15 percent that of G-7 countries, the stock of human capital has a positive relationship with the migration rate, indicating brain gain. For the entire sample (which also includes upper-middle-income countries such as Brazil, Mexico, and South Africa), they find no evidence of a loss of human capital accumulation as a result of migration.[a] In a more recent study, Angel-Urdinola, Takeno, and Wodon (2008) find a negative relationship between emigration of students from Latin American countries to the United States and tertiary enrollment rates in the countries of origin, indicating an absence of any brain gain.[b] There are some positive experiences of brain gain in the health and information technology (IT) sectors. The expectation of emigrating may have increased the incentive to invest in higher education and specialized training such as IT (in India and Taiwan, China) and nursing (in Ghana and the Philippines) (Solimano 2008).

a. The authors used a cross-section of 37 developing countries in 1998 to examine the relationship between an indicator for the level of educational attainment and the rate of migration to the United States, controlling for other variables, such as public education expenditure, wage differentials, and population of the home country.
b. It is difficult to conclude that these results—based on annual data—are evidence of brain drain and not merely the absence of brain gain. Even if there were some brain gain effect, there would typically be a considerable lag between the migration of high-skilled individuals and the incentive for those remaining behind to acquire higher education.

tries. With the exception of the Caribbean and Central America regions, all developing regions had migration rates of 3 percent or less of their total labor force in 2000 (Global Skilled Migration database, described in Docquier and others 2010). Sub-Saharan Africa had the third-lowest migration rate among developing regions, with only 1 percent of its labor force residing in OECD countries or South Africa in 2000 (figure 3.1). Only South and East Asia had migration rates lower than Africa, at less than 1 percent of the labor force. Still, all developing regions saw their overall migration levels increase by about 20 percent between 1990 and

Figure 3.1 Share of Migrants in Labor Force, by Region, 1990 and 2000

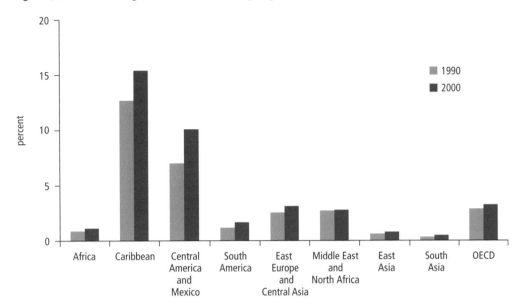

Source: Authors, based on data from the Global Skilled Migration database (described in Docquier and others 2010).

2000, suggesting increased labor mobility from developing countries to OECD destinations.

Highly educated workers are more likely to emigrate than less educated workers. In all developing regions, in both 1990 and 2000, the migration rate for tertiary-educated workers (the number of tertiary-educated migrants divided by the total number of tertiary-educated workers) far exceeded the migration rate for less educated workers. In 2000, the migration rates of the tertiary educated ranged from about 5 percent in South America, South Asia, and Eastern Europe to more than 41 percent in the Caribbean (figure 3.2). Africa had the third-highest migration rate of tertiary-educated workers, after the Caribbean and Central America and Mexico. South Asia had the lowest and East Asia the second-lowest migration rates among the tertiary educated.

Another important statistic is the share of tertiary-educated workers in the total stock of migrants, which exceeds the share of tertiary-educated workers in the domestic labor force in every developing region of the world (figure 3.3). In South Asia, for example, tertiary-educated workers accounted for 5 percent of the labor force and 51 percent of all migrants. In Sub-Saharan Africa, the tertiary educated accounted for less than 3 percent of the labor force but more than 35 percent of all migrants.

There are numerous economic and policy-induced reasons why tertiary-educated workers in developing regions are more likely than less

Figure 3.2 Migration Rate among Tertiary-Educated Workers, 1990 and 2000

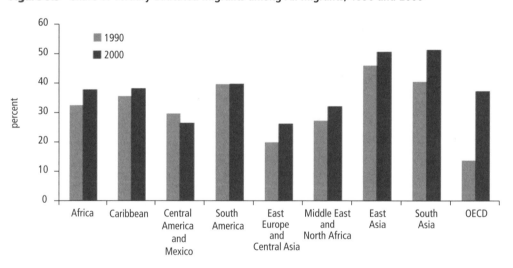

Source: Authors, based on data from the Global Skilled Migration database (described in Docquier and others 2010).

Figure 3.3 Share of Tertiary-Educated Migrants among All Migrants, 1990 and 2000

Source: Authors, based on data from the Global Skilled Migration database (described in Docquier and others 2010).

educated workers to emigrate. First, wage gaps (in absolute terms) increase with education, which implies that the overall income gains from emigration are higher (Clemens, Montenegro, and Pritchett 2008). Second, tertiary-educated workers are more likely to possess skills (such as languages) that enable them to adapt to the destination countries' labor markets and social environments relatively easily and rapidly. Third, educated workers are better able to overcome the financial costs

Figure 3.4   Share of Tertiary-Educated Workers in the Labor Force, 2000

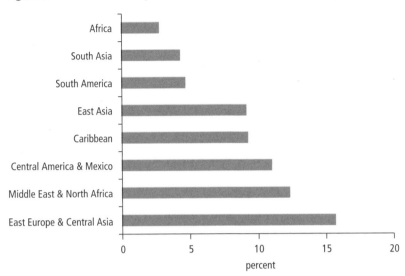

Source: Authors, based on data from the Global Skilled Migration database (described in Docquier and others 2010).

and legal barriers of immigration. Fourth, selective migration policies in many OECD countries strongly favor tertiary-educated migrants.

Migration rates for tertiary-educated workers are particularly high in Africa. In 2000, one out of every eight tertiary-educated Africans lived in an OECD country, the highest rate among developing regions except the Caribbean and Central America and Mexico. These relatively high skilled immigration rates reflect the fact that Africa has the lowest rate of tertiary education of any developing region (figure 3.4). In 2000, only 3 percent of Africa's labor force had tertiary education—a far lower figure than in the Caribbean (11 percent) or Central America and Mexico (9 percent), the other two regions with high migration rates among tertiary-educated workers. Despite significant increases in tertiary education in many African countries since 2000, Sub-Saharan Africa still lags other regions.

The small share of the labor force with tertiary education and the relative inability of the unskilled to migrate make skilled migration rates in Africa look especially high relative to other regions. A comparison of Africa and South America provides a useful illustration. In 2000, South America's labor force of 170 million was much smaller than Sub-Saharan Africa's of 240 million. However, South America had more than 21.5 million tertiary-educated workers (12.6 percent of the labor force) compared with only 6.6 million (2.8 percent of the labor force) in Africa. About 1.2 million tertiary-educated migrants from South America and a little more than 1 million from Africa were living in OECD countries in 2000. The migration rate among the tertiary educated in South America (5.5 percent) was about one-third of Africa's (15.2 percent), because of the much larger number of tertiary-educated workers in South America. The migration rate to OECD countries of less educated workers was much higher in South America than in Africa, a reflection of the lower transportation costs to the United States and the availability of social networks that reduce assimilation costs and legal barriers (Beine, Docquier, and Ozden 2011). At the same time, superior business climates and stable social/political environments in Latin American countries increase the incentives to stay at home for tertiary-educated workers (Fajnzylber and Lopez 2007; Grogger and Hanson forthcoming). Both of these factors led to a lower ratio of migrants with tertiary education among all migrants.

HIGH-SKILLED MIGRATION ACROSS AFRICA

Most African countries resemble the regional average, with low levels of human capital and high rates of tertiary-educated migration. Tertiary-educated workers accounted for less than 10 percent of the labor force in the vast majority of African countries in 2000 (figure 3.5, panel a). They represented at least 10 percent of migrants in almost every country, however, and more than 30 percent in more than half of the countries.

One of the mistakes often made in discussions of skilled migration is to treat Africa as a single homogenous entity. Aggregate migration rates mask wide disparities among country groups and individual countries. The share of migrants among tertiary-educated workers in Africa ranged from a very low rate of 3 percent in Burkina Faso to a staggering 82 percent in Cape Verde. By contrast, overall migration rates range from 1 to 35 percent, with the vast majority of countries below 7 percent (figure 3.5, panel b). The wide divergence between tertiary-educated and other workers stems from the fact that most workers are unable to leave Africa, mainly because of financial and physical barriers.

On average, small countries in Africa have higher migration rates than large countries. In 2000, the share of migrants in the labor force in small countries (populations of less than 3 million) was four times the share in large countries. The average migration rate among the tertiary educated in small countries (30 percent) was three times that of large countries and 1.5 times the skilled migration rate in medium-size countries (figure 3.6). This pattern of higher overall migration and higher-skilled migration in smaller countries is not limited to Africa but is found in many small countries in the Caribbean and the Pacific (Docquier and Marfouk 2007).

Figure 3.5   Tertiary-Educated Migration Rates in Selected African Countries

a. Percentage of migrants with tertiary education

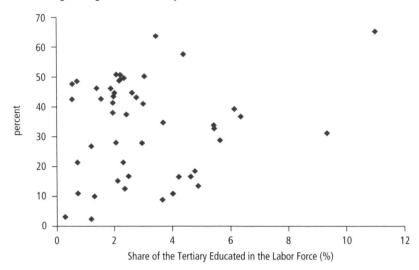

b. Percentage of migrants among people with tertiary education

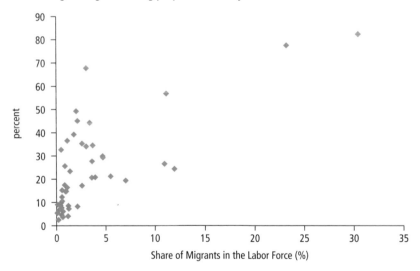

Source: Authors, based on data from the Global Skilled Migration database (described in Docquier and others 2010).

Low-income African countries tend to have higher migration rates than middle-income countries. The migration rate among the tertiary educated in low-income African countries is twice that of middle-income countries (figure 3.7). Although the tertiary educated accounted for less than 2 percent of the labor force in low-income countries in 2000, they made up almost one-third of total migrants.

Figure 3.6   Migration Rates in Africa, by Country Size, 1990 and 2000

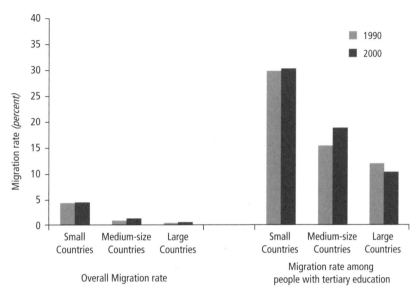

Source: Authors, based on data from the Global Skilled Migration database (described in Docquier and others 2010).

The high rates of tertiary-educated migration from small and low-income countries reflect their small pools of tertiary-educated workers. In 2000, less than 900,000 of the 64 million workers in low-income African countries were tertiary educated. The migration of 200,000 tertiary-educated workers from these countries—a relatively small number considering that in 2000 there were 173,000 tertiary-educated migrants in the OECD countries from South Africa alone—results in a very high level of skilled migration rate for this group. The return on human capital in these countries tends to be relatively low, given the limited opportunities for specialization. The scope for highly skilled workers to generate economic spillovers in more developed countries leads to higher economic gains and strong incentives to migrate.

Ten medium-size countries and nine middle-income countries also had high tertiary-educated migration rates in 2000. Three small countries and three low-income countries had low tertiary-educated migration rates (table 3.1).

At the individual country level, South Africa boasts some of the highest living standards on the continent and has a relatively skilled labor force. Yet in 2000, the migration rate among tertiary-educated workers in South Africa was only twice that of Burkina Faso, one of the world's poorest nations. Meanwhile, Mauritius—often touted as an African success story—had more than 60 percent of its tertiary-educated labor force residing in OECD countries in 2000. This rate is more than seven times the

Figure 3.7 Migration of Tertiary-Educated Workers in Africa, by Country Income Level, 2000

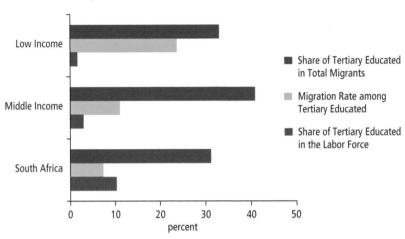

Legend:
- Share of Tertiary Educated in Total Migrants
- Migration Rate among Tertiary Educated
- Share of Tertiary Educated in the Labor Force

Source: Authors, based on data from the Global Skilled Migration database (described in Docquier and others 2010).

migration rate of similar workers in Madagascar, another francophone island nation with a per capita GDP one-tenth that of Mauritius. High tertiary-educated migration rates from middle-income African countries are likely to reflect the greater ability to overcome financial and legal barriers to migration.

Political conflict can affect the migration of tertiary-educated workers, but it does not always result in the massive migration of the tertiary educated. Migration rates in 2000 among the tertiary educated in seven African countries that suffered from civil conflicts during the 1990s ranged from a mere 4 percent (in Angola) to 42 percent in (Liberia). Various country-specific factors account for this variation. For example, Portuguese-speaking Angolans are less likely to migrate than English-speaking Liberians, because most destinations for skilled migrants are also English speaking. The presence of an established diaspora in the destination is another key determinant of migration flows, even for skilled workers (Beine, Docquier, and Ozden 2011).

DESTINATIONS OF HIGH-SKILLED MIGRANTS

Tertiary-educated migrants from Africa go predominantly to English-speaking countries such as the United States, Australia, and Canada. In 2000, 53 percent of all tertiary-educated emigrants from African countries to OECD countries went to these three countries, down slightly from 57 percent in 1990 (figure 3.8). These countries, on the other hand, account for only 28 percent of total African emigrants to the OECD countries.

Table 3.1 High-Skilled Migration Rates in Sub-Saharan African Countries of Different Sizes and Income Levels, 2000

Migration rate < 10 percent			Migration rate 10–25 percent			Migration rate > 25 percent		
Country	Size	Income	Country	Size	Income	Country	Size	Income
Angola[a]	Medium	Middle	Cameroon	Medium	Middle	Cape Verde	Small	Middle
Benin	Medium	Middle	Comoros	Small	Middle	Congo, Rep.[a]	Medium	Middle
Botswana	Small	High-middle	Congo, Dem. Rep.	Large	Middle	Eritrea	Medium	Middle
Burkina Faso	Medium	Middle	Equatorial Guinea	Small	Middle	Gambia, The	Small	Middle
Burundi[a]	Medium	Middle	Gabon	Small	High-middle	Ghana	Medium	Middle
Central African Republic	Medium	Middle	Lesotho	Small	Middle	Guinea-Bissau	Small	Low
Chad	Small	Middle	Mali	Medium	Middle	Kenya	Large	Low
Côte d'Ivoire	Medium	Middle	Nigeria	Large	Middle	Liberia[a]	Medium	Low
Djibouti	Small	Middle	Senegal	Medium	Middle	Malawi	Medium	Low
Ethiopia	Large	Middle	Swaziland	Small	Middle	Mauritius	Small	High-middle
Guinea	Medium	Middle	Tanzania	Large	Low	Mozambique[a]	Medium	Low
Madagascar	Medium	Low	Togo	Medium	Low	Namibia	Small	High-middle
Mauritania	Medium	Low	Zambia	Medium	Low	Rwanda[a]	Medium	Low
Niger	Medium	Low	Zimbabwe	Medium	Low	São Tomé and Príncipe	Small	Middle
South Africa	Large	High-middle				Seychelles	Small	High-middle
Sudan[a]	Large	Middle				Sierra Leone	Medium	Low
						Somalia[a]	Medium	Low
						Uganda	Medium	Low

Source: Authors, based on data from the Global Skilled Migration database (described in Docquier and others 2010).
a. Experienced civil conflict during the 1990s.

The importance of the United States, Australia, and Canada for tertiary-educated African migrants is the outcome of several factors. First, migration policies in these countries tend to favor educated migrants in general. Second, these destinations have more flexible labor markets than other OECD countries. Third, these countries are widely perceived to offer better career and assimilation prospects than other OECD destinations. Fourth, these countries are farther from Africa than European destinations, which implies higher costs of migration and, hence, works against unskilled workers, who are generally unable to overcome these costs.

A closer look at 10 diverse African countries reveals more detailed information about emigrants' destination countries. Colonial links feature prominently as a determinant of destinations.[3] For example, France accounts for the largest shares of migrants from Côte d'Ivoire, Madagascar, and Senegal, and the United Kingdom receives the largest shares of migrants from Kenya and Zambia (outer circles in figure 3.9).

Colonial links appear less important for tertiary-educated migrants. In 2000, the United States accounted for the largest shares of tertiary-educated migrants from Ghana and Nigeria. The dominance of the United States, Canada, and Australia as destinations for tertiary-educated migrants is evident even among some francophone countries: in 2000 the United States received 37 percent of tertiary-educated migrants from Côte d'Ivoire, just slightly less than France's share of 40 percent (inner circles in figure 3.10).

Figure 3.8 **Distribution of Total Migrants and Skilled Migrants from Africa by Destination, 1990 and 2000**

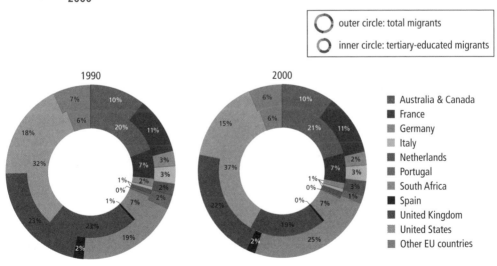

Source: Authors, based on data from the Global Skilled Migration database (described in Docquier and others 2010).
Note: Outer circle shows total migrants. Inner circle shows tertiary-educated migrants.

Figure 3.9 Distribution of Migrants and Skilled Migrants from Selected Anglophone Countries in Africa, 2000

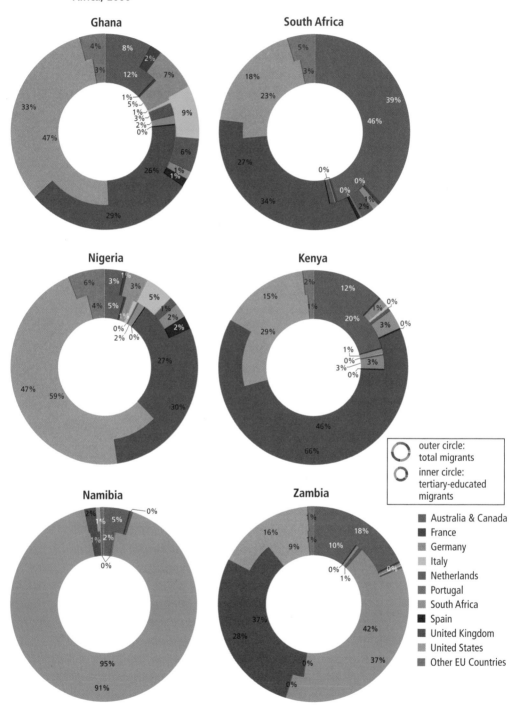

Source: Authors, based on data from the Global Skilled Migration database (described in Docquier and others 2010).
Note: Outer circle shows total migrants. Inner circle shows tertiary-educated migrants.

Figure 3.10 Distribution of Total Migrants and Skilled Migrants from Selected Francophone Countries in Africa, 2000

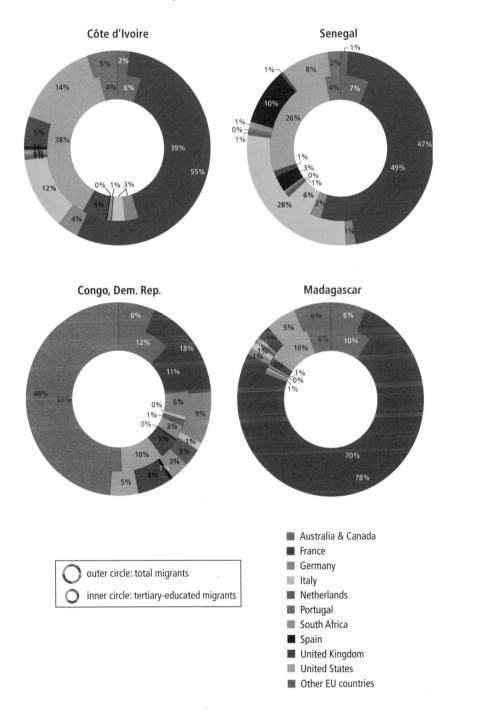

Source: Authors, based on data from the Global Skilled Migration database (described in Docquier and others 2010).
Note: Outer circle shows total migrants. Inner circle shows tertiary-educated migrants.

EARNINGS OF TERTIARY-EDUCATED MIGRANTS IN DESTINATION LABOR MARKETS

The professional placement and performance of tertiary-educated migrants in their destination labor markets have important implications for the policy debate on skilled migration. The type of job a migrant has influences his or her performance in the destination country and, thus, the overall welfare gains from migration.

One concern is "brain waste," which occurs when highly educated migrants accept positions that require little training or education (or do not find employment at all), eroding the benefits of migration to them and their home country. Mattoo, Neagu, and Ozden (2008) argue that this issue is more important for people whose quality of education and skills do not match the standards expected in the destination countries' labor markets. They estimate the probability that a foreign-born bachelor's degree holder will obtain a skilled job (a job that on average requires tertiary education) and the probability that a foreign-born professional-degree holder (for example, law, medicine, pharmacy) will obtain a science-oriented or professional job in the United States. They find evidence of significant variation across origin countries and especially low rates of professional placement among educated migrants from several African countries (figure 3.11). Migrants with bachelor's degrees from 7 of 15 African countries have less than a 40 percent chance of ending up in a skilled job. The pilot project in Ghana (box 3.2) indicates that brain waste is not a problem for top students.

In most cases, the probability of obtaining a skilled job is higher for an African-born migrant with a professional degree than one with a bachelor's degree. For example, the probability of obtaining a skilled job for an Eritrean- or Ethiopian-born migrant with a professional degree is three times that of a bachelor-degree holder. Among the 15 countries listed in figure 3.11, only bachelor's degree holders from Senegal and Sierra Leone had higher probabilities of landing a skilled job than holders of professional degrees.

The factors that influence the probability that a tertiary-educated migrant obtains a skilled job or a professional job in the United States vary significantly by country of origin. Factors such as expenditure on tertiary education and the use of English as a medium of instruction have a tremendous impact on the quality of education. Mattoo, Neagu, and Ozden (2008) show that they strongly influence whether a migrant obtains a professional or other high-skilled job. In a related study, Coulombe and Tremblay (2009) compare the skill intensity and schooling levels of Canadian immigrants and natives who were submitted to the same standardized tests

Figure 3.11 Probability That an African-Born Migrant Holding a Bachelor's or Professional Degree Obtains a Skilled Job in the United States

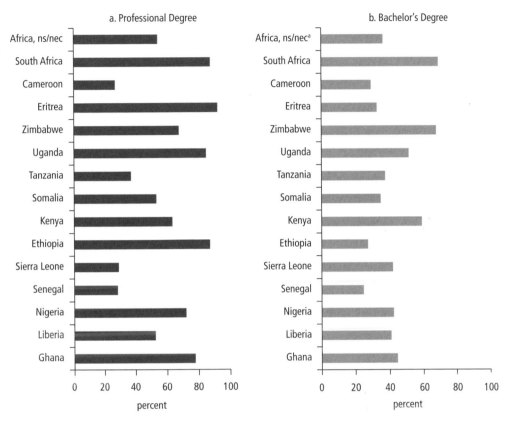

a. Professional Degree

b. Bachelor's Degree

percent

percent

Source: Mattoo, Neagu, and Ozden 2008.
a. ns/nec = not specified/not elsewhere classified.

in literacy, math, and problem solving. They estimate a skill-schooling gap for each origin country, defined as the difference between the mean years of schooling of the immigrant subgroup and the typical Canadian native with the same skill proficiency level. The larger the skill-schooling gap, the lower the quality of education in the country of origin. In simple regressions, they show that the skill-schooling gap is a decreasing function of per capita income of the origin country. The estimate of the slope coefficient indicates that the skill-schooling gap declines by one year for every $10,000 increase in annual per capita income in the origin country.

Migrants with bachelor's degrees from the three francophone countries studied (Cameroon, Senegal, and Sierra Leone) face lower probabilities of obtaining professional jobs than other skilled jobs in the United States. The probabilities that migrants from these countries obtain professional jobs are lower than those for their counterparts from anglophone countries. But the probabilities of obtaining either a skilled or a professional

Box 3.2 Migration Patterns of Ghana's Best and Brightest

Concerns about loss of human capital are greatest in the case of the most highly skilled and talented individuals. Yet very little information exists about migration patterns at different levels of education and skill. Original research undertaken for this report provides a first glimpse of these patterns for Ghana. In 13 of the top high schools in Ghana (based on performance in A-level and senior secondary school examinations), the top five students graduating each year between 1976 and 2004 were tracked. About one-third of these students were located and a third of those students (283 students) were surveyed. Any nonresponse bias should lean toward surveying the more successful of this already elite group.

Migration rates were extremely high among these top academic achievers. Three-quarters had migrated abroad at some point between secondary school and age 35 (box figure 3.2.1). But there was also significant return migration, with 43 percent of those who migrated returning to Ghana by age 45. Migration rates were very similar for men and women.

Box figure 3.2.1 Migration Status by Age of Ghana's Top High School Students

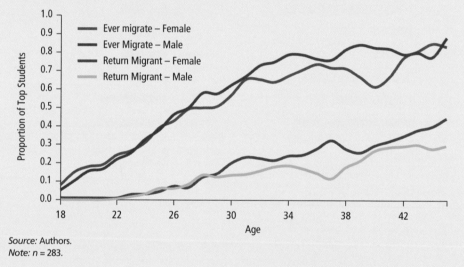

Source: Authors.
Note: n = 283.

The United States and United Kingdom were the top destination choices and together accounted for more than 80 percent of all migrants (box figure 3.2.2). Only 8 percent were in other African countries.

job vary among the three francophone countries as well. The probability that a Sierra Leone–born migrant with a bachelor's degree will obtain a skilled job is 42 percent compared with only 24 percent for a Senegalese migrant with the same qualifications and 29 percent for a Cameroonian (Mattoo, Neagu, and Ozden 2008).

Country differences reflect more than just language. The probability that a migrant from Ethiopia (where Amharic is the official language but

Box 3.2 Migration Patterns of Ghana's Best and Brightest *(continued)*

Box figure 3.2.2 Migration Destinations of Top Students from Ghana Living Abroad

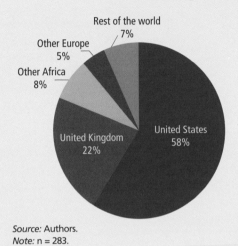

Source: Authors.
Note: n = 283.

Migrant students earned more than five times as much as top students who never migrated (box figure 3.2.3). After controlling for age, parental education, and family wealth status at the end of high school, a migrant who was abroad earned about $74,000 a year more than a non-migrant. There was no significant difference between the incomes of nonmigrants and return migrants, after controlling for various personal attributes. Assuming a discount rate of 5 percent, the net present value of the lifetime earnings gained from working abroad rather than in Ghana exceeded $1 million per migrant.

Box figure 3.2.3 Annual Earnings of Elite Nonmigrants, Migrants, and Return Migrants in Ghana

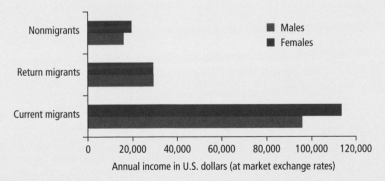

Source: Authors.
Note: n = 283.

(Box continues on next page)

Box 3.2   Migration Patterns of Ghana's Best and Brightest *(continued)*

Another key observation emerging from these data is the difference between women and men. Labor market data from many different countries indicate that on average women earn more than men (although the difference is not statistically significant) for identical levels of education and other qualifications. The data on this elite group point show that women, especially elite migrants, earn significantly more than men. There are many possible reasons for this gap, including potential selection biases in migration and education decisions. Examination of these issues was beyond the scope of this research but worth noting for future rounds of analysis.

Migrants abroad are working in broadly similar occupations as those in Ghana. Typical occupations include management consultants, engineers, information technology specialists, academics, doctors, lawyers, and bankers. Elite migrants do not appear to be working in occupations far beneath their qualification levels.

Almost all of these top professionals have bachelor's degrees (box table 3.2.1). Among current migrants 41 percent obtained their bachelor's degree abroad. In contrast, only 9 percent of return migrants had foreign degrees. Current migrants are significantly more likely to have obtained an advanced degree than nonmigrants, and in the majority of cases these advanced qualifications were obtained abroad. Among all former top students currently living in Ghana, 32 percent with an advanced degree obtained it abroad.

Box table 3.2.1   Educational Achievements of Former Top Ghanaian Students Currently 25–45 *(percent)*

Migration status	Bachelor's degree		Masters degree, law degree, medical degree, or doctorate	
	Proportion with degree	Proportion of degree holders who earned it abroad	Proportion with degree	Proportion of degree holders who earned it abroad
Migrant	85	41	68	72
Return migrant	78	9	70	50
Nonmigrant	92	n.a.	32	n.a.
Nonmigrant and return migrant	86	4	49	32

Source: Authors.
Note: n = 293. n.a. = not applicable.

What are the effects of high-skilled migration on Ghana? Among current migrants surveyed who were not students, 93 percent were sending remittances, and most were sending about $5,000 a year. There was little involvement in trade: only 3 percent of migrants helped a Ghanaian firm make a trade deal or exported goods from their home country in the past year. About 19 percent made investments in Ghanaian businesses, with a mean investment of $3,700 per migrant. The most common knowledge transfer that current migrants engaged in was providing advice on study and work options abroad to other Ghanaians, which about half of migrants reported doing. There were also some limited interactions with companies and businesses: 16 percent of current

Box 3.2 Migration Patterns of Ghana's Best and Brightest *(continued)*

migrants had advised a Ghanaian company, and 14 percent had carried out research with people in Ghana in the past year.

All of the individuals surveyed received their secondary education in Ghana, and many received their undergraduate education there, too. The main fiscal cost of migration is the lost income and sales taxes that the country would have earned as a return on this educational investment. The fiscal benefit consists of sales taxes on any cash remittances spent in Ghana and the fiscal expenditure saved by not having to provide government services to migrants. Taking these factors into account, the net fiscal loss to Ghana of each of these high-skilled individuals living abroad rather than at home is estimated to be about $5,500–$6,300 a year. This is about equal to the amount migrants are remitting each year and less than the sum of their remittances and investments made in home companies. The amount is also small in comparison to the enormous gains in income that the migrants enjoy from migrating. That said, remittance flows and the income gains accrue to private individuals rather than the government.

Source: Gibson and McKenzie 2010.

English is the medium of instruction in secondary schools) with a bachelor's degree will obtain a skilled job in the United States is about 20 percent. The same probability for a migrant from South Africa or Zimbabwe is more than 65 percent. Variations for holders of professional degrees are also wide. For example, the probability that a Tanzanian holder of bachelor's degree obtains a professional job is less than 40 percent, compared with 60 percent for a migrant born in Kenya and more than 80 percent for a migrant born in Eritrea (Mattoo, Neagu, and Ozden 2008).

MIGRATION OF HEALTHCARE PROFESSIONALS

Among the highly educated people who leave Africa each year, none has triggered more widespread emotion and, at times, controversy than healthcare professionals. Some argue that the exodus of healthcare professionals, especially physicians, has contributed to a decline in healthcare outcomes in many African countries (Bundred and Levitt 2000). There is no question that many African countries with large numbers of emigrant healthcare professionals face severe shortages of healthcare workers. For example, the vacancy rate in Ghana's public sector health was 47 percent for doctors and 57 percent for nurses in 2002 (Dovlo 2003). Moreover, given the technological and institutional constraints on substitution among medical personnel, the departure of doctors may result in the underemployment of nurses and other auxiliary staff (Commander, Kangasniemi, and Winters 2004). The number of physicians per hundred

Figure 3.12 Stock of Migrant Physicians in OECD Countries as Percentage of Locally Trained Physicians in Source Region, by World Region

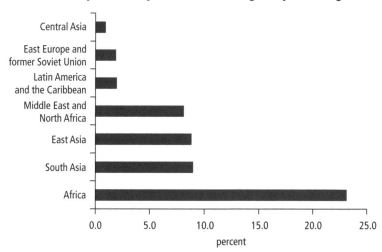

Source: Authors, based on data in Bhargava, and Docquier 2008 and the Medical Skilled Migration database (described in Bhargava, Docquier, and Moullan 2010).

thousand people is less than 5 in many African countries, compared with more than 250 in many OECD countries (the destination for the majority of African physician emigrants) (Bhargava and Docquier 2008). In 2004, there were about 25,000 Africa-trained physicians in OECD countries (Bhargava and Docquier 2008), almost one-fourth the total number of physicians practicing medicine in Sub-Saharan Africa—three times the rate in the next-highest region (figure 3.12).

Emigration of African physicians has risen significantly since the early 1990s. The number of physicians in Africa increased 61 percent while the number of migrant physicians rose 91 percent. This increase reflects the increased capacity and improved quality of medical education in Africa, mainly as a result of the intensive focus by domestic governments and the international community on healthcare problems in Africa (figure 3.13).

Factors causing African physicians to leave their home countries are similar to those driving other skilled workers from developing countries to migrate to OECD countries. Some issues are more important for healthcare delivery, however, such as the lack of professional development prospects, insufficient postgraduate training opportunities, and poor practice conditions at home, especially regarding facilities, equipment, medical supplies, and support staff (Clemens 2007; Bhargava and Docquier 2008). Ghanaian doctors who live abroad cite income and career development as their main reasons for emigrating (box 3.3).

Figure 3.13 Number of African-Trained Physicians in Africa and in OECD Countries, 1991–2004

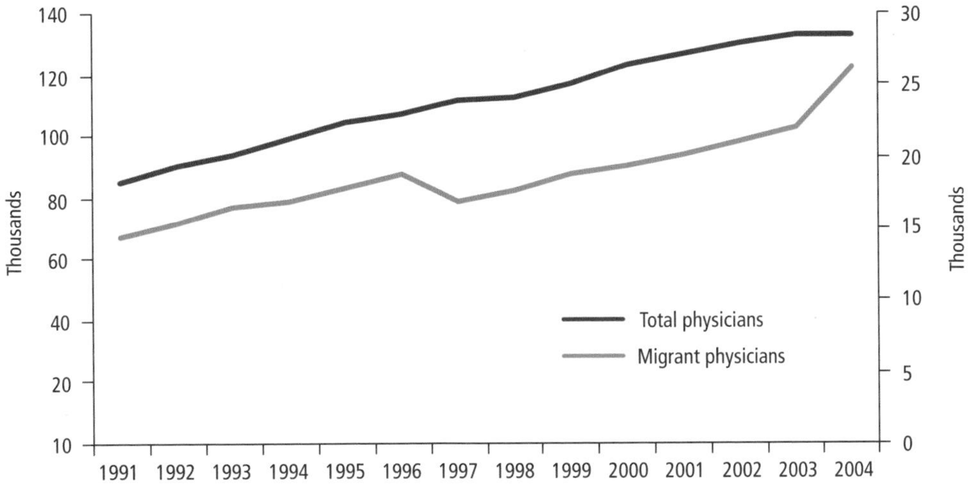

Source: Authors, based on data in Bhargava and Docquier 2008 and the Medical Skilled Migration database (described in Bhargava, Docquier, and Moullan 2010).

The destination choices of African physicians are similar to those of other African professionals but even more biased in favor of English-speaking countries. The United Kingdom, the United States, Canada, and Australia account for more than 85 percent of African physicians in OECD countries, with the United Kingdom alone accounting for 55 percent (figure 3.14). Ireland is the fifth-largest destination for African physicians among OECD countries. A larger number of physicians in developing countries are trained in or fluent in English when compared to other languages. The practice of medicine requires interaction with other professionals and patients. As a result, English-speaking countries become natural destinations for physicians from developing countries. The principal language still has some influence: France and Belgium, for example, are the dominant destinations for physicians from francophone countries. The fact that the United States receives a significant share of physicians from francophone countries suggests that, in some cases, economic prospects and selective immigration policies can supersede language and colonial links as determining factors.

Policies also play an important role in influencing destination choices. Destination countries that emphasize the attraction of high-skilled labor tend to receive more emigrant physicians. Profession-specific laws and regulations regarding foreign-trained doctors are also important; regulatory criteria that discriminate against foreign-trained doctors impede

Box 3.3   Ghana: A Case Study of Emigrant Physicians

The exodus of Ghanaian doctors is not new. Its roots go back to the 1930s, when a scholarship scheme that was established to train African medical doctors in the United Kingdom planted the seeds for the first physician migration from Ghana. For at least 20 years, medical schools in Ghana included study in the United Kingdom as an official component of the medical program. As a result, in 2004 nearly one of every three Ghanaian doctors worked in an OECD country, mostly in the United States and the United Kingdom. A 1999 study estimates that of the 489 physicians who graduated from the University of Ghana between 1985 and 1994, less than 40 percent remained in the country; more than half went to the United Kingdom and about a third to the United States (Dovlo and Nyonator 1999). The number of migrant physicians grew steadily from 1991 to 2004, albeit at a slower pace than that of domestic physicians (box figure 3.3.1).

Box figure 3.3.1   Number of Ghanaian Physicians at Home and Abroad, 1991–2004

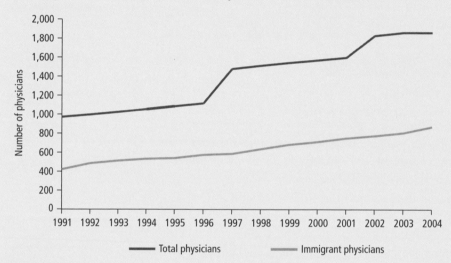

Source: Bhargava and Docquier 2008.

The United States is the largest destination, accounting for 41 percent of all Ghanaian doctors abroad, followed by the United Kingdom, with 39 percent (box figure 3.3.2). The large share of the United States and the United Kingdom is to be expected given the language factor and the colonial links to the United Kingdom. Data on Ghanaian doctors in Australia and South Africa, other likely destination countries, were not available and are not included in these figures.

migration. For example, in the United States, foreign-trained doctors need to complete their residency there, regardless of their prior specializations. Despite this requirement the United States is the most important destination for foreign-trained doctors; without it, the number of foreign-trained doctors would be even greater.

Box 3.3   Ghana: A Case Study of Emigrant Physicians *(continued)*

Box figure 3.3.2   Distribution of Ghanaian Physicians in OECD Countries, 2004

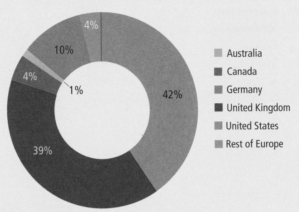

Source: Ozden 2010.

A World Bank survey of Ghanaian physicians in the United Kingdom and the United States offers important insights not only into the demographic attributes of the migrant doctors but also about factors that influenced their decision to migrate. The top reasons cited by Ghanaian doctors for leaving their home country were related to income and career development. More than 90 percent of respondents said they left the country to pursue their specialization. More than 40 percent of respondents cited concerns about instability in Ghana as one of the top five reasons for leaving the country.

Sub-Saharan Africa experienced high emigration rates by health professional between 1991 and 2004. But rates varied widely across countries. In absolute numbers, a small group of countries—generally the largest in terms of population—are the source of the vast majority of migrant physicians in OECD countries. The main reason is that these countries also have the largest supply of physicians. Five countries—South Africa, Nigeria, Sudan, Ghana, and Ethiopia—accounted for more than 87 percent of all African physicians in OECD countries; South Africa alone accounted for 60 percent of the total stock of migrant physicians in 2004 (Docquier and Marfouk 2007).

These countries are not necessarily the ones facing the highest rates of migration as a share of the existing physician stock. Most countries with high emigration rates for physicians (rates of more than 10 percent) experienced an increase in migration rates between 1991 and 2004 (figure 3.15). Small countries were most affected. Cape Verde had the highest rate

Figure 3.14 **Number of African Physicians Working in Selected OECD Countries, 1991 and 2004**

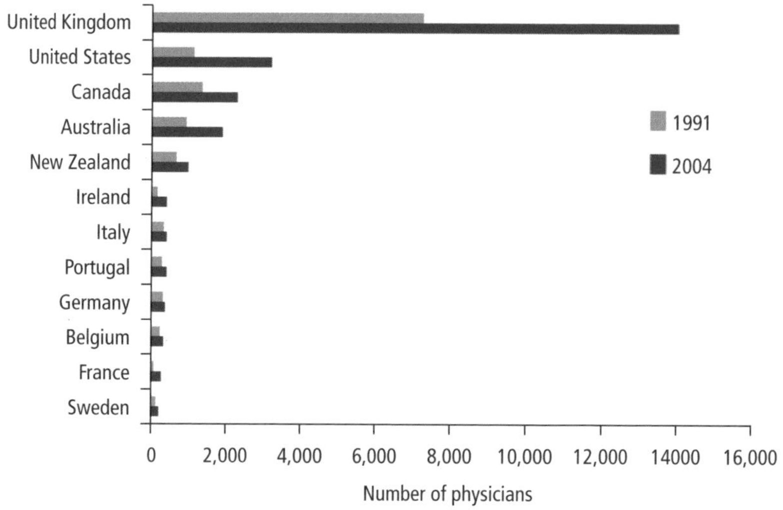

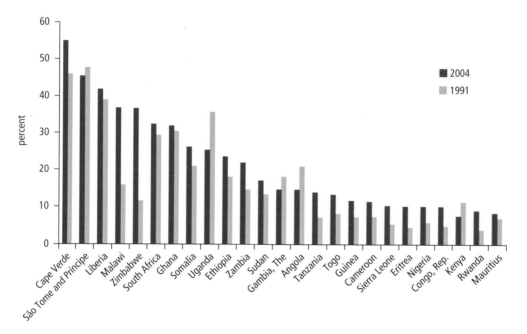

Source: Authors, based on data in Bhargava and Docquier 2008 and the Medical Skilled Migration database (described in Bhargava, Docquier, and Moullan 2010).

Figure 3.15 **African Countries with Highest Rates of Physician Emigration, 1991 and 2004**

Source: Authors, based on date in Bhargava and Docquier 2008 and the Medical Skilled Migration database (described in Bhargava, Docquier, and Moullan 2010).

of physician migration (55 percent), followed by São Tomé and Príncipe (45 percent).

The reasons behind these variations are similar to those for overall tertiary-educated flows. Smaller and poorer countries provide fewer professional and financial opportunities; in many cases, they do not even have medical schools and thus have to send their students abroad for medical training, at a great fiscal expense in many cases.

Data on the migration behavior of nurses are more limited, but studies indicate that their migration rates are also very high. In 2004, 17 Sub-Saharan African countries saw emigration rates of 20 percent or higher among locally trained nurses (figure 3.16). Many of the countries with high physician emigration rates also have high nurse emigration rates, suggesting that the same factors may influence the migration decisions of all healthcare professionals. For example, emigration rates of nurses from Cape Verde and São Tomé, which have the two highest rates of migration among physicians, were about 40 percent. In Liberia, 40 percent of doctors and 80 percent of nurses emigrated.

IMPACT OF MIGRATION OF HEALTHCARE PROFESSIONALS

Consensus is slowly emerging on the extent of migration of physicians and other healthcare professionals from Africa. There is much less agreement on the overall impact on Africa's health outcomes. Anand and Bärnighausen (2004) performed a cross-country analysis of maternal mortality, infant mortality, and under-five mortality rates. Their results suggest that the density of human resources for healthcare is significant in accounting for the three mortality rates tested, with elasticities ranging from –0.39 to –0.17. A later study by the same authors using a similar method suggests that healthcare worker density is correlated with the coverage of three vaccinations (MCV, DTP3, and polio3).[4] When the impact of doctors and nurses is assessed separately, Anand and Bärnighausen find that only nurse density is positively associated with the three vaccinations.

Clemens (2007) tests the hypothesis that decreases in emigration raise the number of domestic healthcare professionals, increases the mass availability of basic primary care, and improves a range of public health outcomes. His results suggest that Africa's generally low staffing levels and poor public health conditions are the result of factors—such as the segmentation of labor markets for healthcare workers—entirely unrelated to international movements of health professionals. He argues that emigration has increased the production of healthcare workers in

Figure 3.16 Migration Rates among Nurses, by Country, 2000

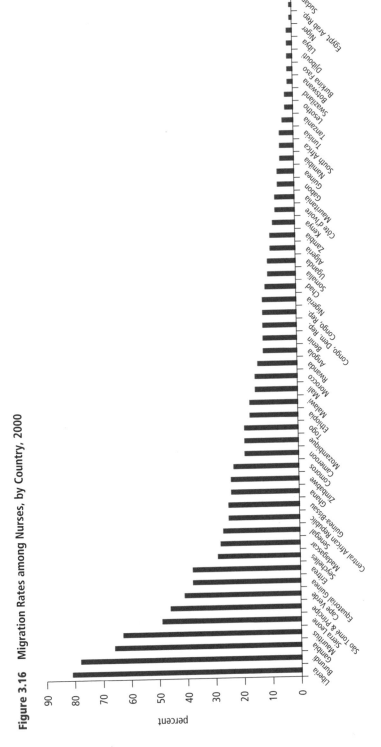

Source: Clemens and Pettersson 2006.

Africa. He highlights the various benefits associated with migration, such as remittances.

Bhargava, Docquier, and Moullan (2010) analyze the effect of physician migration on child mortality and vaccination levels, using a random effects model. Their more nuanced results indicate that many health indicators improve with physician levels when adult literacy levels exceed 55 percent. They demonstrate the importance of the complex linkages among migration, development, and the overall social and economic environment of the country in question and show that the number of physicians in a country is only one of the inputs into the provision of health services. Stopping their migration, they conclude, would have a positive but small impact on the overall human development indicators they analyze.

POLICY OPTIONS

One of the main developmental challenges African countries face—more critical than high-skilled emigration—is low levels of human capital. How to increase human capital, given limited resources, is a complex problem, well beyond the scope of this book. The main focus in this section is on policy choices governing tertiary-educated migration. These choices can be divided along two main dimensions: What stage of a migrant's professional career should be targeted by the policies—before or after education is obtained? Who implements the policies—sending countries or destination countries, mostly in the OECD?

Two educational issues are most relevant for international migration: tuition policies and the type of education offered. In regard to policies governing tuition, a dilemma exists. Careers in medicine, engineering, and other technical subjects are fast becoming global, and professionals in these fields are in high demand in destination countries. Training in these fields also tends to be the most costly. Requiring students to pay for a portion of the cost of their training seems only fair, especially if the students will migrate soon after graduation. This option is frequently recommended, especially on economic efficiency grounds (Clemens 2009). Tuition levels that reflect the actual cost of education would sharply restrict the number of graduates and limit eligibility to the rich, however, because most of the origin countries lack credit markets to finance education. Limited access to finance, which is especially acute in African countries (Gurgand, Lorenceau, and Melonio 2011), would result in many highly qualified African students being unable to obtain professional education. Furthermore, as professionals in science, technology, and medicine are the ones generating positive externalities, it would make sense to subsidize their education from public funds.

One potential solution is a two-tiered tuition system, similar to the one currently implemented in medical schools in Ghana. It involves partial (or full) cost recovery for a portion of students and free tuition for the rest, where eligibility depends on academic merit, public service requirements, or both. This system may generate extra revenue, which, in turn, would raise the supply of students, reduce the reliance on government funding, or both. Because a large portion of the financial gain from migration accrues to migrants and their social networks, a partial ex ante recovery of the cost of the education is also economically efficient.

Another alternative is for governments to offer merit-based scholarships for students who otherwise could not afford education. Scholarships could substitute for direct public funding; if structured to include certain conditions, they could help stem emigration.

The potential for migration may also influence the type of education provided. A frequently suggested policy is to change the education mix—for example, by training physicians' assistants rather than physicians or health aides rather than nurses. One example concerns "health surveillance assistants" in Malawi, who require limited training. The first effect of such change is to increase the overall number of healthcare workers, as the training costs per student are significantly lower than the costs of training higher-level healthcare workers. Because many critical services, such as the immunization of children, can be provided by nurses or other healthcare workers, an increase in the number of healthcare professionals may increase the delivery of such services and improve certain outcomes. The second effect is that migration rates may decline, because the demand for such professionals is likely to be lower in the destination OECD countries. Such policy suggestions can be controversial and may have serious negative welfare implications, however, such as prompting an explicit trade-off between quantity and quality (Soucat and Scheffler forthcoming). Such a trade-off is found in many countries where services are of high quality only in rich and urban areas, at the cost of poor and rural areas.

Another group of policies takes effect after the education of potential migrants is completed. South Africa requires several years' service in rural areas after graduation from medical schools. Ghana has experimented with bonding schemes to require some medical professionals to pay back a part of the government-funded tuition if they fail to serve for a number of years after graduation. Except for nursing, however, payment levels were set so low that they did not cover the cost of the education and did not discourage doctors from immigrating—most doctors working abroad

Box 3.4 Incentives to Retain Health Professionals in Ghana

The Ghanaian Ministry of Health established incentive schemes to keep medical professionals in the country. The program consisted of several components. First, it reduced the need for specialized training outside the country by establishing the Ghana College of Physicians and Surgeons. The college has increased the supply of labor in remote districts, as part of the training is conducted in hospitals outside of Accra.

Second, since 1999 a program called the Additional Duty Hours Allowance (ADHA) has, for the first time, compensated doctors and nurses for hours worked beyond their normal schedules. The program was initially successful among doctors, but it was considered demotivating for nurses, whose salaries were low, in particular in comparison with what doctors earned (Buchan and Dovlo 2004). Moreover, the program became too expensive: by 2005, ADHA payments and salaries accounted for 97 percent of total government health expenditures and 67 percent of total government and donor health expenditures. As a result, in 2006 ADHA was replaced by a comprehensive salary regime (the health sector salary scheme) that removed the health sector from the general Ghanaian salary structure and raised overall salaries.

Third, the government provided health professionals in deprived districts an additional allowance equal to 20–35 percent of their monthly salaries. Each district's level of deprivation was based on the lack of electricity, potable water, all-weather roads, and adequate basic education. The policy did not succeed in attracting more health professionals to the targeted districts, largely because healthcare workers in urban areas could supplement their government salaries by taking highly paid, part-time jobs at private health clinics.

Source: Awumbila 2010.

simply paid off the bond instead of completing the service requirements (Awumbila 2010). Such bond requirements, if imposed at all, should be structured so that they do not significantly reduce the demand for education or encourage immediate migration to escape from the requirement.

An alternative is to impose additional taxes/payments on migrants (generally referred to as the Bhagwati tax).[5] Although such a practice sounds efficient and fair, in practice it may be difficult to impose and enforce, because the cooperation of destination countries' government or courts may be needed (see Wilson 2009 for a detailed analysis).

Ghana has sought to curb the emigration of medical professionals by offering higher salaries and professional opportunities (box 3.4). But there is no convincing evidence of the cost-effectiveness of such policies, given the vast wage gaps between the destination and origin countries.[6]

Another alternative that has been suggested is to restrict travel, by refusing to issue passports or diplomas to students and recent graduates. These policies are not likely to be effective; they also violate basic principles of human rights.

Other policies that repeatedly appear in policy discussions aim to encourage the return of professionals. Among the incentives provided are efforts to help returnees find jobs and to subsidize housing or return expenses. To stem the loss of its healthcare workers, Kenya provided incentives including paid leave, overtime pay, housing support, car loans, transport allowances, life insurance, shortened working hours, and better healthcare coverage (Ndetei, Khasakhala, and Omolo 2008). In Zambia, more training opportunities may have led to higher retention rates (Mathauer and Imhoff 2006).

Migration policies to provide subsidies or other incentives to return migrants are popular, but there is no systematic evidence of their effectiveness. Thorn and Holm-Nielsen (2008) find that although adequate pay is necessary, the primary determinants of decisions to return include the quality of the research environment, professional reward structures, and access to state-of-the-art equipment. Financial incentives are also likely to create distortions, such as penalizing professionals who never migrated or subsidizing returnees who were planning to return even in the absence of the incentives. In addition, such policies may result in adverse selection, with the least skilled returning and the more skilled remaining abroad. One simple policy that can provide significant benefits at low fiscal cost would be to remove certain biases against returning professionals that exist in professional regulations or government employment, by, for example, adequately recognizing qualifications and experience obtained abroad.

Destination-country policies are also important in determining the size and composition of migrant flows. Many OECD countries implement selective policies that target highly skilled and educated migrants, making their entry and assimilation as easy as possible. Such policies range from providing special visas for the highly educated to citizenship laws, recognition of professional qualifications, and provision of access to public services such as education and healthcare. The increase in demand for high-skilled workers in the United States has been filled through permanent employer-based resident permits ("green cards") for individuals with advanced degrees in science and technology, temporary H-1B visas for high-skilled workers, and intracompany transfer (L1) visas. Australia, Canada, and New Zealand award higher points for highly educated applicants for work permits. And the European Union (EU) is considering creating a "blue card," which would grant high-skilled professionals selected through a points-based system unrestricted access to EU labor markets after an initial period in the host country.

Because OECD countries are the main beneficiaries of the migration of professionals trained by public funds in African countries, there is some justice in asking them to subsidize the education expenses in the origin countries. Provision of such assistance must be additional to other forms of assistance if it is to compensate countries of origin for the fiscal loss associated with high-skilled emigration.[7] A similar scheme might involve the provision of scholarships for students from developing countries to study at universities in destination countries. Most students, however, use such programs as entry points into the labor markets of the destination countries, as current experience shows.

Among the most popular postgraduation policies debated are the ones centered on the recruitment policies of destination countries. As a result of public pressure, many OECD governments (such as that of the United Kingdom) impose "ethical" recruitment policies, especially for medical professionals. Such policies have had limited effectiveness (Bach 2008). Inflows of nurses from some of the poorest countries in Sub-Saharan Africa (such as Malawi and Swaziland), which are prohibited by the U.K. code of practice, have continued.[8]

A potential policy measure is a cooperation arrangement under which OECD governments would agree to help African governments enforce their service or taxation requirements or impose their own additional taxes to be remitted to African governments. No destination country would want to impose such taxes unilaterally, however, for fear of diverting migrant professionals to other destination countries that do not implement them. Furthermore, enforcement in many countries might face institutional and legal obstacles.

The debate on policies regarding skilled migration takes place in the absence of detailed and systematic empirical analysis. Not only is it unclear what the policy parameters need to be, in many cases it is not obvious whether any migration-related policy should be implemented at all. For example, if the main constraints in the delivery of healthcare are equipment and facilities, then any policy aiming to limit migration of physicians or other professionals is unlikely to generate an improvement in welfare. In this case, the remittances sent home by migrants or the professional links they establish may benefit their country of origin.

Policies restricting mobility directly or through educational restrictions are extremely distortionary and violate simple human freedoms. Moreover, anecdotal evidence suggests that they are unlikely to work. In cases where limited mandatory service requirements are imposed, the terms and duration need to be carefully chosen in order not to create the perverse effect of encouraging migration to avoid such burdens. Where the goal is cost recovery, such policies should probably be implemented ex ante rather than ex post through additional taxation, which is difficult to enforce.

Policies set by destination countries are even less likely to be effective, but additional subsidies to educational institutions in origin countries are likely to be the least distortionary. The feasibility of hiring institutions (for example, public or private hospitals) in receiving countries opening training facilities in Africa should be examined to increase the supply of professionals.

The multitude of constraints facing Africa's health sector as a whole need to be addressed. Poor working conditions, limited opportunities for professional progress, and shortages of equipment and support staff are some of the main reasons driving African physicians to migrate to wealthier countries in the North. A forthcoming World Bank publication (Soucat and Scheffler) tackles various human resource challenges faced in the health sector in Africa and provides detailed analysis.

The problems facing the healthcare sector in Africa are complex. Addressing them requires country-specific, detailed, multifaceted approaches that incorporate policies on education, compensation, private sector participation, and financing of healthcare expenditures. Analysis and debate, based on much better data collection, will be needed before sustainable solutions can be found.

NOTES

1. The terms *highly skilled, highly educated,* and *tertiary educated* are used interchangeably in the academic and policy literature.

2. The term *brain drain* is often used to refer to high-skilled migration, especially when the goal is to highlight the negative effects of skilled migration. This chapter refrains from using this term, as a more neutral expression probably leads to more objective discussion.

3. Exceptions exist: the dominant destination for migrants from Mozambique—a former colony of Portugal—was South Africa, mainly because of proximity.

4. It is important to keep in mind that correlation does not imply causation. Healthcare worker density may be correlated with limited vaccine coverage but not cause it. Indeed, a plethora of other factors could be responsible for both the scarcity of healthcare workers and poor health outcomes.

5. Clemens (2009) discusses the ethical dimensions of the Bhagwati tax.

6. Melonio (2008) proposes the concept of migration balances between countries adjusted for education level and expenditure. He suggests making transfers directly from destination countries to origin countries without involving individuals in the process, thus minimizing the administrative burden.

7. Training financed directly by OECD governments for courses geared toward OECD licensing requirements or OECD–focused job search assistance may encourage migration.

8. The code of practice of the U.K. National Health Service (NHS) applies only to the active recruitment of health professionals from developing countries by the NHS in the absence of a bilateral agreement.

BIBLIOGRAPHY

Acosta, Pablo, Pablo Fjanzylber, and J. Humberto Lopez. 2007. "The Impact of Remittances on Poverty and Human Capital: Evidence from Latin American Household Surveys. In *International Migration, Economic Development and Policy*, ed. Caglar Ozden and Maurice Schiff. Washington, DC, and New York: World Bank and Palgrave MacMillan.

Anand, Sudhir, and Till Bärnighausen, 2004. "Human Resources and Health Outcomes: Cross-Country Econometric Study." *Lancet*. 364 (9445): 1603–09.

Angel-Urdinola, Diego F., Taizo Takeno, and Quentin Wodon. 2008. "Student Migration to the United States and Brain Circulation-Issues, Empirical Results, and Programmes in Latin America." In *The International Mobility of Talent: Types, Causes and Development Impacts*, ed. Andres Solimano. Oxford: Oxford University Press.

Awumbila, Mariama. 2010. *Mobility of Health Professionals from Selected African Countries to the European Union (MOHPROF) Project*. Revised Ghana National Report (Macro Research) submitted to the International Organization for Migration, Regional Office for Southern Africa, South Africa.

Bach, Stephen. 2008. "International Mobility of Health Professionals: Brain Drain or Brain Exchange?" In *The International Mobility of Talent: Types, Causes and Development Impacts*, ed. Andres Solimano. Oxford: Oxford University Press.

Beine, Michel, Frédéric Docquier, and Caglar Ozden. 2001. "Diasporas." *Journal of Development Economics* 95 (1): 30–41.

Beine, Michel, Frédéric Docquier, and Hillel Rapoport. 2001. "Brain Drain and Economic Growth: Theory and Evidence." *Journal of Development Economics* 64 (1): 275–89.

Bhargava, Alok, and Frédéric Docquier. 2008. "HIV Pandemic, Medical Brain Drain, and Economic Development in Sub-Saharan Africa." *World Bank Economic Review* 22 (2): 345–66.

Bhargava, Alok, Frédéric Docquier, and Yasser Moullan. 2010. "Modeling the Effect of Physician Emigration on Human Development." http://www.ncbi.nlm.nih.gov/pubmed/21288783.

Buchan, James, and Delanyo Dovlo. 2004. *International Recruitment of Health Workers to the UK: A Report for DFID*. London: Department for International Development Health Systems Resource.

Bundred, Peter E., and Cheryl Levitt. 2000. "Medical Migration: Who are the Real Losers?" *Lancet* 356 (8225): 245–46.

Chand, Satish, and Michael Clemens. 2008. "Skilled Emigration and Skill Creation: A Quasi-Experiment." Working Paper 152, Center for Global Development, Washington, DC.

Clemens, Michael. 2007. "Do Visas Kill? Health Effects of African Health Professional Emigration." Working Paper 114, Center of Global Development, Washington, DC.

———. 2009. "Skill Flow: A Fundamental Reconsideration of Skilled-Worker Mobility and Development." Working Paper 180, Center of Global Development, Washington, DC.

Clemens, Michael, Claudio E. Montenegro, and Lant Pritchett. 2008. "The Place Premium: Wage Differences for Identical Workers across the U.S. Border." Working Paper 148, Center for Global Development, Washington, DC.

Clemens, Michael, and Gunilla Pettersson. 2006. "New Data on African Health Professionals Abroad." Working Paper 95, Center for Global Development, Washington, DC.

Commander, Simon, Mari Kangasniemi, and L. Alan Winters. 2004. "The Brain Drain: Curse or Boon? A Survey of the Literature." In *Challenges to Globalization: Analyzing the Economics*, ed. Robert E. Baldwin and L. Alan Winters, 235–78. Cambridge, MA: National Bureau of Economic Research.

Coulombe, Serge, and Jean-François Tremblay. 2009. "Migration and Skills Disparities across the Canadian Provinces." *Regional Studies* 43 (1): 5–18.

Docquier, Frédéric, and Abdeslam Marfouk. 2007. "International Migration by Education Attainment, 1990–2000." In *International Migration, Remittances and the Brain Drain*, ed. Ozden Caglar and Maurice Schiff. Washington, DC, and New York: World Bank and Palgrave Macmillan.

Docquier, Frédéric, Abdeslam Marfouk, Caglar Ozden, and Christopher Parsons. 2010. "Geographic, Gender and Skill Structure of International Migration." Université Catholique de Louvain, Belgium.

Docquier, Frédéric, and Hillel Rapoport. 2009. "Skilled Immigration: The Perspective of Developing Countries." *Skilled Immigration Today*, ed. Jagdish Bhagwati and Gordon Hanson. New York: Oxford University Press.

Dovlo, Delanyo. 2003. "The Brain Drain and Retention of Health Professionals in Africa." Case study prepared for the Regional Training Conference "Improving Tertiary Education in Sub-Saharan Africa: Things That Work!" World Bank, Accra, Ghana, September 23–25.

Dovlo, Delanyo, and Frank Nyonator. 1999. "Migration by Graduates of the University of Ghana Medical School: A Preliminary Rapid Appraisal." *Human Resources for Health* 3 (1): 40–51.

Dustmann, Christian, Itzhak Fadlon, and Yoram Weiss. 2010. "Return Migration, Human Capital Accumulation, and the Brain Drain." April. Draft paper prepared for the Multi-Donor Trust Fund on Labor Markets, Job Creation, and Economic Growth administered by the World Bank's Social Protection and Labor Unit, Washington, DC.

Easterly, William, and Yaw Nyarko. 2009. "Is the Brain Drain Good for Africa?" *Skilled Immigration Today*, ed. Jagdish Bhagwati and Gordon Hanson. New York: Oxford University Press.

Fajnzylber, Pablo, and J. Humberto Lopez. 2007. *Close to Home: The Development Impact of Remittances in Latin America.* World Bank, Washington, DC. http://www.almendron.com/politica/pdf/2006/8845.pdf

Gibson, John, and David McKenzie. 2010. "The Economic Consequences of "Brain Drain" of the Best and Brightest: Microeconomic Evidence from Five Countries." World Bank Policy Research Working Paper 5394, Washington, DC.

Grogger, Jeffrey, and Gordon Hanson. Forthcoming. "Income Maximization and the Selection and Sorting of International Migrants." *Journal of Development Economics.*

Gurgand, Marc, Adrien Lorenceau, and Thomas Melonio. 2011. *Student Loans: Liquidity Constraint and Higher Education in South Africa.* Paris: Agence Française de Développement.

Mathauer, Inke, and Ingo Imhoff. 2006. "Health Worker Motivation in Africa: The Role of Non-financial Incentives and Human Resource Management Tools." *Human Resources for Health* 4 (24): 1–17.

Mattoo, Aaditya, Ileana Cristina Neagu, and Caglar Ozden. 2008. "Brain Waste? Educated Immigrants in the U.S. Labor Market." *Journal of Development Economics* 87 (2): 255–69.

Melonio, Thomas. 2008. "Migration Balances Concept, Hypotheses and Discussion." Working Paper 74, Agence Française de Développement, Paris.

Mountford, Andrew. 1997. "Can a Brain Drain Be Good for Growth in the Source Country?" *Journal of Development Economics* 53 (2): 287–303.

Ndetei, David M., Lincoln Khasakhala, and Jacob O. Omolo. 2008. "Incentives for Health Worker Retention in Kenya: An Assessment of Current Practice." Equinet Discussion Paper 62, Harare, Zimbabwe.

Ozden, Caglar. 2010. "Ghanaian Physicians Abroad and at Home." Development Economics Research Group, World Bank, Washington DC.

Solimano, Andres. 2008. *The International Mobility of Talent: Types, Causes and Development Impacts*. Oxford: Oxford University Press.

Soucat, Agnes, and Richard Scheffler. Forthcoming. *Human Resource for Health in Africa: A New Look at the Crisis*. World Bank, Washington, DC.

Stark, Oded. 2004. "Rethinking the Brain Drain." *World Development* 32 (1): 15–22.

Stark, Oded, C. Helmenstein, and A. Prskawetz. 1997. "A Brain Gain with a Brain Drain." *Economics Letters* 55 (2): 227–34.

Thorn, Kristian, and Lauritz B. Holm-Nielson. 2008. "International Mobility of Researchers and Scientists: Policy Options for Turning a Drain into a Gain." In *The International Mobility of Talent: Types, Causes and Development Impacts*, ed. Andrés Solimano. Oxford: Oxford University Press.

Wahba, Jackline. 2007. "Returns to Overseas Work Experience: The Case of Egypt." In *International Migration, Economic Development and Policy*, ed. Caglar Ozden and M. Schiff. Washington, DC, and New York: World Bank and Palgrave Macmillan.

Wilson, John. 2009. "Income Taxation and Skilled Migration: The Analytical Issues." In *Skilled Immigration Today*, ed. Jagdish Bhagwati and Gordon Hanson. New York: Oxford University Press.

World Bank. 2006. *Global Economic Prospects: Economic Implications of Remittances and Migration*. Washington, DC: World Bank.

4

Harnessing the Resources
of the Diaspora

African countries have large diaspora groups living in and outside Africa. The potential contribution of the diaspora to the continent's development goes far beyond the personal remittances discussed in chapter 2. These contributions range from collective remittances that fund philanthropic activities to knowledge exchange, increased trade links, and better access to foreign capital markets (for example, through diaspora bonds). This chapter reviews the evidence on how the African diaspora contributes to the economic development of countries of origin and offers recommendations on how African governments can support these efforts.

Several important findings emerge from this chapter:

- *Efforts to understand the size and characteristics of the diaspora should be a high priority for developing countries interested in harnessing diaspora resources.* Lack of adequate data impairs efforts to increase the contributions diasporas can make to origin countries. The size of the African diaspora is larger than the official estimate of 30.6 million migrants. Many migrants are not counted in national surveys, especially within Africa, and many descendants of migrants still have emotional ties to the country of their ancestors. Case studies indicate that networks of diaspora families and friends send funds for development purposes, such as constructing schools, providing supplies to schools or hospitals, supporting orphans, and supporting small-scale projects, but little is known about the scale or impact of such activities.
- *Diasporas facilitate cross-border trade, investment, and access to advanced technology and skills.* Diaspora networks play an important role in cross-border exchanges of market information about trade and regulations. Diaspora members may also invest directly in origin countries

or provide their expertise to assist investments by multinational firms. Compared with other foreign investors, members of diasporas may accept lower interest rates on loans to home countries, because they have emotional ties to home countries, because better access to information may allow them to discount the risk premium relative to other foreign investors, and because they may have local currency liabilities that make them less worried than other investors about the potential for currency devaluation or the forced conversion of assets denominated in foreign currencies to local currencies. Diaspora bonds targeted to nationals residing abroad can open opportunities for investment and facilitate investment in their home countries.

- *Diasporas may also provide origin countries access to advanced technology and scarce skills.* The role of the diaspora in technology transfer is well documented in many countries, particularly China and India. In contrast, the evidence for African countries is limited.

- *Harnessing diaspora contributions to trade, investment, and technology requires a supportive business climate.* Diaspora members may be more willing than other investors to take risks in their own country. Investment by them nevertheless requires a conducive business environment, including property rights, security, elimination of red tape, and good infrastructure. Providing voting rights and dual citizenship to migrants can help maintain their ties to origin countries. Dual citizenship can also encourage trade and investment, by enabling migrants to avoid constraints on business activities faced by foreigners. The devotion of more staff in embassies to diaspora issues and adequate training of these staff would facilitate better services and enhance linkages. Better coordination among different departments within embassies and governments would increase efficiency in building relationships with diasporas and their networks.

The chapter is organized as follows. The first section presents a short overview of where the African diaspora is located. The second section discusses how countries benefit from diasporas, though trade, finance, and the transfer of technology. The third section recommends policies that African countries and destination countries could consider to increase the diasporas' contribution to development.

LOCATING THE AFRICAN DIASPORA

Estimating the size of the African diaspora is difficult, because of incomplete data and differences in the definitions of migrants and the diaspora

Box 4.1 Defining Diasporas

A diaspora can be defined as people who have migrated and their descendents who maintain a connection to their homeland. The U.S. Department of State defines diasporas as migrant groups that share the following features:

- dispersion, whether voluntary or involuntary, across sociocultural boundaries and at least one political border
- a collective memory and myth about the homeland
- a commitment to keeping the homeland alive through symbolic and direct action
- the presence of the issue of return, although not necessarily a commitment to do so
- a consciousness and associated identity, expressed in diaspora community media, the creation of diaspora associations or organizations, and online participation (U.S. Department of State 2010).

This definition is different from the definition used by the African Union, which defines the African diaspora as "consisting of people of African origin living outside the continent, irrespective of their citizenship and nationality and who are willing to contribute to the development of the continent and the building of the African Union" (African Union 2005, p. 6).

Estimating the size of a diaspora is complicated by several factors, including place of birth, time of emigration, citizenship, and questions of identity (Ionescu 2006). For example, estimates of U.S.–based diasporas are constructed using the "place of birth for the foreign-born population" available from the U.S. census. Most European countries in the Organisation for Economic Co-operation and Development (OECD), Japan, and the Republic of Korea classify immigrants based on the ethnicity of the parent, which results in higher estimates of the stock of immigrants than does classification based on place of birth. Temporary immigrants may be considered as part of a diaspora but may not be captured in immigration statistics. Origin countries also use different definitions of diasporas. India, for example, uses three categories: nonresident Indian (NRI), person of Indian origin (PIO), and overseas citizenship of India (OCI).

(box 4.1). This chapter uses a narrow but convenient definition of the diaspora as "people born in another country." This definition captures only first-generation migrants; it excludes children and grandchildren, who may have ties to the origin country. The chapter's conclusions should hold, however, irrespective of the definition of the diaspora.

As noted in chapter 1, official data estimate the stock of international emigrants from African countries at 30.6 million in 2010. Of these migrants, more than 14 million African migrants live within Africa. For example, large numbers of immigrants from Burundi and the Democratic Republic of Congo live in Tanzania; Somalis are still living in Kenya; and Lesotho, Mozambique, and Zimbabwe have many migrants in South Africa.

A large number of African migrants are also living in high-income OECD countries. France, Saudi Arabia, the United States, and the United

Figure 4.1 Top Countries of Origin of African Immigrants in the United States, 2010

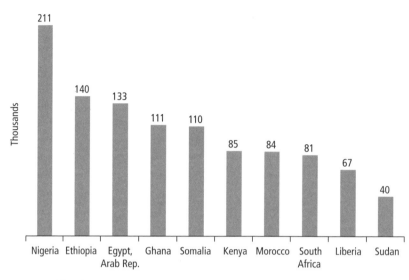

Source: World Bank 2010.

Kingdom are major destination countries for African migrants (see figure 1.1 in chapter 1). Historical colonial ties continue to be a major factor affecting the patterns of migration from Africa, although Italy, Qatar, Spain, and the United Arab Emirates have become new countries of destination for some African emigrants.

The African diaspora in the United States is relatively small.[1] Nigerians are the largest group, followed by Ethiopians and Egyptians (figure 4.1). In Canada the top 12 source countries (Algeria, the Democratic Republic of Congo, Egypt, Ethiopia, Ghana, Kenya, Morocco, Nigeria, Somalia, South Africa, Tanzania, and Uganda) make up 75 percent of the African migrant stock (Crush 2010).

BENEFITING FROM DIASPORAS

Much of the literature on diaspora contributions focuses on skilled migrants and how trade, technology, and capital formation are facilitated by migrants with advanced degrees. But both low-skilled and high-skilled migrants make contributions to their homeland. A growing body of research suggests that skilled migrants and country networks abroad are important reservoirs of knowledge (Pack and Page 1994; Khadria 1999; Meyer and Brown 1999; Saxenian 2002a, 2004, 2006; Barré and others 2003; Kuznetsov 2006; Westcott 2006; Wickramesakara 2009). Other studies highlight the contributions of all migrants, including low-skilled diaspora (Orozco 2003, 2006a, 2006b; Lowell and Genova 2004; Lucas 2004; Portes, Escobar, and Radford 2007; Crush 2011). Other studies analyze how members of the African diaspora contribute to their countries of origin (Chikezie 2000; Mohamoud 2003, 2010; Mohan and Zack-Williams 2002; Bakewell 2008). This section describes the contributions of the diaspora, including Africans living within and outside Africa, without distinguishing between skilled and unskilled emigrants.

TRADE

Migration can affect trade through two channels. First, immigrants have a preference for their native country's goods (supporting "nostalgic trade" in ethnic products) (Light, Zhou, and Kim 2002), partially offsetting the loss of these sales associated with migration (if emigrants had stayed at home, they presumably would have demanded the same products) (Gould 1990, 1994). The effect is difficult to estimate, because migrants presumably have more income than they would have had in the origin country but relocation to the destination country reduces the efficiency with which home country goods are supplied (by adding transport costs, for example).

Second—and more important—migrants can increase the availability of market information essential for trade by helping origin-country exporters find buyers, understand the market, and comply with government requirements and market standards. Migrants facilitate bilateral trade and investment between host and source countries by helping overcome information asymmetries and other market imperfections (Gould 1994; Rauch and Trindade 2003). Transnational networks can help producers of consumer goods find appropriate distributors and assemblers find the right component suppliers. Sharing the same language or a similar cultural background eases communication and facilitates better understanding of transport documents, procedures, and regulations.

The literature emphasizes the role of ethnic networks in overcoming inadequate information about international trading opportunities, which drives down trade costs (see Rauch 2001 for a review of business networks). Gould (1994) and Rauch and Casella (1998) find that ethnic networks promote bilateral trade by providing market information and by supplying matching and referral services. Empirical studies of Australia, Canada, Spain, the United Kingdom, the United States, and the OECD countries generally find that immigration increases bilateral trade flows.[2] But these effects differ by type of good (for example, differentiated goods

Figure 4.2 Migration and Trade Go Hand in Hand: African and OECD Countries

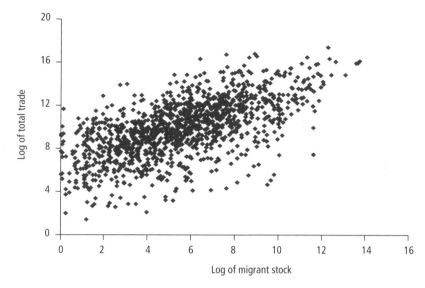

Source: Authors, based on data on migrant stocks from World Bank 2010; 2007 trade data from World Integrated Trade Solution (WITS); and methodology in Dolman 2008.

versus more uniform commodities) and the skill level of the migrants. Estimates of the size of these effects vary widely, and it is difficult for the models used to account for endogeneity. Studies for the United States (Gould 1994; Dunlevy and Hutchinson 1999; Rauch 1999; Dunlevy 2004; Herander and Saavedra 2005; Bandyopadhyay, Coughlin, and Wall 2008) and Canada (Head and Reis 1998) find a positive relationship between trade flows and migration, although export and import elasticities vary across countries and products.

Some governmental agencies and private firms in Africa are tapping their diasporas to provide market information (see annex table 4A.1). Activities include the establishment of diaspora trade councils and participation in trade missions and business networks. The embassies of Ethiopia, Kenya, and Uganda in Washington, DC, and in London support business and trade forums to attract diaspora investors and try to match suppliers with exporters. Some case studies of activities in Sub-Saharan Africa have been conducted (Riddle 2006), but there has not been a proper assessment of whether these contacts generate additional exports.

Countries appear to trade more with countries from which they have received immigrants. Figure 4.2 shows a positive relationship between the size of migrant populations living in OECD countries and the level of bilateral merchandise trade between OECD countries and all African trading partners for which data are available. This relationship could, of course, reflect other variables that affect trade flows between the OECD and Africa.[3]

DIRECT INVESTMENT

Diasporas can increase investment flows between sending and receiving countries, because they possess important information that can help identify investment opportunities and facilitate compliance with regulatory requirements. Language skills and similar cultural backgrounds can greatly contribute to the profitability of investment in unfamiliar countries.[4] Diasporas may use the information they have regarding their countries to invest directly. Alternatively, investors can improve their profitability by tapping the expertise of a diaspora member. A major barrier for a multinational or a foreign firm setting up a production facility in another country is uncertainty and lack of information regarding the new market. For this reason, professionals and managers from Taiwan, China are very much sought after by multinationals for their operations in China.

Members of a diaspora may be more willing than other investors to take on risks in their origin country, because they are better placed to evaluate investment opportunities and possess contacts to facilitate this process (Lucas 2001). Emotion, sense of duty, social networks, the strength of diaspora organizations, and visits to the origin country may also be important determinants of diaspora investment (Nielsen and Riddle 2007).

Some studies find a significant relationship between migrants, particularly skilled ones, and investment inflows to origin countries. Kluger and Rapoport (2005); Javorcik and others (2006); Docquier and Lodigiani (2007); Murat, Pistoresi, and Rinaldi (2008); and Leblang (2011) find that migration facilitates foreign direct investment.

Some government agencies in Africa are attempting to improve their contacts with diasporas to generate investment opportunities for origin-country firms. Ethiopia, Ghana, Kenya, Nigeria, Rwanda, and other African countries are looking to tap into their diasporas for investments in their homeland countries (see annex table 4A.1). Recognizing the need to create suitable mechanisms to encourage diaspora members to channel remittances toward investment projects in partnering states, the East African Community is developing a proposal to attract diaspora financing.[5] Both governments and the private sector have supported business forums to attract diaspora investors. One of the new roles of African investment promotion agencies in Ethiopia, Ghana (Riddle 2006), Nigeria, and Uganda is to provide accurate information and linkage opportunities to investors, including from diasporas.

Some private firms and African diaspora associations also provide information on investment opportunities and sourcing in their homeland countries. They also facilitate contacts between traders in destination and origin countries.

INVESTMENTS BY HOUSEHOLDS

Many migrants transfer funds to households in origin countries for the purpose of investment (see table 2.3 in chapter 2). Data from household surveys reveal that households receiving international remittances from OECD countries have been making productive investments in land purchases, building houses, businesses, improving the farm, agricultural equipment and other investments (36 percent in Burkina Faso, 55 percent in Kenya, 57 percent in Nigeria, 15 percent in Senegal, and 20 percent in Uganda; figure 4.3). Households receiving transfers from other African

Figure 4.3 Investments in Business and Housing Funded by Remittances from within and outside Africa

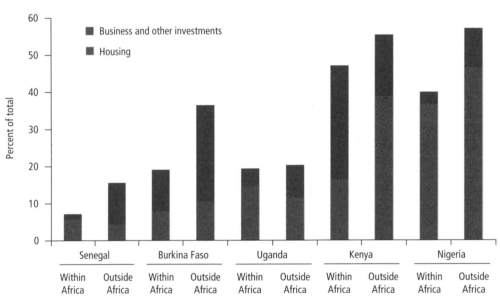

Source: Authors, based on results of Africa Migration Project Household surveys in Burkina Faso, Kenya, Nigeria, Senegal, and Uganda in second half of 2009, Plaza, Navarrete, and Ratha 2011.
Note: "Other investments" includes purchases of land, livestock, and agricultural equipment and investment in agriculture.

countries are also investing a significant share of remittances in business activities, housing, and other investments in Kenya (47 percent), Nigeria (40 percent), Uganda (19 percent) and Burkina Faso (19 percent).

Osili (2004) uses a data set from Nigeria to analyze migrants' housing investments in their communities of origin. She finds that older migrants are more likely to invest in housing in their hometown and to devote a larger share of household income to housing investments. She concludes that "housing investments may be the first stage of a broader investment relationship between migrants and their countries of origin" (p. 844). Survey data indicate similar patterns of investment by households receiving transfers from abroad in Latin America (de Haas 2005), with the difference that Latin American migrants and their family members invest in agriculture and other private enterprises as well.[6] The evidence for Africa from household surveys for investment in agriculture equipment is somewhat limited.

African migrants in other African countries set up small-scale businesses, such as restaurants and beauty salons. They also invest in housing. The African diaspora has invested in service sector activities, such as import/export companies, telecommunications, and tourism and transport companies (examples include Databank, in Ghana; Geometric Power Limited, in Nigeria; Teylium, in Senegal; and Celtel, in Sudan).

Some governments have eased restrictions on foreign land ownership to attract investments from diasporas. Credit Financier de Cameroon offers housing loans to migrants to attract investment in real estate.[7] The Ethiopian government allowed holders of yellow cards (the identification card for the Ethiopian diaspora) to lease land parcels at low rates for the construction of residences in Addis Ababa (see annex table 4A.1). Because of the high demand for land, in 2008 the city of Addis Ababa officially suspended allocation of residential land for the diaspora. The Rwanda Diaspora General Directorate allows groups of 15 or more people to acquire land in Kigali for the purpose of house construction, provided the project is approved by the Kigali City Council based on the Kigali Master Plan.[8]

There is some evidence that returning migrants use savings accumulated while abroad to invest in small businesses when they return (King 1986; Gitmez 1988; Murillo Castaño 1988; Massey and others 1987; Ahmed 2000; Murphy 2000; McCormick and Wahba 2003). Based on surveys conducted in 2006, Gubert and Nordman (2011) find that one-third of returnees to Algeria, Morocco, and Tunisia invested in businesses. They do not find a correlation between migration duration and entrepreneurship. The results of a survey of 302 returnees conducted in

2001 indicate that more than half of Ghanaian and 23 percent of Ivorian returnees reported returning with more than $5,000 in savings (Black and Castaldo 2009). Both studies indicate that many return migrants invest in business activity and that work experience and the maintenance of communication with friends and family while abroad facilitates the opening a business upon return. Cassini (2005) concludes that the most successful Ghana-based businesses of Ghanaian migrants were owned by migrants who visited home frequently and developed social networks.

INVESTMENTS IN CAPITAL MARKETS

Diaspora members can act as catalysts for the development of financial and capital markets in their countries of origin by diversifying the investor base (many countries' capital markets are dominated by investments from government and large companies), introducing new financial products, and providing a reliable source of funding. Diaspora connections with markets in destination and origin countries are important. This subsection presents some estimates of the savings of the African diaspora and describes two vehicles—diaspora bonds and diaspora investment funds—for encouraging diaspora investments in Africa.

Wealth and savings of the African diaspora in host countries

Ketkar and Dora (2009) use the New Immigration Survey data on the United States to understand the wealth and asset diversification behavior of recent immigrants from Asia, Sub-Saharan Africa, Latin America, and the Middle East and North Africa. They find that the region of origin is not a significant determinant of savings levels once length of stay, educational attainment, and number of children are taken into account. African immigrants in the United States tend to have lower levels of savings than immigrants from Asia and Latin America, largely because they have been in the country for a shorter period of time and have lower levels of education.

Ratha and Mohapatra (2011) estimate the annual savings of the African diaspora to be about $52 billion. About $30 billion of this amount—equivalent to 3.2 percent of Sub-Saharan Africa's GDP—is saved by African migrants in Sub-Saharan African (table 4.1).[9] These estimates are based on assumptions that members of the African diaspora with tertiary education earn the average income of their host countries, that migrants without tertiary education earn a third of the average household incomes

Table 4.1   Estimated Savings by Migrants from Selected African Countries, 2009

Country	Emigrant stock (millions)	Estimated savings by migrants	
		Billions of dollars	Percent of GDP
Egypt, Arab Rep.	3.7	6.0	3.2
Morocco	3.0	9.6	10.5
Zimbabwe	1.3	1.6	34.4
Algeria	1.2	4.2	3.0
Côte d'Ivoire	1.2	0.6	2.6
Nigeria	1.0	3.5	2.0
Sudan	1.0	1.3	2.3
South Africa	0.9	3.8	1.3
Congo, Dem. Rep.	0.9	1.1	10.5
Ghana	0.8	2.0	7.5
Somalia	0.8	1.8	..
Uganda	0.8	0.6	4.0
Tunisia	0.7	2.0	5.1
Ethiopia	0.6	1.9	6.5
Senegal	0.6	0.9	7.0
Kenya	0.5	1.8	6.1
Angola	0.5	0.9	1.1
Liberia	0.4	0.6	66.8
Cameroon	0.3	0.8	3.8
Mauritius	0.1	0.6	7.2
Other	10.2	7.1	2.5
Total	30.5	52.7	3.6
Sub-Saharan Africa	21.8	30.4	3.2
North Africa	8.7	22.3	4.3

Source: Ratha and Mohapatra 2011.
Note: .. = negligible.

of the host countries, and that both skilled and unskilled migrants have the same personal savings rates as in their home countries. Not surprisingly, savings are higher for countries that have more migrants in high-income OECD countries. Most of these savings are invested in the host countries of the diaspora. It is plausible that a fraction of these savings could be attracted as investment in Africa if African countries designed proper instruments and incentives.

Diaspora bonds

A diaspora bond is a retail savings instrument marketed only to members of a diaspora. It can be an effective tool for tapping diaspora wealth (Ketkar and Ratha 2010). By retailing diaspora bonds in small denominations ($100–$1,000), a government or reputable private corporation in a developing country can tap into the wealth of relatively poor migrants. Diaspora bonds can also be sold in larger denominations to institutional and foreign investors. Investment bankers may be needed to structure these bonds and ensure compliance with securities regulations in the United States and other jurisdictions. Diaspora bonds can be sold globally through national and international banks and money transfer companies. They can be marketed through churches, community groups, ethnic newspapers, stores, and hometown associations in countries and cities where large numbers of migrants reside.

In addition to patriotic reasons and the desire to give back, a diaspora investor may be willing to buy diaspora bonds at a lower interest rate than the rate demanded by foreign investors. The cost of retailing diaspora bonds can be high, but it can be absorbed if the interest rate offered is lower than the rate typically paid to pension funds and other institutional investors. The bond can be made even more attractive by offering tax breaks and credit enhancements (first-loss guarantee, relatively senior creditor status).

Migrants are expected to be more loyal than the average investor in times of distress. They likely have better knowledge of their origin country and legal recourse in the event of a default. They are also less likely to worry about the risk of currency devaluation, as they can find ways to spend money back home if the bonds are repaid in local currency terms.

The governments of India and Israel have issued diaspora bonds, raising about $40 billion, often in times of financial crisis.[10] In 2009 and 2010, Ethiopia and Nepal issued diaspora bonds, but neither was successful in mobilizing funds.[11] One problem was limited marketing and publicity. In Nepal, "foreign employment bonds" were issued mostly to low-skilled migrants in the Gulf Cooperation Council countries rather than to the richer diaspora groups in OECD countries. The interest rates offered on the bonds, which were denominated in local currency, were low relative to the rates on comparable instruments, which were already lower than the rate of inflation.

Like other investors, diaspora investors are concerned about the government's willingness and ability to service its debt. Factors such as government reputation, the rule of law, and the protection of property rights affect their decision to invest in their home countries. Countries in which diaspora groups are politically opposed to the government and countries facing governance problems may find it difficult to issue diaspora bonds.

Diaspora bonds have a greater chance of success if the proceeds are earmarked to finance projects in which diaspora members are interested. Such projects could include housing, schools, hospitals, and other community infrastructure projects that benefit the migrants, their families, or their region in the home country. Before launching a bond, therefore, it is advisable that the borrowing government or corporation hold consultations with diaspora groups. To be able to do so, countries need to build a knowledge base about the size, income, and wealth characteristics of diaspora groups in key destination countries. Currently, such information is not easily available.

It is plausible that the issuance of diaspora bonds may reduce the volume of remittances. This does not appear to have been the case for India, where there was additionality of inflows from diaspora bonds rather than substitution of workers' remittances (Debabrata and Kapur, 2003). After the maturity of the India Resurgent Bonds, a large part of the proceeds were converted to local currency deposits and began to be counted as remittances (World Bank 2005). In the case of Israel as well, diaspora investors have tended to roll over their capital to newer diaspora bonds after the maturity of the diaspora bonds.

Preliminary estimates suggest that Sub-Saharan African countries could potentially raise $5–$10 billion a year by issuing diaspora bonds (Ratha, Mohapatra, and Plaza 2009). Countries that could potentially issue diaspora bonds include Ethiopia, Ghana, Kenya, Liberia, Nigeria, Senegal, Uganda, and Zambia in Sub-Saharan Africa and Egypt, Morocco, and Tunisia in North Africa.[12] These countries have large diasporas abroad, especially in high-income countries.

Ratha and Ketkar (2011) underscore three reasons why there are still very few issuances of diaspora bonds. First, there is limited awareness of this financing vehicle. Developing country policy makers would benefit from technical assistance aimed at improving their understanding of how to structure bond offerings, register them with regulatory agencies such as the U.S. Securities and Exchange Commission, and determine whether such instruments need to be rated by rating agencies. Second, many countries still have little concrete knowledge of the capabilities and resources of their diasporas. Third, in some cases diaspora members may not trust their home country government. In addition, some Sub-Saharan African countries may face difficulties because of the absence of national banks in destination countries.

The donor community and multilateral development banks can facilitate the piloting and mainstreaming of such innovative financing tools (Ratha 2010). Their involvement could include granting or lending seed money for investment banking and credit rating services and providing legal help, financial guarantees, and technical assistance in project design. Potential issuers of diaspora bonds should be reminded of the risks associated with debt denominated in foreign currency. Considerations must be given to prudential risk management before taking on additional debt. Volatility in migrants' incomes and disruption in relationships with the diaspora can occur quickly in some countries where political risks are high. Large foreign currency inflows after a bond issuance require careful macroeconomic management, especially of the exchange rate in order to avoid Dutch disease.

Diaspora investment funds

Developing countries, especially in Sub-Saharan Africa, suffer from a shortfall of private equity capital. Portfolio equity flows to Sub-Saharan Africa have gone mainly to South Africa (Ratha, Mohapatra, and Plaza 2009). Foreign investors appear to be averse to investing in Africa because of lack of information, the perception of high risk, and the small size of the market, which makes stocks relatively illiquid. One way to encourage greater private investment in these markets could be to tap the African diaspora.

Several African investment funds have been proposed to attract investments from wealthy African migrants abroad; examples include the Liberian Diaspora Social Investment Fund, the Rwandan Diaspora Mutual Fund, and the Zambia First Investment Fund. Such funds can take the form of regional funds, mutual funds, or private equity to be invested in African companies and pension funds.[13] Persuading diaspora investors to invest in African diaspora funds may require strengthening investor protections to ensure proper management of the funds. Some of the options for building diaspora investors' confidence proposed by Aydagul, Ketkar, and Ratha (2010) apply to investment funds: management of funds by a state agency, management of funds by a private company,[14] and management of funds by a combination of a private company but with participation of members from the diaspora.

COLLECTIVE REMITTANCES

The African diaspora has begun to collectively contribute financial and nonfinancial resources to homeland countries, albeit not yet on a large scale. Organizations have been created in Europe, the United States, and some African countries, based on religion, ethnicity, and geographic ties.[15] These groups include hometown associations, ethnic associations, alumni associations, religious associations, professional associations, nongovernmental organizations, investment groups, national development groups, welfare/refugee groups, and Internet-based virtual organizations. The number of associations appears to be roughly correlated with the size of the diaspora in each country.[16]

In contrast to similar groups of Asian (particularly Filipino) and Latin American diasporas, little is known about the scope, scale, patterns, and impact of African diaspora associations.[17] Data are not collected on contributions sent by formal migrant associations, and there is no information on collective remittances by undocumented immigrants.

Hometown associations and other voluntary associations of migrants from the same geographical area have provided substantial funds to some African communities. This financing is often equal to or greater than the municipal budget for public works, particularly in towns with small populations (Orozco 2003). Some twinning projects have also been established. Burundians in a town in France, for example, have partnered with a town in Burundi (Turner and Mossin 2008).

Interviews conducted for this study provide insight into collective remittances from the African diaspora:[18]

- Networks of families and friends pool resources and support their villages or friends. In some cases they send funds for development purposes, such as constructing a school, providing supplies to schools or hospitals, supporting orphans, or training new migrants arriving in the destination country. In other instances they send funds to support funerals or weddings. These transactions are not documented.
- Diaspora organizations rely on the skills of members, volunteers' time, donations, and fundraising events for project financing.
- Collective remittances appear to be motivated by migrants' sense of identity and feeling of solidarity with their home countries, as well as by sociocultural and political bonds and the feeling of being useful and powerful (Guarnizo 2003 reaches similar conclusions).
- The most frequent activity of African diaspora organizations in Denmark (where 123 associations covering 22 African countries and 18 associations with regional coverage were surveyed) is the shipment of used equipment in containers, typically destined for schools, universities, orphanages, or hospitals (41 associations), followed by the sending of collective remittances (27 associations) and educational

campaigns, including campaigns to increase awareness of HIV/AIDS, discourage female circumcision, and advance civil rights. Other projects involve construction or support for schools, orphanages, and activity centers and small-scale projects, such as the construction of wells, implementation of farming or smaller business projects, and provision of microcredit loans. In some cases the money goes to private entities; in other cases it goes to public institutions.[19] Box 4.2 describes some of the challenges facing African diaspora organizations in Denmark.

It is difficult to gauge the impact of diaspora-financed development projects based on these case studies and surveys. Most of the projects involved are small, and their economic impact has not been evaluated. Many organizations appear to lack the capacity, funds, leadership, and information required to manage projects or understand and navigate procedures in either their origin or their destination country. Such problems are not unique to Africa: Paul and Gammage (2005) find similar findings on El Salvadoran associations in the United States. The interviews conducted for this study underline the difficulties facing development work in Africa: a poor investment climate, inadequate ports and customs facilities, excessive red tape, and lack of trust in governments.

Box 4.2   A Case Study of African Associations in Denmark

African migrant associations in Denmark developed following the influx of African migrants in the early 1990s. Government funds, most often from the Danish Association for International Co-operation (Mellemfolkeligt Samvirke) and the Project Advice and Training Centre (PATC), are provided to almost three-quarters of these associations for development activities. Migrant associations can apply for these funds on equal terms with other Danish associations. Both programs require contact with a partner nongovernmental organization in the destination country.

The lack of language skills is the main impediment to these organizations' activities in Denmark. Other issues include inadequate access to financing and insufficient knowledge of Danish laws and regulations. Measures that would enhance the impact of these organizations include providing access to information about funding opportunities, offering training to key members from associations with few or no members of Danish origin, and encouraging collaboration between Danish and ethno-national associations, which would give such associations access to Danish networks and resources.

Source: Trans and Vammen 2011.

Governments in a number of large labor-sending countries have attempted to develop schemes to channel collective remittances into public revenue, investment, or community development. Given the private nature of these transactions, policy interventions have focused either on appropriating some of the flows, largely without success, or on creating incentives to change individual or household behavior. For example, a few governments have offered matching grants for remittances from diaspora groups or hometown associations, in order to attract funding for specific community projects. The best known of these matching schemes is Mexico's 3-for-1 program, under which the local, state, and federal governments each contribute $1 for every $1 of remittances sent to a community for a designated development project (Page and Plaza 2006). Colombia also provides government funding to match migrant group funds for local projects benefiting vulnerable populations (IOM 2004).

Little evaluation of the impact of these programs has been conducted. Resources have gone primarily to rural areas, where they have increased the supply of essential services (health, education, roads, and electricity) (World Bank 2005). In some cases hometown associations have funded the construction of soccer fields and community halls but have not funded the ongoing maintenance of these facilities. It is difficult to assess whether these investments—and the matching grants—have gone to the highest-priority projects or have been diverted from other regions with a great need of assistance from fiscally constrained governments (World Bank 2005). Proponents of hometown associations argue that their involvement ensures that programs are focused on community needs and that the associations promote increased accountability and transparency of local and national authorities (Page and Plaza 2006).

The potential of hometown associations to serve as conduits for broader development projects is limited by at least three factors. First, they may not have the best information on the needs of the local community, or they may have different priorities. Second, the capacity of hometown associations to scale up or form partnerships is limited by the fact that their members are volunteers and their fundraising ability is weak.[20] Third, hometown associations can become divided, weakening their advocacy potential (Newland and Patrick 2004; Kuznetsov 2006). In the context of Africa, support based on regional ties may exacerbate income disparities, particularly as outmigration is concentrated in a few areas in many African countries. The fact that volunteer initiatives are often driven by individuals, without institutionalized support, could also threaten the sustainability of projects.

TRANSFERS OF TECHNOLOGY AND SKILLS

A diaspora can be an important source and facilitator of research and innovation, technology transfer, and skills development. Japan, the Republic of Korea, and Taiwan, China are examples of economies that have relied on their diasporas as knowledge sources. The governments in these economies promoted the return of foreign-educated students or established networks of knowledge exchange with them (Pack and Page 1994). Other developed labor-sending countries with large, skilled emigrant populations (Australia, Ireland, Israel) have also been able to tap their expatriates and develop mentor-sponsor models in certain sectors.

Diaspora involvement in origin countries' economies can take several forms (Kuznetsov 2006; Plaza 2008a):

- licensing agreements to facilitate the transfer of technology and know-how between diaspora-owned or -managed firms in origin and destination countries
- direct investment in local firms through joint ventures
- knowledge spillovers (which occur, for example, when diaspora members assume top managerial positions in foreign-owned firms in their country of origin)
- involvement in science or professional networks that promote research in destination countries directed toward the needs of origin countries
- temporary or virtual return, through extended visits or electronic communication in professional fields such as medicine and engineering
- return to permanent employment in the sending country after work experience in the host country.

Diaspora knowledge networks refer to the "skilled personnel who migrate every year from their home countries to join thousands and millions of their countrymen and women residing in countries other than their own" (Mahroum, Eldridge, and Daar 2006, p. 26; see also Kuznetsov 2006 and Meyer and Quattiaus 2006).[21]

There are three types of diaspora knowledge networks:

- Scientists and research and development (R&D) personnel networks provide knowledge, mentoring expertise, and finance (venture capital).
- Professional and business networks are regional or local networks of skilled diaspora members located in larger cities (Saxenian 2002b).[22] Relevant associations provide technical assistance and organize conferences, investment forums to match investors with counterparts at home, and recruitment fairs. African examples include the Ghanaian

Doctors and Dentists Association United Kingdom (GDDA–UK) and the Association of Kenyan Professionals in Atlanta (AKPA).
• Global knowledge networks are transnational networks linking global regions with origin countries (see Plaza 2008a for a description of Chile Global).

Several African countries are attempting to organize their diasporas in order to gain more benefits from their nationals abroad. Diaspora members sometimes maintain residences in both their origin country and their destination country or return to their origin countries every year to support specific activities. These movements and exchanges of knowledge and skills benefit the origin countries (Easterly and Nyarko 2008). Increasing these benefits will require efforts to survey diasporas' human resources, create active networks, and develop specific activities and programs, such as those of small pilot initiatives that invite diaspora members to teach courses at African universities.[23]

AN EMERGING POLICY AGENDA TO MAXIMIZE THE BENEFITS OF DIASPORAS

Both sending and receiving countries are beginning to implement policies to boost flows of financial resources, information, and technology from the diaspora. Several developing countries (including the Philippines, India, China, and several African countries) have set up agencies and initiatives to engage with their diasporas.

Such efforts and initiatives have met with little success in Armenia, Colombia, Mexico, Moldova, Peru, and South Africa. Some initiatives—such as Conectandonos al Futuro, in El Salvador, Red Caldas, in Colombia, and Red Científica Peruana, in Peru—lost momentum and faded away (Dickinson 2003; Chaparro, Jaramillo, and Quintero 1994). The South African Network of Skills Abroad (SANSA) has experienced a reduction in the number of new members since its inception in 1998 (Marks 2004). Several high-income countries (including Australia, Ireland, Israel, and the United Kingdom) have implemented initiatives to strengthen engagement with their diasporas (Kingslye, Sand, and White 2009; Finch, Andrew, and Latorre 2010).

DUAL/MULTIPLE CITIZENSHIP

Holding dual (or multiple) citizenship can improve both a diaspora's connection with its origin country and its integration into the destination country.[24] Dual citizenship provides an important link between diasporas and their home countries (Ionescu 2006). Citizenship and residency rights are important determinants of a diaspora's participation in trade, investment, and technology transfer with its origin country (Cheran 2004) and make it easier to travel to and own land in the origin country.

Origin countries that allow for dual citizenship benefit, because their migrants are more willing to adopt the host country's citizenship, which can improve their earnings and thus their ability to send remittances to and invest in the origin country. Immigrants from some countries that adopted the policy of allowing dual citizenship during the 1990s and 2000s (Brazil, Colombia, Costa Rica, the Dominican Republic, and Ecuador) experienced a rise in earnings in the United States (Mazzolari 2007), because citizenship allowed them to acquire legal status and gain access to better jobs. Immigrants from countries that were granted dual citizenship during the 1990s experienced a 3.6 percentage point increase in the probability of full-time work relative to other Latin American immigrant groups. Destination countries can also benefit by providing dual citizenship, which can help foster the assimilation of immigrants.

Origin countries have increased their acceptance of dual citizenship. For example, 10 Latin America countries (Brazil, Colombia, Costa Rica, the Dominican Republic, Ecuador, El Salvador, Mexico, Panama, Peru, and Uruguay) passed new laws on dual nationality or citizenship in the 1990s and 2000s (Jones-Correa 2001). In some countries, such as Kenya, the policy was adopted under pressure from diaspora groups.[25] Other countries, including most of the former Soviet republics, oppose dual citizenship status.

About half of the African countries on which information is available allow dual citizenship (table 4.2). Interest has increased in providing dual citizenship to the children or grandchildren of migrants, in order to encourage their ties to origin countries. The potential gains for origin countries are limited, however, because many destination countries do not permit dual citizenship.

Chiswick (1978) was the first to show a positive impact of naturalization on earnings. More recent studies show that the integration of migrants in destination countries amplifies their involvement in the development of their countries of origin (de Haas 2006). Studies of Canada and the United States seem to support the existence of a citizenship premium; European studies show mixed results (Bevelander and Pendakur 2009). According to Cheran (2004), citizenship or residency

Table 4.2 African Countries Permitting and Prohibiting Dual Citizenship for Adults

Country	Dual citizenship		Country	Dual citizenship	
	Yes	No		Yes	No
Algeria	X		Libya		X
Angola	X		Madagascar		X
Benin	X		Malawi		X
Botswana		X	Mali		X
Burkina Faso	X		Mauritania		X
Burundi	X		Mauritius	X	
Cameroon		X	Morocco	X	
Cape Verde	X		Mozambique		X
Central African Republic	X		Namibia	X	
Chad	—		Niger		X
Comoros	—		Nigeria	X	
Congo, Dem. Rep.		X	Rwanda	X	
Congo, Rep.		X	São Tomé and Principe	—	
Côte d'Ivoire	X		Senegal		X
Djibouti		X	Seychelles		X
Egypt, Arab Rep.	X		Sierra Leone	X	
Equatorial Guinea		X	Somalia		X
Eritrea		X	South Africa	X	
Ethiopia		X	Sudan	—	
Gabon		X	Swaziland		X
Gambia, The	X		Tanzania	X (in process)	
Ghana	X		Togo	X	
Guinea		X	Tunisia	X	
Guinea-Bissau	—		Uganda	X	
Kenya	X		Zambia (in draft constitution)		X
Lesotho		X	Zimbabwe		X
Liberia		X			

Source: Authors, based on Brown 2009; information collected from interviews with African countries' embassies and consular services in Washington, DC, Paris, London, and Pretoria; http://www.multiple citizenship.com/countrylist.html; http://www.cic.gc.ca/english/resources/publications/dual-citizenship. asp; and http://allafrica.com/stories/201001200400.html.
— = not available.

rights are important in determining immigrants' participation in trade, investment, and knowledge transfer.

Some origin countries do not allow dual citizenship but offer identification card schemes in destination countries. In some countries these cards grant visa rights to migrants. Ethiopia, India, and Mexico offer special identification cards that entitle migrants to specific rights. In 2002, the Ethiopian government enacted a law permitting Ethiopian migrants with foreign citizenship to be treated as nationals if they hold a "person of Ethiopian origin" identification card, known locally as a yellow card. The yellow card entitles its holder to most of the rights and privileges of an Ethiopian citizen, such as entry into Ethiopia without a visa, the right to own residential property, and the right to live and work in the country without additional permits. Yellow card holders may not vote or be elected to political office, and they cannot be employed in national defense, security, or foreign affairs (Federal Negarit Gazeta 2002). India issues a Person of Indian Origin (PIO) card, which allows for entry without a visa during the period of its validity.[26] Mexico issues a *matrícula consular* to Mexicans living in the United States; this document not only serves as an identity card, it is also accepted by many states as a valid document for issuance of a driver's license and by many banks for opening accounts (World Bank 2005).

VOTING RIGHTS

Origin countries can strengthen their ties to the diaspora by allowing citizens who reside abroad to vote without returning (box 4.3). Some countries give nationals abroad voting rights, and some reserve a specific number of seats in parliament for diaspora representatives.

Some African countries that confer voting rights on their diasporas require advanced registration or allow voting in person only. In other

---

Box 4.3   Educating the Rwandan Diaspora about Elections in Rwanda

Interviews with diaspora groups and individuals indicate that granting voting rights to the diaspora is an important means of encouraging greater engagement with origin countries. Rwanda provides a useful example of an effort to engage the diaspora by reaching out and encouraging voting by foreign citizens. In August 2010, Rwandans living abroad participated in presidential elections for the first time since the civil war. In preparation for the elections, a delegation of the National Electoral Commission (NEC) visited Belgium, Burundi, Denmark, France, Germany, Kenya, Norway, Sweden, Switzerland, and Uganda to inform emigrants about the electoral process. Of the 17,824 registered voters in the diaspora, 14,242 (78 percent) cast valid votes.

Source: http://global.factiva.com/redir/default.aspx?p=sta&ep=AE&an=AFNWS00020100810e68 a000n7&fid=300516908&cat=a&aid=9JOI000500&ns=53&fn=diaspora&ft=g&OD=V2AUbjNaqd 6b6yKMegonfnoY9oOdATkhWR19knPBTvmljPNVjs%2fEl5nw%3d%3d.

countries, voting by mail is possible. Migrants who permanently live abroad can register with an embassy or consulate in the country of their permanent residence and vote there, but the costs of registration may be high. For example, South Africa approved voting rights for South Africans living abroad in 2009, but only about 16,000 voters (out of the estimated 1.2 million South African citizens in the diaspora) who had been registered well in advance were able to participate in the 2009 elections. Members of the Nigerian diaspora asked the Independent National Electoral Commission (INEC) to register Nigerians abroad so they could participate in the 2011 elections.[27] The extent of participation also depends on whether voting is required (as it is in Peru) or voluntary (as it is in most countries).

DESTINATION COUNTRIES' SUPPORT FOR DIASPORAS

Some destination countries are devoting resources to helping diasporas promote the development of their countries of origin. Canada, France, Germany, Italy, Spain, the United States, and the European Union, among other governments and institutions, are becoming more interested in working with the diasporas residing in their countries. Some of their initiatives are at the initial stage of implementation. Other programs, such as those promoting return, have been unsuccessful.[28]

One area of focus has been the reduction in fees for transferring remittances (see chapter 2). There are few well-defined programs that facilitate diaspora trade, investment, and technology operations apart from small grants or matching grant initiatives (for example, the Development Marketplace for the African Diaspora in Europe, the African Development Marketplace, and the Joint Migration and Development Initiative). There is little information on initiatives and few external evaluations of their effectiveness (de Haas 2006). The United States has focused on engaging with diaspora communities as a core element of its foreign policy, with an emphasis on the role diasporas can play in their origin countries (an example is the role Haitian-Americans played in providing relief to Haiti following the earthquake). The U.S. Department of State and the U.S. Agency for International Development (USAID) have sponsored a new initiative called the Diaspora Networks Alliance (DNA).[29] Canada, France, the Netherlands, and the European Commission have funded development projects implemented by diaspora groups. The Netherlands has awarded grants to projects aimed at building the capacity of migrant organizations. In 2007, France added cofunding of diaspora projects to its menu for codevelopment. At the 25th Annual Africa-France Summit, participating heads of state decided "to place the African diasporas living in France at the center of the migration and development strategies, promoting their involvement in the economic and social development of their country of origin by means of codevelopment programs, encouraging migrant business projects and mobilizing their savings for social and productive investment."[30]

The governments of France, Italy, the Netherlands, Spain, the United States, and the United Kingdom are working with developing country diaspora groups to promote development in origin countries and support their own foreign policy objectives. Such initiatives (for example, the French codevelopment policy or the European mobility partnership agreements) often aim to "better manage migration flows, and in particular to fight illegal migration" (EU 2007).

INCENTIVES FOR RETURN BY HOST COUNTRIES

Since the 1970s, some European countries (France, Germany, the Netherlands, and recently Spain) have encouraged return migration by providing money to immigrants and financing projects to employ returnees in their home countries (Constant and Massey 2002; Panizzon 2011).[31] Few migrants have participated, and most projects have been unsuccessful. The French local development migration program provided assistance, though mostly on a small scale, to projects by Malian and Senegalese returnees in their countries of origin (Lacroix 2003).

In the late 1990s, countries changed their approach by encouraging the return of not only unskilled but also skilled immigrants. The approach encouraged circular migration, codevelopment, reintegration of temporary workers in their home countries, and the return of skilled migrants to Africa. For example, France entered into agreements with migrants' origin countries to facilitate return (Panizzon 2011). Its pact on concerted migration management with Senegal seeks the voluntary return of medical doctors and other health professionals in France by offering research equipment or the prospect of joint university appointments (French Senate 2007). The new mobility partnership agreements also establish circular migration schemes for professional education and expert missions by members of the diaspora (Plaza 2009).

Temporary labor migration is seen by origin countries as a way for migrants to acquire skills abroad and bring them home upon return. Examples include France's pact with Benin in 2006 and Senegal's government-run Retours vers l'agriculture plan in 2007, which includes an initiative to reintegrate returning migrants (Panizzon 2011).

European governments, often in cooperation with the International Organization for Migration (IOM), have been implementing assisted voluntary return programs for almost three decades. The majority of these programs target irregular migrants. According to the IOM, about 1.6 million migrants returned to more than 160 countries with the help of these programs. About 32,000 migrants returned under the IOM Assisted Voluntary Return programs in 2009, up from about 23,000 in 2008. In the United Kingdom, there were 4,945 returns in 2009, 4,301 in 2008, and 4,157 in 2007. The costs of assisted voluntary returns are less than the costs of forced returns (Council of Europe 2010). In the United Kingdom, for example, in 2005 compulsory removals cost British taxpayers £11,000 per person, whereas voluntary returns cost £1,000 per person. Factoring in reintegration assistance, voluntary returns cost less than one-third the cost of forced returns (National Audit Office 2005).

The IOM is helping skilled migrants return to Africa, hoping that the returnees' financial resources and technical skills will further development. The Return of Qualified African Nationals Program attracted more than 2,000 highly skilled persons back to 41 African countries over a 16-year period (1974–90). Support for the return of migrants has expanded to include various forms of contact with origin countries. The IOM's Migration for Development in Africa (MIDA) program supports a variety of return options, including virtual return (through, for example, teaching courses and leading seminars online); repeated visits; investment; temporary return; and permanent reallocation (Ndiaye 2011).[32] The MIDA Great Lakes project involves missions, workshops, and roundtables to facilitate the exchange of knowledge between institutions in Burundi, the Democratic Republic of Congo, and Rwanda with the diaspora in Belgium.[33]

The United Nations Development Programme's (UNDP) Transfer of Knowledge through Expatriate Nationals (TOKTEN) projects support three-week to three-month development assignments for expatriates, at much lower costs than hiring professional consultants. A recent evaluation of a TOKTEN program in Sri Lanka indicates that these services have not had a significant impact on local institutions, because expatriate involvement was not sustained (TOTKEN provides two visits at most) (Wanigaratne 2006). An evaluation of the Rwandan TOTKEN program in 2005–07, which involved visits by 47 volunteers to teach and provide technical assistance, noted that an average stay of less than two months and the variety of responsibilities constrained the transfer of knowledge to counterparts in host institutions (Touray 2008).

According to the OECD (2010), diaspora knowledge flows could increase if barriers to short-term and circular mobility were removed. There has been an increase in mobility partnership pacts between EU and origin countries. For example, an agreement with Cape Verde focuses on visa and border control policies. India has initiated discussions with the European Union on the export of high-skilled professionals (Plaza 2009b). More data and research are needed to develop effective policies to encourage circular migration. The Swedish government has appointed an independent parliamentary committee to examine the connection between circular migration and development, with a report to be presented in March 2011 (Swedish Ministry of Justice 2010).

RETURN INITIATIVES BY SENDING COUNTRIES

A number of origin countries have introduced measures to encourage return by skilled migrants. The most successful efforts have been in Asia. China offers attractive salary packages, multiple-entry visas (for migrants who have lost their Chinese citizenship), and access to foreign exchange. The Hsinchu Industrial Park initiative, by the government of Taiwan, China, attracted more than 5,000 returning scientists in 2000 alone (Saxenian 2002b, 2006). Thailand has offered generous research funding and monetary incentives for return (Pang, Lansang, and Haines 2002). Many programs to encourage return have met with only limited success, and studies of return migration suggest "that those who return may be those that have performed relatively poorly when abroad, while those who stay are the best and the brightest" (Lodigiani 2009, p. 21).

Less information is available on African policies to encourage return. A study on return migrants in Côte d'Ivoire and Ghana finds that policies that favor returnees above those who never left the country are likely to be counterproductive and to cause resentment (Ammassari 2006).

Experiences from many of the government initiatives implemented by developing countries in Latin America, Asia, and Africa have demonstrated that it is difficult to promote return, particularly permanent return. Some returnees were not able to reenter local labor markets at a level appropriate for their skills and knowledge. The lack of laboratories and equipment makes it difficult for scientists and researchers to keep up to date on the latest scientific developments worldwide. Some members of the diaspora may return with unrealistic expectations or find it hard to readjust to local norms (OECD 2010).

AFRICAN GOVERNMENTAL INITIATIVES TO ENGAGE THE DIASPORA

African governments are reaching out to the diaspora. Ghana, Nigeria, Senegal, and South Africa have launched plans to incorporate their diaspora communities as partners in development projects. Ethiopia, Ghana, Mali, Nigeria, Rwanda, Senegal, Tanzania, Uganda, and other countries have established institutions (at the agency or ministerial level) to interact with the diaspora (see annex table 4A.1).

These initiatives have taken various forms, ranging from the creation of dedicated ministries to deal with migrant communities to the addition of specific functions to the ministries foreign affairs, interior, finance, trade, social affairs, youth, and so on. Some governments have set up institutions such as councils or decentralized institutions that deal with migrant community issues. Several of these initiatives have not maintained their momentum or have been discontinued with a change of government.[34]

To date, the interest of African governments in their diasporas has focused largely on migrants living outside Africa, such as in OECD countries. Conferences and investment seminars, either at home or in the capitals of major OECD countries, target the diaspora outside Africa.

There have been some proposals to take a more harmonized and integrated approach to the diaspora within each regional economic community. There is a proposal for the creation of a regional diaspora office within the East African Community (EAC). The Economic Community of West African States (ECOWAS) has proposed establishing a dedicated financial instrument at the regional level to facilitate business contributions of the diaspora. These proposals focus on the diaspora outside Africa. Some other initiatives focus on establishing an integrated approach to cross-border payment systems, including the transfer of remittances within ECOWAS and the Economic and Monetary Community of Central Africa (CEMAC). Government institutions abroad, especially embassies and consulates, can play a key role in reaching out to the diaspora (Ionescu 2006). A survey of embassies in Abu Dhabi, Pretoria, Paris, London, and Washington, DC, indicates the need to improve African governments' capacity and increase their resources in order to sustain the activities of the ministries and institutions dealing with diaspora communities abroad (box 4.4). Steps that could improve embassies' engagement with diasporas include creating outreach programs to gain more information on diaspora communities, training embassy staff in contacting diaspora members and facilitating investment and trade contacts, and using embassies as vehicles for marketing investment and financial mechanisms such as diaspora bonds. Governments

Box 4.4   The Role of Embassies in Enabling Diasporas

The authors conducted 48 interviews with government officials and diplomats of embassies in Abu Dhabi, Pretoria, Paris, London, and Washington, DC, to understand the role embassies are playing in enabling their diasporas to make economic contributions to their countries. They found few differences across embassies in this respect. Most origin countries have only a limited engagement with the diaspora, although some embassies are implementing initiatives to reach their diaspora. Embassies provide consular services to their expatriate community but little information on trade and investment opportunities.

Some of the difficulties that embassies are facing in reaching their diaspora include the following:

- lack of coordination among departments, especially between the embassy and consular offices
- lack of information on the number of nationals in the diaspora
- reluctance of migrants from politically unstable countries to engage with the embassy
- inadequate staff dedicated to working with the diaspora
- insufficient capacity to reach out to the diaspora and facilitate investment, trade, and skill transfers.

Source: Plaza 2009a.

can help facilitate diaspora networks through the Internet, professional associations, embassies, and cultural events. Some origin countries are supporting long-term and long-distance linkages between emigrants and their countries of origin (Ghai 2004).

African governments are also working through the African Union (AU) on diaspora issues. In 2003, the AU executive council agreed to actively engage the African diaspora.[35] In 2005, the African Union formally designated the African diaspora as the "sixth region" of the AU's structure. It allocates 20 seats for the African diaspora in the Economic, Social and Cultural Council of the Africa Union (ECOSOCC).

In September 2008, the African Union Commission (AUC) launched the Africa Diaspora Health Initiative to provide a platform through which health experts from the diaspora can transfer information, skills, and expertise to their counterparts in Africa. It created the African Citizens Directorate to deal with overarching issues in the relationship between overseas diasporas and homeland governments.

The African Union's approach is to enable the diaspora to organize itself with AU support within the framework provided by executive organs of the union, the council, and the assembly, with the guidance of member states. The mechanisms and the process for diaspora engagement are still being worked out, causing some frustration among diaspora communities, which in recent forums have expressed a reluctance to wait for AU directions before organizing themselves.[36]

The World Bank is supporting many of the diaspora activities of the AU and African governments.[37] Its African Diaspora Program (launched in September 2007) partners with the African Union, client countries, donors, and diaspora professional networks and hometown associations to enhance the contributions of the African diaspora to the development of their home countries.

Improving the business environment

Like other potential investors and trading partners, migrants seeking to invest in or trade with African countries are often constrained by the poor business environment. Interview results stress the impediments of excessive red tape and customs delays.

The diaspora requires a conducive business environment, a sound and transparent financial sector, rapid and efficient court systems, and a safe working environment (Page and Plaza 2006). De Haas (2005) emphasizes that bad infrastructure, corruption, red tape, lack of macroeconomic stability, trade barriers, lack of legal security, and lack of trust in government institutions affect migrants' decisions to invest in their home countries and to return. A survey of skilled South African migrants identifies crime, the cost of living, taxation, and the quality of public and commercial services as the main barriers to conducting business (Kuznetsov 2006). Black and Castaldo (2009) report policies, laws, and regulations as the biggest obstacles facing diaspora members and return migrants in establishing a business. Case studies and interviews with members of the African diaspora indicate that procedures governing business licenses, registrations, and exports and imports remain complicated. Indeed, some diaspora associations report barriers to shipping donated goods, citing, for example, cumbersome import procedures for donated books.[38] Some African governments are providing incentives to attract investment from the diaspora. Ethiopia offers investment incentives for both foreign investors and the diaspora that include income tax exemption for two to seven years, 100 percent duty exemption on the import of machinery and equipment for investment projects, and 100 percent customs exemption on spare parts whose value does not exceed 15 percent of the total value of capital goods imported (Federal Negarit Gazeta 2003). Such policies have encouraged many in the Ethiopian diaspora to invest in small businesses in Ethiopia, including cafes, restaurants, retail shops, and transport services in big cities and small towns that were otherwise restricted to Ethiopian nationals living in the country (Chakco and Gebre 2009).

The treatment of potential investors from the diaspora remains controversial. Some diaspora members have complained that certain countries (for example, Burundi) have more favorable policies for foreign investors than for members of the diaspora. It may be better to provide efficient procedures for all investors, without requiring proof of the investor's origin and nationality. However, origin countries could still benefit from focusing their scarce resources on providing services to members of the diaspora and to move beyond consular services to a broader range of support for diaspora investors.

Encouraging participation in savings and social security schemes

Governments can mobilize resources from diasporas by encouraging their participation in social security, housing, and microfinance programs. Bangladesh has created a number of schemes tailored to investors and nonresidents, such as saving accounts in foreign currency. The Philippines allows its citizens to enroll in or continue their social security coverage while abroad. Workers from the Philippines can also continue contributing to the Pag-IBIG Fund (Home Development Mutual Fund), which Filipinos can access through embassies and consulates abroad (ADB 2004). Some of these initiatives could be implemented in Africa to generate savings.

ANNEX 4A   EXAMPLES OF AFRICAN GOVERNMENT INSTITUTIONS DEALING WITH DIASPORA COMMUNITIES ABROAD

Table 4A.1   African Government Institutions Dealing with Diaspora Communities Abroad

Country	Diaspora institutions	Activities
Algeria	• Ministry of National Solidarity, Family and the National Community Abroad	
Benin	• Ministry for Foreign Affairs, African Integration, the Francophone Community • Beninese Abroad Subagency (Directorate for Relations with Beninese Abroad)	• Contributes to periodic census of Beninese abroad, in coordination with other agencies.
Burkina Faso	• High Council of Expatriate Burkinabé • Ministry of Foreign Affairs and Regional Cooperation	
Cape Verde	• Ministry of Emigrant Communities • Focal Points for Migration, established in each of Cape Verde's 22 municipalities	
Ethiopia	• Ethiopian Investment Agency • Ethiopian Expatriate Affairs, Ministry of Foreign Affairs • Diaspora Coordinating Office, Ministry of Capacity Building, in each of Ethiopia's nine regional states and in three administrative cities • Embassies abroad	• Ensures the well-being, safety, security, rights, and privileges of Ethiopians abroad. • Disseminates information to the Ethiopian community abroad through media outlets. • Conducts research to identify problems faced by the diaspora in order to improve legislation for its increased participation. • Keeps diaspora informed of relevant issues. • Support events involving the diaspora. High Commission in London organizes annual events. Ghanaian Embassy in Rome works with Council of Ghana Nationals Associations in Italy.
Kenya	• Diaspora technical team formed by government of Kenya, Kenya Private Sector Alliances (KEPSA), and diaspora representatives (2007) • Multiministerial commission, including ministries of interior, labor, youth, and foreign affairs and the central bank • Diaspora Committee within the Ministry of Planning, Development (moved to Ministry of Foreign Affairs in 2009) • Diaspora desk within the Ministry of Foreign Affairs (this ministry also has representation in the Kenya Diaspora Association) • National Diaspora Council of Kenya (2004)	• Prepared report entitled "Maximizing the Potential and Input of the Kenyan Diaspora in the Political Process, Wealth Creation, Employment Generation and Poverty Reduction," as background for the Kenya Diaspora Bill 2007 (still not passed into law). • Kenyan diaspora proposed creation of a Kenyans Abroad Investment Fund (KAIF) in 2004. • Consultations with diaspora on how best to facilitate their participation in national development (2002–07).

continued

Table 4A.1 African Government Institutions Dealing with Diaspora Communities Abroad *(continued)*

Country	Diaspora institutions	Activities
	• Embassies abroad	• Organized series of investments forums to promote investments in the United States and United Kingdom (for example, Kenya Diaspora Investment EXPO 2010). Ministers of finance and foreign affairs participated. Consular affairs/ diaspora desk established in London to facilitate networking in United Kingdom
Mali	• Ministry of Malians Abroad and African Integration	• Distributes a *Practical Guide for Malians Abroad* (2003). Assists in administration of skill transfer programs, such as the United Nations' Transfer of Knowledge through Expatriate Nationals (TOKTEN) program.
	• Guichet Unique of the Agency for Promotion of Investments (API)	
	• High Council of Malians Abroad	• Provides information to Malians considering emigrating.
Morocco	• Ministry Charged with the Moroccan Community Residing Abroad • Ministerial Delegate for the Prime Minister Responsible for Moroccans Resident Abroad	• Provides advice on investment, financial planning, diaspora tax, customs, commerce and transportation, social security, remittances/ banking references, and cultural events.
	• Hassan II Foundation for Moroccans Resident Abroad	• Provides social and legal assistance, including partial funding for the repatriation of the deceased.
	• Council of the Moroccan Community Abroad	• Monitors public policies regarding emigrant nationals, ensuring the protection of their rights and enhancing their participation in the political, economic, cultural, and social development of Morocco.
Nigeria	• Ministry of Foreign Affairs Unit of the Nigerians in Diaspora Organization (NIDO)	• Oversees the interests of Nigerian nationals living abroad. • Organizes annual diaspora conference.
	• National Volunteer Service • One Stop Investment Centre (OSIC) of the Nigerian Investment Promotion Commission (NIPC)	
Senegal	• Ministry of Senegalese Abroad and Tourism • Senegalese Diaspora Foundation (Fundation des Senegalais de l'extérieur) • Guichet Unique of Investment Promotion and Major Works Agency (APIX) • Superior Council of Senegalese Abroad	

Table 4A.1   African Government Institutions Dealing with Diaspora Communities Abroad *(continued)*

Country	Diaspora institutions	Activities
Tunisia	• Ministry of Social Affairs, Solidarity and Tunisians Abroad Subministry: Office for Tunisians Abroad • Guichet Unique of Agency for the Promotion of Industry (API) • Guichet Unique of the Export Promotion Centre (CEPEX) • Guichet Unique of Agricultural Investment • Promotion Agency (APIA) • Regional delegations in 17 regions of Tunisia (under the Office of Tunisians) • Ministry of Social Affairs, Solidarity and Tunisians Living Abroad	• Provides social workers at consulates to address family issues in the diaspora. • Organizes exploratory and study visits and summer camps in Tunisia for diaspora youth. • Registers highly skilled expatriates.
Zambia	• Diaspora desk at President's Office	• Encourages and coordinates dialogue with Zambians living abroad.

Source: Authors, based on data from Rannverg 2009; ICMPD–IOM 2010; Mohamoud 2010; http://www.mfa.gov.et/Ethiopians_Origin_Abroad/Ethiopia_Origin.php; and meetings with embassies and consular services officials; http://www.ccme.org.ma/en/Presentation/council-for-the-moroccan-community-abroad.html.
Note: Table is not exhaustive. It is intended to provide only relevant examples.

NOTES

1. According to Wickramasekara (2009, 6), "The African diasporas can be broadly classified into two categories: (a) Africans in America, the United Kingdom, Brazil/Latin American/Caribbean as a result of involuntary migration and (b) the new African immigrants, mainly in North America and Europe, and to a smaller extent in Australia and Japan, among others, as a result of voluntary migration for education and for employment." The African Union uses a similar classification.

2. A growing body of research suggests that diasporas and country networks abroad are an important reservoir of knowledge of trade and investment opportunities. This literature emphasizes that trade and migration are complements rather than substitutes. See Gould (1990, 1994); Helliwell (1997); Head and Ries (1998); Dunlevy and Hutchinson (1999); Rauch and Trindade (1999, 2002); Hutchinson and Dunlevy (2001); Girma and Yu (2002); Light, Zhou, and Kim (2002); Wagner, Head, and Ries (2002); Combes, Lafourcade, and Mayer (2003); Dunlevy (2003); Rauch (2003); Bardhan and Guhathakurta (2004); Blanes Cristóbal (2004); Bryant and Law (2004); Co, Euzent, and Martin (2004); Blanes (2005); Herander and Saavedra (2005); Blanes and Martín-Montaner (2006); Dunlevy (2006); Bandyopadhyay, Coughlin, and Wall (2008); Bettin and Lo Turco (2008); Dolman (2008); Foad (2008); and Morgenroth and O'Brien (2008).

3. Countries that are far apart trade much less than countries that are near one another. Colonial ties are important. Landlocked countries trade less than countries with coasts.

4. Transnational companies often make investments based on their ethnic ties (Aykut and Ratha 2003). For example, some ethnic Korean companies invest in Kazakhstan and some ethnic Chinese companies invest in the East Asia and Pacific Region.

5. http://www.eac.int/invest/index.php?option=com_content&view=article&id=53:eac-diaspora&catid=39:global-east-africans.

6. Data from African household surveys conducted in Burkina Faso, Kenya, Nigeria, Senegal, South Africa, and Uganda do not indicate that African migrants invest in agricultural equipment (Plaza, Navarrete, and Ratha 2011).

7. http://www.slideshare.net/ifad/vincent-okele.

8. http://www.rwandandiaspora.gov.rw/rwanda-investment/housing.html.

9. These estimates—which update the estimates in Ratha, Mohapatra, and Plaza (2009)—are based on the assumptions that members of the African diaspora with tertiary education earn the average income of their host countries, that migrants without tertiary education earn a third of the average household incomes of the host countries, and that both skilled and unskilled migrants have the same personal savings rates as in their home countries.

10. According to Ketkar and Ratha (2009a), the Development Corporation for Israel (DCI) raised more than $25 billion from diaspora bonds. Jewish diaspora investors pay a steep price premium (perhaps better characterized as a large patriotic yield discount) when buying DCI bonds. The State Bank of India raised $11.3 billion through three issues of diaspora bonds, issued after ordinary sources of funding had all but vanished in 1991, following the balance of payments crisis], and in 1998, after the country conducted nuclear tests.

11. See Negash (2009) and Mersha (2009) for a description of the Ethiopian Diaspora Investment Potential and the millennium bond issued by the Ethiopian Electric Power Corporation.

12. Countries outside Africa that can issue diaspora bonds include Bangladesh, Colombia, El Salvador, Haiti, India, Jamaica, Mexico, Nepal, Pakistan, Philippines, Romania, Sri Lanka, and Tajikistan.

13. Several diaspora investment funds have been created or are in the process of being created and registered. One example is the Diaspora Unit Trust Funds Schemes (DUTFS), a collective investment scheme licensed by the Capital Markets Authority of Kenya. See http://www.mobilepay.co.ke/tangaza/2010/04/kenyans-abroad-to-benefit-from-the-diaspora-investment-fund/.

14. A private company, PHB Asset Management Limited, a subsidiary of Bank PHB Plc, manages the $200 million diaspora investment fund set up by the Nigerians in Diaspora Organisation Europe (NIDOE) in 2008 (http://timbuktuchronicles.blogspot.com/2008/03/diaspora-investment-fund.html).

15. Diaspora groups in Africa that have formed organizations include Somalis in Kenya, Zimbabweans in South Africa, and various groups in Côte d'Ivoire. Associations of Zimbabweans in the diaspora contributed fuel, food, and medicines to Zimbabwe during the economic crisis through the Global Zimbabwe Forum.

16. For example, the countries with the largest numbers of Ghanaians are the United States and the United Kingdom (about 100,000 migrants each), Italy (50,000), Germany (34,000), and the Netherlands (20,000). There are about 100 Ghanaian associations in the United Kingdom (Van Hear, Pieke, and Vertovec 2004); 200 in the United States; 21 in Germany; and 70 in the Netherlands.

17. See Alarcon 2002; Goldring 2004; and Orozco and Welle 2006 for a review of Asian and Latin American associations.

18. People interviewed include members of diaspora organizations in Denmark, South Africa, the United Kingdom, and the United States, and embassy officials in France, South Africa, the United Arab Emirates, the United Kingdom, and the United States. In the United States, the interviews covered 10 groups from Ethiopia, Liberia, Mali, and Nigeria and two organizations covering Africa.

19. Trans and Vammen (2011) cite an association that sends regular donations to Eritrea to support development projects.

20. Interviews with African diaspora organizations in the United States indicated that their members volunteer their time and work for the diaspora association's activities after normal work hours. To raise funds, these associations sponsor runners in marathons and organize arts and crafts fairs and other events. Membership fees are low, so they cannot fully cover the associations' activities.

21. Meyer and Brown (1999) describe three categories of diaspora involvement: student networks, local associations of skilled expatriates, and scientific diaspora networks.

22. Arora and Gambardella (2004) and Commander and others (2004) describe the role Indian professionals in the diaspora played in promoting India as an outsourcing destination.

23. Associations of Chinese and Indian scientists and engineers living abroad exchange information and collaborate on research and development projects with scientists in their countries of origin (Saxenian 2002b). Financing local sabbatical stays for researchers living abroad as well providing them with the opportunity to teach short courses or workshops are good measures to promote exchange. African associations that engage in these activities include the International Society of African Scientists (Delaware) and the Ethiopian Scientific Society (Washington, DC). The Carnegie Institute for Advanced Study Regional Initiative in Science and Education (RISE) aims to strengthen higher education

in Sub-Saharan Africa by increasing the number of qualified professors teaching in Africa's universities. Members of the diaspora can contribute by teaching short courses, hosting RISE students at laboratories abroad, and engaging in collaborative research with researchers in their home countries. The Nelson Mandela Research Center sponsors professors from the diaspora who teach in African universities.

24. A person can acquire citizenship by place of birth (the *jus soli* rule of citizenship), by descent according to blood kinship (*jus sanguinis*), or by naturalization. Most countries apply one or a combination of the three rules. Canada and the United States are the only developed countries that still offer birthright citizenship to tourists and undocumented people.

25. For Kenya, see http://www.cnn.com/2010/WORLD/africa/08/05/kenya. elections/index.html.

26. The PIO card also grants holders of Indian passports access to all facilities in acquiring, holding, transferring, and disposing of immovable properties in India, except in matters relating to the acquisition of agricultural/plantation properties. The card does not allow holders to vote.

27. See http://www.afriqueavenir.org/en/2010/08/03/nigerians-in-the-diaspora-demand-voting-rights-in-2011-election/.

28. See the REMPLOD research project (Van Dijk and others 1978).

29. http://www.usaid.gov/our_work/global_partnerships/gda/remittances.html.

30. http://www.ambafrance-uk.org/France-Africa-Summit-conclusions.html.

31. Examples include Germany since 1972, the Netherlands since 1975, France since 1977, and Spain since 2008 (https://blogs.worldbank.org/peoplemove/volunteers-wanted-will-spain-successfully-entice-unemployed-migrants-to-leave).

32. http://www.iom.int/jahia/Jahia/activities/by-theme/migration-development/mida-africa/how-it-works.

33. http://www.migration4development.org/content/mida-migration-development-africa.

34. A 2003–05 Ghanaian poverty reduction strategy paper that proposed establishing a Non-Resident Ghanaian Fund for poverty projects was never implemented. A 2007 Kenya Diaspora bill, designed to increase benefits from the diaspora, was never passed. Nigeria launched a dialogue with Nigerians abroad to incorporate their views in national development policies.

35. This mandate led to the adoption of a new Article 3: "to invite and encourage the full participation of the African diaspora as an important part of our continent, in the building of the AU (Legwaila 2006).

36. See the report from an AU–UN gathering of the diaspora in New York, October 20–21, 2010 (http://kingdomzx.net/forum/topics/report-from-recent-african?xg_source=activity).

37. The World Bank's strategy for engaging the African diaspora involves working with the African Union Commission and country governments to help create enabling environments for diaspora engagement and working with development partners to support diaspora development projects in Africa. In July 2008, the Bank signed an agreement with the African Union.

38. It is necessary that all merchandise meant for charity purposes fulfill the same inspection, quality control, and certification processes required for other imports.

BIBLIOGRAPHY

Abella, M., and F. Alburo. 2003. "Driving Forces of Labour Migration in Asia." In *World Migration 2003*. Geneva: International Organization for Migration.

ADB (Asian Development Bank). 2004. *Technical Assistance for the Southeast Asia Workers' Remittance Study*. http://www.adb.org/Documents/TARs/REG/tar-stu-38233.pdf.

Adepoju, A. 2005a. "Migration in West Africa." Paper prepared for the Policy Analysis and Research Program of the Global Commission on International Migration, Global Commission on International Migration, Geneva. http://www.gcim.org/attachements/RS8.pdf.

———. 2005b. "Patterns of Migration in West Africa." In *At Home in the World: International Migration and Development in Contemporary Ghana and West Africa*, ed. T. Manuh, 24–54. Accra: Sub-Saharan Publishers.

African Union. n.d. "Statement at the African Union Consultation with the African Diaspora in the US: Building Bridges across the Atlantic." http://www.unohrlls.org/en/orphan/791/.

———. 2005. *Report of the Meeting of Experts from Member States on the Definition of the African Diaspora*. Addis Ababa, April 11–12.

Ahmed, S. 2000. *Strange Encounters: Embodied Others in Post-Coloniality*. London: Routledge.

Alarcon, R. 2002. "The Development of Home Town Associations in the United States and the Use of Social Remittances in Mexico." In *Sending Money Home: Hispanic Remittances and Community Development*, ed. R. O. de la Garza and B. L. Lowell. Lanham, MD: Rowman & Littlefield Publishers.

Ammassari, S. 2006. "From Nation-Building to Entrepreneurship: The Impact of Elite Return Migrants in Côte d'Ivoire and Ghana." Paper presented at the International Workshop on Migration and Poverty in West Africa, University of Sussex, United Kingdom, March 13–14.

Arocena, R. A. 2006. "Brain Drain and Innovation Systems in the South." *International Journal on Multicultural Societies* 8 (1): 43–60.

Arora, Ashish, and Alfonso Gambardella. 2004. "The Globalization of the Software Industry: Perspectives and Opportunities for Developed and Developing Countries." NBER Working Papers 10538, National Bureau of Economic Research, Cambridge, MA.

Aydagul, B., Suhas Ketkar, and Dilip Ratha. 2010. "Diaspora Bonds for Funding Education." Paper presented at the Soros Foundation, New York.

Aykut, Dilek, and Dilip Ratha. 2003. "South-South FDI Flows: How Big Are They?" *Transnational Corporations* 13 (1): 149–76.

Ba, H. 2006. "Les statistiques des travailleurs migrants en Afrique de l'Ouest." *Cahier des Migrations Internationales* 79F, Bureau International du Travail, Geneva.

Bakewell, Oliver. 2008. "In Search of the Diaspora within Africa." *Africa Diaspora* 1 (1): 5–27.

Bandyopadhyay, Subhayu, Cletus C. Coughlin, and Howard J. Wall, 2008. "Ethnic Networks and U.S. Exports." *Review of International Economics* 16 (1): 199–213.

Bardhan, Ashok Deo, and Subhrajit Guhathakurta. 2004. "Global Linkages of Subnational Regions: Coastal Exports and International Networks." *Contemporary Economic Policy* 22 (2): 225–36.

Barré, Remi, V. Hernández, J-B. Meyer, and D. Vinck. 2003. *Diasporas scientifiques? Comment les pays en développement peuvent-ils tirer parti de leurs chercheurs et de leurs ingénieurs expatriés?* Institute de Recherche pour le Développement, Paris.

Bettin, Giulia, and Alessia Lo Turco. 2008. "A Cross Country View on South-North Migration and Trade: Dissecting the Channels." Revised March 31, 2010. Department of Economics, Università Politecnica delle Marche, Ancona, Italy. http://ssrn.com/abstract=1233544.

Bevelander, P., and R. Pendakur. 2009. "Citizenship, Co-ethnic Populations and Employment Probabilities of Immigrants in Sweden." IZA Working Paper 4495, Institute for the Study of Labor, Bonn.

Biopact. 2007. "Spain and Senegal to Cooperate on Biofuels as a Way to Curb Illegal Migration." http://biopact.com/2007/08/spain-and-senegal-to-cooperate-on.html.

Black, R., and A. Castaldo. 2009. "Return Migration and Entrepreneurship in Ghana and Côte d'Ivoire: The Role of Capital Transfers." *Tijdschrift voor Economische en Sociale Geografie* 100 (1): 44–58. Oxford.

Black, R., K. Koser, K. Munk, G. Atfield, L. D'Onofrio, and R. Tiemoko. 2004. *Understanding Voluntary Return.* Home Office Online Reports, London.

Blanes, J. V. 2005. "Does Immigration Help to Explain Intra-Industry Trade? Evidence for Spain." *Review of World Economics* 141 (2): 244–70.

Blanes, J. V., and J. A. Martín-Montaner. 2006. "Migration Flows and Intra-Industry Trade Adjustment." *Review of World Economics* 142 (3): 568–85.

Blanes Cristóbal, J. V. 2004. "Does Immigration Help to Explain Intra-Industry Trade? Evidence for Spain." Economic Working Papers at Centro de Estudios Andaluces E2004/29, Seville, Spain.

Brown, Jan H. 2009. "Dual Citizenship: Living on Both Sides of the Global Fence." *NYSBA International Law Practicum* 22 (Autumn): 2.

Bryant, J., and D. Law. 2004. "New Zealand's Diaspora and Overseas-born Population." Working Paper 04/13, New Zealand Treasury, Wellington. http://www.treasury.govt.nz/publications/research-policy/wp/2004/04-13.

Business Asia. 1994. "Human Reunification." 26: 5–6.

Cassini, S. 2005. "Negotiating Personal Success and Social Responsibility: Assessing the Developmental Impact of Ghanaian Migrants' Business Enterprises in Ghana." Master's thesis, International School for Humanities and Social Sciences, University of Amsterdam.

Chakco, Elizabeth, and P. Gebre. 2009. "Leveraging the Diaspora for Development: Lessons from Ethiopia." Paper presented at the International Conference on Diaspora for Development, World Bank, Washington, DC, July 13–14.

Chaparro, Fernando, H. Jaramillo, and V. Quintero 1994. "Role of Diaspora in Facilitating Participation in Global Knowledge Networks: Lessons of Red Caldas in Colombia." Report prepared for the Knowledge for Development Program of the World Bank, Bogota.

Cheran, R. 2004. "Diaspora Circulation and Transnationalism as Agents for Change in the Post-conflict Zones of Sri Lanka." Policy paper submitted to the Berghof Foundation for Conflict Management, Berlin.

Chikezie, Chukwu-Emeka. 2000. "Africans Help Their Homelands." *West Africa* 13 (November): 12–14.

Chiswick, Barry. 1978. "The Effect of Americanization on the Earnings of Foreign-Born Men." *Journal of Political Economy* 86 (5): 897–921.

Co, Catherine Y., Patricia Euzent, and Thomas Martin. 2004. "The Export Effect of Immigration into the USA." *Applied Economics* 36 (6): 573–83.

Combes, Pierre-Philippe, Miren Lafourcade, and Theirry Mayer. 2003. "Can Business and Social Networks Explain the Border Effect Puzzle?" CEPR Discussion Paper 3750, Center for Economic and Policy Research, London.

Commander, Simon, Rupa Chanda, Mari Kangasniemi, and Alan Winters. 2004. "Must Skilled Migration Be a Brain Drain? Evidence from the Indian Software Industry." IZA Discussion Paper 1422, Institute for the Study of Labor, Bonn.

Constant, Amelie, and Douglas Massey. 2002. "Return Migration by German Guestworkers: Neoclassical versus New Economic Theories." *International Migration* 40 (4): 5–38.

Council of Europe. 2010. "Voluntary Return Programmes: An Effective, Humane and Cost Effective Mechanism for Returning Irregular Migrants." Parliamentary Assembly. http://assembly.coe.int/Documents/WorkingDocs/Doc10/EDOC12277.pdf.

Crush, Jonathan. 2010. "Diaspora Networks at Work in SADC." Paper presented at the conference "Africa's New Frontier: Innovation, Technology, Prosperity," Ottawa, February 4.

———. 2011. "Diasporas of the South: Situating the African Diaspora in Africa." In *Diaspora for Development in Africa*, ed. Sonia Plaza and Dilip Ratha. Washington, DC: World Bank.

Debabrata, Patra, and Muneesh Kapur. 2003. "Indians' Worker Remittances: A Users' Lament about Balance of Payments Compilation." Paper presented at the 16th Meeting of the IMF Committee on Balance of Payment Statistics, Washington, DC, December 1–5.

de Bree, June, Tine Davids, and Hein de Haas. "Post-return Experiences and Transnational Belonging of Return Migrants: A Dutch-Moroccan Case Study." *Global Networks: A Journal of Transnational Affairs* 10: 489–509. doi: 10.1111/j.1471-0374.2010.00299.

de Haas, Hein. 2005. "International Migration, Remittances and Development: Myths and Facts." *Third World Quarterly* 26 (8): 1269–84.

———. 2006. "Engaging Diasporas: How Governments and Development Agencies Can Support Diaspora Involvement in the Development of Origin Countries." International Migration Institute, Oxford.

Dickinson, D. 2003. "How Networking Can Help Mitigate the Brain Drain." Science and Development Network SciDevNet. http://unpan1.un.org/intradoc/groups/public/documents/APCITY/UNPAN022377.pdf.

Docquier, Frédéric, and Elisabetta Lodigiani. 2007. "Skilled Migration and Business Networks." Development Working Paper 234, Centro Studi Luca d'Agliano, University of Milano, Milan.

Dolman, B. 2008. "Migration, Trade and Investment." Productivity Commission Staff Working Paper, Canberra, Australia.

Dunlevy, James. A. 2003. "Interpersonal Networks in International Trade; Evidence on the Role of Immigration in Promoting Exports from the American States." Paper presented at the Seventh Annual Meeting of the International Society for New Institutional Economics, Budapest, September 12.

———. 2004. "Interpersonal Networks in International Trade: Evidence on the Role of Immigrants in Promoting Exports from the American States." Working Paper, Department of Economics Miami University, Oxford, OH.

———. 2006. "The Influence of Corruption and Language on the Pro-trade Effect of Immigrants: Evidence from the American States." *Review of Economics and Statistics* 88 (1): 182–86.

Dunlevy, James A., and William K. Hutchinson. 1999. "The Impact of Immigration on American Import Trade in the Late Nineteenth and Early Twentieth Centuries." *Journal of Economic History* 59 (04): 1043–62.

Easterly, W., and Yaw Nyarko. 2008. "Is the Brain Drain Good for Africa?" Brookings Global Economy and Development Working Paper 19, Washington, DC.

ECA (Economic Commission for Africa). 2006. *International Migration and Development: Implications for Africa.* New York: Economic Commission of Africa.

EU (European Union). 2007. "Circular Migration and Mobility Partnerships between the European Union and Third Countries." Press release, May 16. http://europa.eu/rapid/pressReleasesAction.do?reference=MEMO/07/197.

EuropeAid, Unit E3. 2010. "Social and Human Development and Migration." Report circulated at the Global Forum on Migration and Development, Puerto Vallarta, Mexico, November 9–11.

Federal Negarit Gazeta of the Federal Democratic Republic of Ethiopia. 2002. *Proclamation 270/202. Providing Foreign Nationals of Ethiopian Origin with Certain Rights to be Exercised in Their Country of Origin Proclamation.* February 3, Addis Ababa.

———. 2003. Proclamation 84.

Finch, Tim, Holly Andrew, and Maria Latorre. 2010. "Global Brit: Making the Most of the British Diaspora." June, Institute for Public Policy Research, London.

Foad, Hishman. 2008. "FDI and Immigration: A Regional Analysis." Department of Economics, San Diego State University, San Diego, CA. http://papers.ssrn.com/sol3/papers.cfm?abstract_id=1092286.

French Ministry of Foreign Affairs. n.d. *Diplomatie France.* http://www.diplomatie.gouv.fr/fr/pays-zones-geo_833/senegal_355/presentation-du-senegal_1293/index.html)

French Senate. 2007. *Le co-développement à l'essai.* Travaux Parlementaires, Rapports d'information No. 417 (2006–2007) de Mme. Catherine Tasca, MM. Jacques Pelletier et Bernard Barraux, fait au nom de la Commission DES Affaires Etrangères, déposé le 25 juillet, Paris. http://www.senat.fr/rap/r06-417/r06-417.html.

Gao, T. 2000. "Ethnic Chinese Networks and International Investment: Evidence for Inward FDI in China." Working Paper 00-08, Department of Economics, University of Missouri.

Ghai, D. 2004. "Diasporas and Development: The Case of Kenya." Global Migration Perspectives 10, Global Commission on International Migration, Geneva. http://www.gcim.org/attachements/GMP%20No%2010.pdf.

Gillespie, Kate. 1999. "Diaspora Interest in Homeland Investment." *Journal of International Business Studies* 30 (3): 623–34.

Girma, Sourafel, and Zhihao Yu. 2002. "The Link between Immigration and Trade: Evidence from the United Kingdom." *Review of World Economics* 138 (1): 115–30.

Gitmez, A. S. 1988. "The Socio-economic Re-integration of Returned Workers: The Case of Turkey." In *International Migration Today,* ed. C. Stahl. Paris: United Nations Educational, Scientific and Cultural Organization (UNESCO).

Goldring, Luin. 2004. "Family and Collective Remittances to Mexico: A Multi-Dimensional Typology of Remittances." *Development and Change* 35 (4): 799–840.

Gould, David. 1990. "Immigrant Links to the Home Country: Implications for Trade, Welfare and Factor Returns?" Ph.D. diss., Department of Economics University of California, Los Angeles.

———. 1994. "Immigrants' Links to the Home Country: Empirical Implications for U.S. Bilateral Trade Flows." *Review of Economics and Statistics* 76 (2): . 302–16.

Guarnizo, L. 2003. "The Economics of Transnational Living." *International Migration Review* 37 (3): 666–99.

Gubert, Flore, and Christophe J. Nordman. 2011. "Return Migration and Small Enterprise Development in the Maghreb." In *Diaspora for Development in Africa*, ed. Sonia Plaza and Dilip Ratha. Washington, DC: World Bank.

Hansen, P., and N. Kleist. 2008. "Somali Collective Remittances: Diaspora Contributions to Conflict, Peace and Development in the Somali Homelands." Background paper for the Africa Migration Project, Danish Institute for International Studies, Copenhagen.

Head, Keith, and John Ries.1998. "Immigration and Trade Creation; Econometric Evidence from Canada." *Canadian Journal of Economics* 31 (1): 47–62.

Helliwell, J. 1997. "National Borders, Trade and Migration." *Pacific Economic Review* 2 (3): 165–85.

Herander, Mark, and Luz A. Saavedra. 2005. "Exports and the Structure of Immigrant-Based Networks: The Role of Geographic Proximity." *Review of Economics and Statistics* 87(2): 323–35.

Hutchinson, W., and J. Dunlevy. 2001. "The Pro-trade Effect of Immigration on American Exports During the Period 1870 to 1910." Working Paper 0125, Department of Economics, Vanderbilt University, Nashville, TN.

ICMPD–IOM (International Centre for Migration Policy Development–International Organization for Migration). 2010. *Linking Emigrant Communities for More Development. Inventory of Institutional Capacities and Practices.* Joint ICMPD–IOM Project Report. Vienna. http://www.icmpd.org/fileadmin/ICMPD-Website/Emigrant_Communities_Project/Inventory_EN.pdf.

IOM (International Organization for Migration). 2004. "Migration from Latin America to Europe: Trends and Policy Challenges." IOM Migration Research Series No. 16. Geneva.

Ionescu, Dina. 2006. "Engaging Diasporas as Development Partners for Home and Destination Countries: Challenges for Policymakers." Migration Research Series 26, International Organization for Migration, Geneva.

Javorcik, Beata S., Caglar Ozden, Mariana Spatareanu, and Cristina Neagu. 2006. "Migrant Networks and Foreign Direct Investment." Policy Research Working Paper 4046, World Bank, Washington, DC.

Jones-Correa, Michael. 2001. "Under Two Flags: Dual Nationality in Latin America and Its Consequences for Naturalization in the United State." *International Migration Review* 35 (4): 997–1029.

Ketkar, Suhas L., and Manoj K. Dora. 2009. "Wealth of Recent Immigrants to the United States." Paper presented at the International Conference on Diaspora for Development, World Bank, Washington, DC, July 13–14.

Ketkar, S., and D. Ratha. 2009a. *Innovative Financing for Development.* Washington, DC: World Bank.

———. 2009b. "New Paths to Funding." *Finance and Development* (June): 43–45. International Monetary Fund, Washington, DC.

———. 2010. "Diaspora Bonds: Tapping the Diaspora during Difficult Times." *Journal of International Commerce, Economics and Policy* 1 (2): 252.

Khadria, Binod. 1999. *The Migration of Knowledge Workers: Second-Generation Effects of India's Brain Drain.* New Delhi: Sage Publications.

King, Russell. 1986. *Return Migration and Regional Economic Problems.* London: Croom Helm.

Kingslye, Aiking, Anita Sand, and Nicola White. 2009. "The Global Irish Making a Difference Together: A Comparative Review of International Diaspora Strategies." Ireland Funds Report, Dublin.

Kluger, M., and H. Rapoport. 2005. "Skilled Emigration, Business Networks, and Foreign Direct Investment." CESifo Working Paper 1455, Munich.

Kuznetsov, Y. 2006. *Diaspora Networks and the International Migration of Skills: How Countries Can Draw on Their Talent Abroad.* Washington, DC: World Bank.

Lacroix, T. 2003. "Espace transnational et territoires: les réseaux marocains du développement." Ph.D. diss., Université de Poitiers, Poitiers, France.

Leblang, D. 2011. "Another Link in the Chain: Migrant Networks and International Investment." In *Diaspora for Development in Africa*, ed. Sonia Plaza and Dilip Ratha. Washington, DC: World Bank.

Legwaila, L. J. 2006. "The Role of the Diaspora in Support of Africa's Development." African Leadership Diaspora Forum, London.

Light, Ivan, M. Zhou, and R. Kim. 2002. "Transnationalism and American Exports in an English-Speaking World." *International Migration Review* 36 (3): 702–25.

Lindley, A. 2005. "Influence of Remittances and Diaspora Donations on Education." Paper presented at the Conference on Somali Remittances, Washington, DC, December 1–2.

Lodigian, Elizabetta. 2009. "Diaspora Externalities as a Cornerstone of the New Brain Drain Literature." CREA Discussion Paper 2009-03, Center for Research in Economic Analysis, University of Luxembourg.

Lowell, L., and S. Gerova. 2004. *Diasporas and Economic Development: State of Knowledge.* Washington, DC: World Bank.

Lucas, R. B. E. 2001. "Diaspora and Development: Highly Skilled Migrants from East Asia." Institute for Economic Development Working Paper 120, Department of Economics, Boston University, Boston, MA.

———. 2004. *International Migration and Economic Development: Lessons from Low-Income Countries.* London: Edward Elgar Publishing.

Mahroum, S., C. Eldridge, and A. S. Daar. 2006. "Transnational Diaspora Options: How Developing Countries Could Benefit from Their Emigrant Populations." *International Journal on Multicultural Societies* 8 (1): 25–42.

Marks, Jonathan. "Expatriate Professionals as an Entry Point into Global Knowledge-Intensive Value Chains: South Africa." Report prepared for the Knowledge for Development Program, World Bank Institute, Washington, DC. http://siteresources.worldbank.org/EDUCATION/Resources/278200-1126210664195/1636971-1126210694253/South_Africa_Diasporas.pdf.

Massey, D. S., Rafael Alarcon, Jorge Durand, and Humberto Gonzalez. 1987. *Return to Aztlan: The Social Process of International Migration from Western Mexico.* Berkeley: University of California Press.

Mazzolari, Francesca. 2007. "Dual Citizenship Rights: Do They Make More and Better Citizens?" IZA Discussion Paper 3008, Institute for the Study of Labor, Bonn, Germany.

McCormick and Wahba 2003. "Return International Migration and Geographical Inequality: The Case of Egypt." *Journal of African Economies* 12 (4): 500–32.

McKenzie, David J., and Johan Mistiaen. 2007. "Surveying Migrant Households: A Comparison of Census-Based, Snowball, and Intercept Point Surveys." IZA Discussion Paper 3173, Institute for the Study of Labor, Bonn, Germany.

Mersha, Genet. 2009. "The Gilgel Gibe Saga: The Bond and Dilemma of Ethiopian Diaspora for a Description of the Main Features of the Millennium Bond." *Ethio Quest News*, April 5. http://www.ethioquestnews.com/Perspective/Gilgel_Gibe_Saga.html.

Meyer, J-B., and M. Brown. 1999. "Scientific Diasporas: A New Approach to the Brain Drain." Discussion Paper 41, United Nations Educational, Scientific and Cultural Organization (UNESCO), Paris. http://www.unesco.org/most/meyer.htm.

Meyer, J-B., and J-P. Quattiaus. 2006. "Diaspora Knowledge Networks: Vanishing Doubts and Increasing Evidence." *International Journal on Multicultural Societies* 8 (1): 4–24.

Mohamoud, Awil. 2003. "African Diaspora and Development of Africa." Report prepared for the African Diaspora Summit in the Netherlands, Felix Meritis European Centre for Art, Culture and Science, Amsterdam, December 16.

———, ed. 2010. *Building Institutional Cooperation between the Diaspora and Homeland Governments in Africa. The Cases of Ghana, Nigeria, Germany, USA and the UK.* The Hague: African Diaspora Policy Initiative, Africa Diaspora Policy Centre.

Mohan, Giles, and A. B. Zack-Williams. 2002. "Globalisation from Below: Conceptualising the Role of the African Diaspora in Africa's Development." *Review of African Political Economy* 92 (29): 211–36.

Morgenroth, E. L. W., and M. D. O'Brien. 2008. "Some Further Results on the Impact of Migrants on Trade." Working Paper DYNREG26, Economic and Social Research Institute, Dublin. http://ideas.repec.org/p/esr/wpaper/dynreg 26.html.

Murat, M., B. Pistoresi, and A. Rinaldi. 2008. "Italian Diaspora and Foreign Direct Investment: A Cliometric Perspective." Paper presented at the Economic History Society Annual Conference, University of Nottingham, United Kingdom, March 28–30. http://www.eco.unc.edu.ar/ief/workshops/2008/24abril2008_ Murat_Pistoresi_Rinaldi_EHR.pdf.

Murillo Castaño, Gabriel. 1988. "International Labor Migration and Refugees in the Americas: Issues for Hemispheric Cooperation." *In Defense of the Alien: Immigration Reform, Temporary Workers, Supreme Court, Private Sector, Legal Aspects of Detention and Sanctuary Movement* 10: 182–213.

Murphy, Rachel. 2000. "Migration and Inter-household Inequality: Observations from Wanzai County, Jiangxi." *China Quarterly* 164: 965–82.

National Audit Office. 2005. "Returning Failed Asylum Applicants, 19/7/2005." Press Notice.

Ndiaye, Ndioro, Sussane Melde, and Rougui Ndiaye-Coïc. 2011. "The Migration for Development in Africa (MIDA) Experience and Beyond." In *Diaspora for Development*, ed. Sonia Plaza and Dilip Ratha. Washington, DC: World Bank.

Negash, Minga. 2009. "Ethiopian Diaspora Investment Potential and EEPCO's Millenium Bond." University of Witwatersrand, Johannesburg. http://www. ethiopianreview.info/2010/minga-negash-ethiopia-diaspora-investment-potential-article-march-2009.pdf.

Newland, K., and E. Patrick. 2004. "Beyond Remittances: The Role of Diaspora in Poverty Reduction in their Countries of Origin." Scoping study for the Department of International Development prepared by the Migration Policy Institute, Washington, DC.

Nielsen, T. M., and L. Riddle. 2007. "Why Diasporas Invest in the Homelands: A Conceptual Model of Motivation." School of Business, George Washington University, Washington, DC. http://papers.ssrn.com/sol3/Papers.cfm? abstract_id=987725.

OECD (Organisation for Economic Co-operation and Development). 2010. *The Contribution of Diaspora Return to Post-Conflict and Fragile Countries. Key Findings and Recommendations.* Paris: Partnership for Democratic Governance.

Orozco, M. 2003. "The Impact of Migration in the Caribbean and Central American Region." Focal Policy Paper FPP-03-03, Canadian Foundation for the Americas, Ottawa. http://www.focal.ca/pdf/migration.pdf.

———. 2005. "Diasporas, Development and Transnational Integration: Ghanaians in the U.S., U.K. and Germany." Inter-American Dialogue, Georgetown University, Washington, DC.

———. 2006a. "Conceptualizing Diasporas: Remarks about the Latino and Caribbean Experience." Paper presented at the International Forum on Remittances, Inter-American Development Bank, Washington, DC. http://idbdocs.iadb.org/wsdocs/getdocument.aspx?docnum=561695.

———. 2006b. "Diaspora and Development: Some Considerations." June, Inter-American Dialogue, Washington, DC. http://www.thedialogue.org/page.cfm?pageID=32&pubID=1010&s=.

———. 2006c. "Migrant Hometown Associations (HTAs): The Human Face of Globalization." In *World Migration Report 2005.* Geneva: International Organization for Migration.

Orozco, M., and K. Welle. 2006. "Hometown Association and Development: Ownership, Correspondence, Sustainability and Replicability." In *New Patterns for Mexico,* ed. Barbara Merz. Cambridge, MA: Harvard University Press.

Orozco, Manuel, and Rebecca Rouse. 2007. *Migrant Hometown Associations and Opportunities for Development: A Global Perspective.* February, Migration Information Source, Migration Policy Institute, Washington, DC.

Osili, U. 2004. "Migrants and Housing Investments: Theory and Evidence from Nigeria." *Economic Development and Cultural Change* 52 (4): 821–49.

Pack, H., and John Page. 1994. "Accumulation, Exports, and Growth in the High-Performing Asian Economies." *Carnegie-Rochester Conference Series on Public Policy* 40 (1): 199–235.

Page, John, and Sonia Plaza. 2006. "Migration, Remittances and Economic Development: A Review of Global Evidence." *Journal of African Economies* 15 (2): 245–336.

Palmer, C. A. 1998. "Defining and Studying the Modern African Diaspora." *Perspectives* (September). http://www.historians.org/perspectives/issues/1998/9809/9809VIE2.CFM.

Pang, T., M. Lansang, and A. Haines. 2002. "Brain Drain and Health Professionals." *British Medical Journal Online.*

Panizzon, V. 2011. "From Co-development to Solidarity Development: French Policies of Subsidizing Migrant Transmission Mechanisms in a Eurafrican Context." In *Diaspora for Development in Africa,* ed. Sonia Plaza and Dilip Ratha. Washington, DC: World Bank.

Paul, Alison, and Sarah Gammage 2005. "Hometown Associations and Development: The Case of El Salvador." *Destination.* Working paper 3, Washington, DC.

Paulson, A., and U. Okonkwo Osili. 2007. "Immigrants' Access to Financial Services and Asset Accumulation." Working paper. http://www.econ.yale.edu/seminars/labor/lap07/osili-paulson-071105.pdf.

Plaza, Sonia. 2008a. "Mobilizing the Diaspora: Creating and Enabling Environment for Trade, Investment, Knowledge Transfer and Enterprise Development." In *Africa's Finances: The Contribution of Remittances,* ed. Raj Bardouille, Muna Ndulo, and Margaret Grieco. Cambridge Scholars Publishing.

———. 2008b. "Volunteers Wanted: Will Spain Successfully Entice Unemployed Migrants to Leave?" September 23, People Move Blog, World Bank, Washington, DC. https://blogs.worldbank.org/peoplemove/volunteers-wanted-will-spain-successfully-entice-unemployed-migrants-to-leave.

———. 2009a. "Promoting Diaspora Linkages: The Role of Embassies." Conference on Diaspora and Development, July 14, World Bank, Washington, DC.

———. 2009b. "Labor Mobility and Circular Migration: What Are the Challenges of the Stockholm Program." November 2, People Move Blog, World Bank, Washington, DC. https://blogs.worldbank.org/peoplemove/labor-mobility-and-circular-migration-what-are-the-challenges-of-the-stockholm-program.

Plaza, Sonia, Mario Navarrete, and Dilip Ratha. 2011. "Migration and Remittances Household Surveys in Sub-Saharan Africa: Methodological Aspects and Main Findings." Background paper. World Bank, DEC-PREM, Migration and Remittances Unit, Washington, DC.

Portes, A., C. Escobar, and A. W. Radford. 2007. "Immigrant Transnational Organizations and Development: A Comparative Study." *International Migration Review* 41 (1): 242–81.

Rannveg, Dovelyn Agunias, ed. 2009. *Closing the Distance: How Governments Strengthen Ties with their Diasporas*. Washington, DC: Migration Policy Institute.

Ratha, Dilip. 2010. "Diaspora Bonds for Development Financing during the Crisis." October 26, People Move Blog, World Bank, Washington, DC. http://blogs.worldbank.org/peoplemove/diaspora-bonds-for-development-financing-during-a-crisis.

Ratha, Dilip, and Suhas Ketkar. 2011. "Diaspora Bonds: Tapping the Diaspora during Difficult Times:" In *Diaspora for Development in Africa*, ed. Sonia Plaza and Dilip Ratha. Washington, DC: World Bank.

Ratha, Dilip, and Sanket Mohapatra. 2011. "Preliminary Estimates of Diaspora Savings." Migration and Development Brief 14, World Bank, Washington, DC.

Ratha, Dilip, Sanket Mohapatra, and Sonia Plaza. 2009. "Beyond Aid: New Sources and Innovative Mechanisms for Financing Development in Sub-Saharan Africa." In *Innovative Financing for Development,* ed. Dilip Ratha and Suhas Ketkar. Washington, DC.

Ratha, Dilip, and William Shaw. 2007. "South-South Migration and Remittances." World Bank Development Prospects Group Working Paper 102, Washington, DC.

Rauch, James. 1999. "Networks versus Markets in International Trade." *Journal of International Economics* 48 (1): 7–35.

———. 2001. "Business and Social Networks in International Trade." *Journal of Economic Literature* 39 (December): 1177–203.

———. 2003. "Diasporas and Development: Theory, Evidence, and Programmatic Implications." Department of Economics, University of California, San Diego. USAID/TESS–funded project. http://www.tessproject.org/products/special_studies/diasporas.pdf =.

Rauch, James, and Alessandra Casella. 1998. "Overcoming Informational Barriers to International Resource Allocation: Prices and Group Ties." NBER Working Paper 6628, National Bureau of Economic Research, Cambridge, MA.

Rauch, James, and Victor Trindade. 1999. "Ethnic Chinese Networks in International Trade," NBER Working Paper 7189, National Bureau of Economic Research, Cambridge, MA.

———. 2002. "Ethnic Chinese Networks in International Trade." *Review of Economics and Statistics* 84 (1): 116–30.

Riddle, Liesl. 2006. "Export and Investment Promotion Organizations: Bridges to the Diaspora Business Community?" Paper presented at the UN Expert

Convocation "Strengthening the Business Sector and Entrepreneurship in Developing Countries: The Potential of Diasporas," New York, October 5. http://www.un.org/esa/ffd/business/msc/tie/Riddle.ppt.

Saxenian, A. L. 2002a. "Brain Circulation: How High-Skill Immigration Makes Everyone Better Off." *Brookings Review* 20 (1): 28–31.

———. 2002b. "The Silicon Valley Connection: Transnational Networks and Regional Development in Taiwan, China and India." *Science Technology and Society* 7 (1): 117–49.

———. 2004. "Taiwan's Hsinchu Region: Imitator and Partner for Silicon Valley." In *Building High Tech Clusters: Silicon Valley and Beyond*. Cambridge, UK: Cambridge University Press.

———. 2006. *The New Argonauts: Regional Advantage in a Global Economy*. Cambridge, MA: Harvard University Press.

Swedish Ministry of Justice. 2010. "Sweden's Committee for Circular Migration and Development." Fact Sheet, July–September, Stockholm.

Taylor, J. Edward. 1986. "Differential Migration, Networks, Information and Risk." In *Research in Human Capital and Development: Migration, Human Capital and Development*, vol. 4, ed. Oded Stark. Greenwich, CT: JAI Press.

Taylor, J. Edward, and Peri L. Fletcher. 1996. "International Migration and Economic Development: A Micro Economy-Wide Analysis." In *Development Strategy, Employment and Migration*, ed. Edward J. Taylor. OECD Development Centre, Organisation for Economic Co-operation and Development, Paris.

———. 1999. "The New Economics of Labor Migration and the Role of Remittances in the Migration Process." *International Migration* 37 (1): 63–88.

Terrazas, Aaron. 2010. "Diaspora Investment in Developing and Emerging Country Capital Markets: Patterns and Prospects." Diaspora and Development Policy Project, Migration Policy Institute, Washington, DC.

Touray, Katim S. 2008. "Final Evaluation of the Support Project to the Implementation of the Rwanda TOKTEN Program." Final Report for the UNDP Evaluation Center, United Nations Development Programme, New York. http://erc.undp.org/evaluationadmin/reports/viewreport.html;jsessionid=7CB6512829832D08DEA79BA3E36245B5?docid=1814.

Trans, Lars Ove, and Ida Marie Vammen. 2011. "African Diaspora Associations in Denmark: A Study of Their Development Activities and Potentials." In *Diaspora for Development in Africa*, ed. Sonia Plaza and Dilip Ratha. Washington, DC: World Bank.

Turner, S., and B. Mossin 2008. *Diaspora Engagement in Post-Conflict Burundi*. Washington, DC: World Bank.

U.S. Department of State. Telegraph 86401. Washington, DC.

———. 2010. *Engaging with Diaspora Communities. Focus on EAP, EUR, and NEA*. Summary Report, Foreign Service Institute Leadership and Management School Policy Leadership Division and the Global Partnership Initiative, Foreign Policy Institute, Office of the Secretary of State, Washington, DC.

Van Dijk, P. J. C., R. W. Koelstra, Paolo De Mas, Rinus Penninx, Herman van Renselaar, and Leo van Velzen. 1978. "REMPLOD Project. Slotconclusies en Aanbevelingen." NUFFIC/IMWOO REMPLOD, The Hague.

Van Hear, N., Frank Pieke, and Steven Vertovec. 2004. "The Contribution of UK–Based Diasporas to Development and Poverty Reduction." April, Report for the Department for International Development prepared by the ESRC Centre on Migration, Policy and Society (COMPAS), University of Oxford,

Oxford. http://www.compas.ox.ac.uk/fileadmin/files/pdfs/Non_WP_pdfs/
Reports_and_Other_Publications/DFID%20diaspora%20report.pdf.

Wagner, D., K. Head, and J. Ries. 2002. "Immigration and the Trade of Provinces." *Scottish Journal of Political Economy* 49 (5): 507–25.

Wanigaratne, R. D. 2006. "An Evaluation of the UNDP Transfer of Technology through Expatriate National Program (TOKTEN)." Evaluation Resource
Center, United Nations Development Programme, New York. http://erc.undp.
org/evaluationadmin/reports/viewreport.html;jsessionid=C2765F5275DEBA
F69935903CCEE56D57?docid=1863.

Wei, Djao. 2003. *Being Chinese: Voices from the Diaspora*. Tucson: University of
Arizona Press.

Westcott, C. G. 2006. "Harnessing Knowledge Exchange among Overseas Professionals of Afghanistan, People's Republic of China and Philippines." Paper
presented at the Labour Migration Workshop, hosted by the United Nations
Institute for Training and Research, the United Nations Population Fund,
the International Organization for Migration, and the International Labour
Organization, New York, March 15.

Wickramasekara, Piyasiri. 2009. "Diasporas and Development: Perspectives on
Definitions and Contributions." Perspectives on Labour Migration 9, Inter-
national Labour Office, Social Protection Sector, International Migration
Programme, Geneva.

World Bank. 2005. *Global Economic Prospects 2006: Economic Implications of Remittances and Migration*. World Bank: Washington, DC.

———. 2010. *Migration and Remittances Factbook 2011*. Washington, DC: World
Bank.

Index

Boxes, figures, notes, and tables are indicated with *b*, *f*, *n*, and *t* following the page number.